FEMININE
LOST

FEMININE
LOST

Why Most Women
Are Male

Jennifer Granger

New York

Hachette Books
Hachette Book Group
1290 Avenue of the Americas
New York, NY 10104
HachetteBooks.com
Twitter.com/HachetteBooks
Instagram.com/HachetteBooks

First Hachette Books edition 2022

Published by Hachette Books, an imprint of Perseus Books, LLC, a subsidiary of Hachette Book Group, Inc. The Hachette Books name and logo is a trademark of the Hachette Book Group.

The Hachette Speakers Bureau provides a wide range of authors for speaking events. To find out more, go to www.hachettespeakersbureau.com or call (866) 376-6591.

The publisher is not responsible for websites (or their content) that are not owned by the publisher.

Library of Congress Cataloging-in-Publication Data is available for this book.

ISBN 978-1-60286-186-2 (print)
ISBN 978-1-60286-187-9 (e-book)

Editorial production by *Marra*thon Production Services. www.marrathon.net

Book design by Jane Raese
Set in 12-point Adobe Caslon Pro

FIRST EDITION

DEDICATED TO MY HUSBAND IGGY SOOSAY

AND MY SON ROBERT GRANGER.

THANK YOU.

Contents

PART THREE

PART FOUR

PART
ONE

CHAPTER **1**

Just How Lost Are We?

SHE SAYS: "LET'S STOP AND GET DIRECTIONS."
HE SAYS: "NO, I'LL FIGURE IT OUT—WE'LL DRIVE ON."

OUR FEMININE MAY BE LOST—BUT NOT FOREVER

Over the past sixty years, the lines between the sexes have blurred to such a degree that it is not surprising that we are not sure who is on whose team anymore. Women are increasingly competitive and combative, acting more like men in so many ways that it has thrown off any balance today's woman may have hoped to achieve. On the other hand, men are becoming ever more bewildered, not knowing when or where or how to act like a man. Going on a date is not a simple thing anymore. Who knows what is expected or how the other person will respond to a simple gesture? In the boardroom and the bedroom, it's a new world out there. Societal changes have caused the traditional male and female roles to be eroded and transformed to such a degree that supposedly, anything goes! But in truth, very little is actually working. Just ask yourself, or any of your friends, Are you truly content in your intimate and interpersonal relationships? Or ask anyone in the stream of people who have come into my office over the past fourteen years.

Why use my office as a barometer? Well, during the past fourteen years I have been offering transformational coaching not just in my office in an inner suburb of Melbourne, Australia, but over the phone and on Skype, connecting with unhappy, unfulfilled, and unsettled men and women all over the world. I've worked closely with clients from Sydney, New York, Los Angeles, Monaco, Singapore, London, and all kinds of places in between.

Let me hasten to point out that while my clients have some things to resolve, they also tend to be successful and accomplished. Most of them are involved in creative careers, or they're using their considerable talents as leaders within large corporations, charitable entities, or their own vibrant companies that they run as entrepreneurs. They come to me because they are struggling to make sense of their lives in these tumultuous times. They don't know exactly what's missing, but they know it is something important. They seek deeper meaning in their lives, knowing that material success is hollow if it is not partnered with a substantial knowledge of self and satisfying relationships at home.

Over the years, I have seen and heard it all. While my focus with clients almost always starts with what is wrong at work, very quickly we shift to their personal lives and end up doing most of our work in that realm. Nine times out of ten, their struggles seem to center on intimate or interpersonal relationships that are out of balance and creating havoc. Trouble at home or inside themselves bubbles over into struggles at work, and as with so many things, one situation needs to be fixed before the other can improve.

DEFINING A NEW WAY FOR MEN AND WOMEN TO RELATE

As clients explained the issues they were having, I began to see that they fell into different categories, or "types" of people, and when they described the challenges they were having with a spouse, friend, coworker, or boss, I could see those people as "types" as well.

It was easy for me to be sympathetic to my clients and their struggles because I had run into many similar problems, finding myself up against many of the same difficult types of people during my corporate career. I had spent twenty-five years working as a director of marketing for a number of multinational companies, and as I traveled around the world for work I had met all kinds of challenging personalities, many bent on controlling everything and everyone.

Drawing on my years as a corporate insider and more than a decade as a transformational coach, I started seeing the dynamics between men and women ever more clearly, and a new inner male-female paradigm began to unfold. I came to understand why interpersonal relationships had become such a horrendous minefield, and why previous coping mechanisms no longer seemed to work for the men and women I was coaching. They needed a new way to understand and bridge the gender gap that was becoming a canyon. They needed to figure out how to deal with new personality types that had emerged from the seismic societal changes that followed World War II.

This book is my way of sharing what I've learned. I will give you a bit more of my own story as we go along, but the focus here will be on how your life can and will improve when you start seeing the people around you for what and who they really are. This knowledge will help you get to know yourself and your own motivations too, because there is both inner and outer work involved in understanding this new paradigm.

LEARNING TO SPEAK THIS NEW LANGUAGE

New ideas demand new language, and I will be explaining my terminology more fully in chapter 4. You will also see that the foundations for the new concepts I describe are as old as our most ancient civilizations. Over the centuries, spiritual wisdom and insight have shone a light on the true internal workings of the human beings that we are. When I take those universal concepts and overlay them on what we're seeing today, much of the way men and women interact on a daily basis becomes clear.

As you learn about these archetypes, you will start to see yourself, your associates, your spouse, family members, and friends in a different light. You'll see a new way of understanding men and women and how they interact, and you may react in the same way so many of my clients do: "Oh, that explains a lot!"

OUR TRUE NATURE DOES NOT LIE

In my work I've identified several modern categories of men and women in our world today. Other archetypes do exist but my focus is on the various types of male-oriented women and on taking a broad view of their male counterparts who are more femininely oriented than ever before. It's like a soap opera: what goes on between these modern archetypes! Bad behavior? Bullying? Manipulation? Playing the martyr? It's all there. You might wonder how some people live through each day as takers and fakers, but by the end of the book you'll understand what's going on. You will be much more able to see through the freeloaders, the abusers, and the power grabbers. You will be able to identify someone's essence when you first meet them, so you can pursue meaningful connections while avoiding a host of bad dates and unwanted heartache.

As we proceed archetype by archetype I will provide real-life examples, with some key details modified, of course, but you'll probably know people in your life just like the ones I describe. For ease of explanation, I've chosen people who exemplify almost all of each archetype's qualities. People are not always so easy to type right away, but if you watch them carefully, you will see the qualities of a given archetype emerge.

Before I describe these categories briefly in this chapter, you need to know that underlying this inner male-female paradigm is an assumption made since ancient times: namely that each and every one of us has both a feminine and a masculine aspect inside us, regardless of whether we choose to present as straight, gay, bisexual, or transgendered in our lives. This means that each of us falls somewhere along the arc of masculine and feminine, depending on how those forces balance within us.

In everyday life we exhibit more or less of our feminine and masculine essence, depending on our natural inclination and what needs to be done. I will explain this in more depth in the next few chapters, but for now let me give you a brief overview of the basic archetypes I have discovered so you can get a sense of where we're going.

INTRODUCING THE NEW WORLD OF WOMEN AND MEN

The first modern gender archetype is the Andro Woman, who was born female and uses her masculine aspect to achieve dominance, to the near-exclusion of her feminine aspect. She may be dressed like a woman, power suit and hair coifed just so, but she is ready to take on anyone who gets in her way. She may present as a Virtuous or Villainous Andro, and once you learn more about these variations, you will know how best to deal with this kind of woman in your daily life.

Next is the Good Doer. She was born into a female body and is actually quite flexible about moving between her feminine and masculine aspects, but she still tends to call upon her male side to a great degree in her relentless drive to get things done. Usually she's doing those things for everyone else, seldom for herself. Living out of balance leads to trouble for this archetype, but she is often the last to realize the danger because she is just too busy.

Next comes a woman who desires power but has no intention of directly working to earn it; I call this archetype the Faux Feminine Woman. This Faux Fem can and will find someone to take care of her, someone she can keep around to do her bidding. It is very difficult to shift this woman's behavior because this archetype is resistant to change. Why work when you don't have to, right?

The fourth archetype is the Cougar. This woman is a predator, stealthy like a cat, older, well connected, well dressed, and very often wealthy. She is on the prowl for a younger man who will make her feel alive, but the one-sided relationship usually ends badly for both the Cougar and her boy toy. You'll find out why as we explore her true inclinations and motivations, and see what is going on in the mind of the young man captivated with her.

Now let's look at the men in our world. First up is the Sensitive Man, a person born male who operates as a male, but owns his feminine aspect without apology. He has found a balance between his yin and yang, and he knows how to express his feminine side. He is the best of both worlds, a champion among men and a sympathetic ear for women, but unfortunately he is so rare as to qualify for the endangered species list. He is hard to find but worth the search. Read on and you will see how best to attract a mate like this.

In the meantime you'll keep running into other men, such as the Pseudo-Masculine Man or the Highly Feminine Man. The first can look rather macho and the second is more likely to appear metrosexual. Both types dress like men, whether in dungarees or gabardine, and they *will* chase women, but you might not want to be caught by either one! Until she understands what's going on, any woman can be vulnerable to their deceptions.

IT'S A JUNGLE OUT THERE, BUT YOU CAN FIND YOUR WAY

So now you have a glimpse of this inner male-female paradigm. We have well-dressed women in the workplace acting like men on a power trip and taking no prisoners. We have men who look like rugby players but are acting out of their feminine side. So who is modeling any kind of healthy male-female relationship? You have every right to ask, What's going on and how did we get here? How bad is it?

I believe that today we are experiencing a dynamic between men and women that has never existed before. Until we understand it and fully grasp the process that has caused it, I fear that we are doomed to live in unhappy relationships, both at work and at home. Fortunately, once you grasp the new information I present, you will be able to make better choices in all aspects of your interpersonal and intimate relationships.

The next chapter presents one of our most common archetypes, the Good Doer, who is facing a drastic situation, experiencing a breakdown that I would not wish on anyone. But as you read it, you will see that it can happen to anyone. I expect you may see yourself in this case study, or someone you know well. This kind of breakdown is happening to thousands of women all over the developed world, creating chaos in their lives and deeply affecting their partners and children.

CHAPTER **2**

Waking Up Wondering

SHE SAYS: "ARE YOU ASLEEP?"
HE SAYS: "YES."

DANGER SIGNS FLASHING BUT NO RESPONSE

Stretched out on her lounge chair on the exclusive beach of Palm Cove in the heart of Australia's Great Barrier Reef, Jen wondered, *If I'm in paradise, then why do I feel so awful?* The aching exhaustion that wracked her body had been with her for a couple of months. Regretfully it was not dissipating in the slightest, despite the two weeks of vacation she had forced herself to take. Every day, she lay on the beach waiting patiently for a sign that whatever ailed her was preparing to leave her body. But it didn't happen that way.

Instead, as she tried to relax she noticed a saltwater crocodile, almost ten feet long, start to amble up the beach from under the pier heading right in her direction. *Yes, I did say crocodile!* The predator had been forced to abandon its hideaway due to recent tropical rains, which is not an unusual occurrence in far-north Queensland. The other beachgoers saw the danger, hastily packed up their things, and hustled off as quickly as they could.

Jen, however, was so exhausted and burnt out that she didn't think it unusual to see an enormous crocodile coming her way. Finally she was roused from her reverie by a stranger frantically motioning for her to get off the beach. Realizing how close she was to becoming the crocodile's next meal, Jen got herself out of harm's way. That close call underscored for her just how far she had sunk from the health and vitality she had enjoyed most of her life.

HITTING THE WALL

Her deterioration had become obvious when Jen collapsed in the shower while preparing for work three weeks before the above scene. It was as if she had hit a cosmic deadline without realizing she even had one. It wasn't that she did not know much about health. On the contrary, she had studied energy work for years and was well versed in the nature of the body, mind, and soul, and their interconnectedness. Despite this, Jen had a history of pushing the envelope, and this time she had pushed it too far. She thought she could handle her very stressful job, but her most recent assignment had been in a truly hostile work environment in a remote part of the country, and finally it all proved too much for her. No amount of sand and sun was going to heal her this time.

To top it all off, Jen was also a single mother to a teenage son and she worried that all her frequent traveling for work was leaving her son without enough structure and support. And she still nursed wounds from a disastrous divorce. After her collapse in the shower, doctors put her through a battery of tests, repeated them, and still came up with nothing. Finally they concluded that she must have chronic fatigue syndrome. They suggested antidepressants, but Jen didn't like the idea of taking drugs and she couldn't help but think that there must be something else she could do to improve her condition.

MOVING FROM JEN'S STORY TO YOUR OWN

As you may have guessed, Jen and I are one and the same. Her story is my story, but I thought I would tell it in the third person so you could see that it is a scenario very similar to that of millions of women in the world today who are doing too much. I'm guessing that if you're a woman reading this page right now you're seeing parts of yourself in my story, and if you're a man it is quite likely that you know any number of women like me. Women who don't even realize they are doing way too much by taking on the roles of wife and mother, full-or part-time work outside the home, plus any number of additional roles that might be required. Only when they crash from stress does anyone really take notice.

So, yes, I was the person who collapsed in the shower and who stared unmoving at that crocodile on the beach. Those were wake-up calls that I will never forget, alarms screaming in my head: *Danger! Danger! Danger!* I knew I had to regain control of my life, once and for all. You may have had similar experiences, coming to a crossroad that forced you to take stock of your life and choose a new direction. I found myself feeling stuck in a remote northern region of Australia, wondering what to do next. I knew that I was not in the right career, but being a single parent I was too scared to step off the corporate track. I needed to provide for my son at least until he'd completed his education, or so I had thought. But now I knew I would have to give up that plan or take a chance on not being able to provide for either one of us. I had well and truly entered a dark night of the soul.

SEEKING THE ROOTS OF MY OWN MALAISE

I began to think back over my life. When did all this begin, this total lack of balance in my life? My mother was an intuitive, very psychic, and by the time I was seven years old we both knew that I shared her gifts. This was not a happy realization for her. Not knowing how to handle them in the context of being normal, my mother had denied her abilities for most of her life. My grandmother, on the other hand, was adept at incorporating her valuable talents into her day-to-day existence, but unfortunately for me she died when I was very young. I was left with a gift but no mentor, so I coped the way my mother had: by denying what I saw or felt and pretending I didn't know more than anyone else. Now that posture was going to have to change.

Taking a spiritual perspective, I decided that my chronic fatigue syndrome was an illness of the soul; it was sending me an undeniable message that the only way I could get better was to stop leading an unexamined life. I had to take responsibility for my talent and begin to do the inner work I had neglected for so long.

HEALING FROM THE INSIDE OUT

My first decision was to study what was known about the dynamics of psychosomatics, the role the mind plays in creating illness. I couldn't find much literature on the topic but ultimately I was guided to find the sources I needed. In particular, I was very interested to discover that the health of a person's psyche is directly related to how vulnerable they are to physical illness. Through further reading and examination I also learned that family members tend to share similar views and beliefs, and this plays an important role in familial diseases and genetic conditions. It was fascinating to realize that it was the shared, limiting belief systems that created similar disease conditions within families.

I continued to dig deeper, which naturally led me to new explorations of myself, and I found a strong basis for a new way of thinking about disease. As I adopted the strategies I was reading about, I internalized them and began processing my every single thought. Sure enough, I soon found that my condition was gradually beginning to improve!

However, it was not easy and there were no shortcuts to this approach. For example, my digestive system was not working properly, so I had to delve deeply into why this was the case. I discovered that my inability to extract nutrition from the food I was eating correlated directly to my belief that my current life experiences were not offering me anything of value. I had to face up to the fact that I no longer found meaning in corporate life and that I had been thinking that way for years. I had hidden those feelings out of necessity and fear, but it was painfully clear that my career path was proving useless to me. Once I came to this realization, I had to not only *own* that thought process but do something about it.

Fortunately the tools were right at hand. My new approach to health and wellness became a major catalyst for challenging every aspect of my thinking. If any thought was determined to be unhelpful, I investigated and put it into right order. No thought or condition was too minor for my investigative curiosity. This process, when I finally embraced it, proved to be completely transformative. Slowly but ever so surely, my vitality started to return. As I felt my life force restored, I realized that now was the time to make some challenging and exciting choices.

THE ESSENCE OF A NEW CAREER PATH

With renewed energy I embarked on a journey of discovery more interesting than any job I had ever done. As I improved, I began to think of how many other people must be hitting the wall in much the same way I had. As I found ways through the suffering and fatigue, I realized that perhaps the solutions I was uncovering could work for them too.

Years earlier I had studied meditation as part of a spiritual practice that was as rewarding as it was demanding. I had even taught small meditation classes before moving north. Now that I had new insight into my life, this seemed like a good time to begin teaching meditation again, this time enhanced by everything I had learned in the interim. I knew firsthand that denial was poison, but I had also learned that shedding such a toxic approach to life had to be a gentle process. I announced to my first class that this was to be the foundation of our practice. We would not deny or bury our emotional baggage but face it head on. We began with something I knew very well, the chakra system of energy points in the body, and used it as part of a strategy for supporting people seeking the full truth about themselves.

Being in service to them was a perfect match for my intuitive gifts and my years of spiritual training. My life was so different now because the tug-of-war between my professional world and my internal self was a thing of the past. I exuded a new confidence and vitality, and without even realizing it I was becoming a role model for women looking for the sense of well-being missing from their busy lives. One by one these people, mostly women to begin with, started asking me if I could help them find a balance between their personal and professional lives, in order to reclaim some calm within the confines of their busy, overcrowded existences. As my classes kept growing in size, my students grew in their ambitions. They loved feeling better, but they also wanted to go deeper inside themselves to resolve those intensely personal issues that blocked their path to true peace.

BECOMING A TRANSFORMATIONAL COACH

As far as I knew there was no name for what I was doing, but it was fun and exciting. I loved the people who came to me for help, perhaps because they reminded me so much of myself only a few years earlier. These were my peers I was attracting, busy businesspeople, corporate climbers, creative entrepreneurs, and generally frazzled women.

In Australia at the time, in the late 1990s, there were only a handful of people calling themselves "life coaches." I knew that was not exactly what I was doing, but when someone referred to me as their coach I thought, Okay, I'm helping people make changes in their lives so maybe I'm a transformational coach. That was the new profession I'd been looking for, and it felt like a perfect fit.

Through a combination of coaching and helping my clients balance their energetic bodies, I was able to help them transform their lives. In the process they became happier and more at peace in their personal lives, which I had hoped they would. But to my surprise, they were also experiencing huge breakthroughs with regard to their careers and financial well-being. Once they were in balance and felt integrity within themselves, they felt they could take on the world.

As my coaching practice expanded, I continued to notice similarities in many of the issues women and men were experiencing. I also noticed that my female corporate clients fell into groups that had very similar ways of thinking. This was the beginning of my development of the archetypes I am presenting here; it took another ten years to fully develop the content for this book. Thanks to my spiritual studies I had been aware for a long time that we humans have energetic bodies as well as physical bodies, and that our energetic bodies have a dual nature: each of us has aspects of the feminine and the masculine within ourselves, and we do best when there is a balance between the two.

ACTIONS SPEAK LOUDER THAN WORDS

I also began to notice that practically all my female clients were behaving in rather stereotypically male ways, although they did not seem aware of it at all. I grew up in a particularly macho environment in South Africa and knew firsthand that high-testosterone men make sure they occupy all the masculine space available in their environment; any women who share that environment have to temper their behavior accordingly. Even as a child I found these patterns of behavior fascinating, and these early experiences growing up gave me a special window on masculinity.

Many younger women today are unaware of how dramatically the feminist movement changed the way men and women interact with each other. This is not surprising since most of them were born onto a more level playing field; why should they care about that history? But from my perspective, they need to be more aware of this key aspect of their history. My female clients were educated and successful, but they seemed to have little notion of how they had arrived at the "feminine" life they were living. When I gave them a bit of history and demonstrated the value of tapping into both their masculine and feminine aspects, they were definitely intrigued.

Having this new understanding allowed my clients to explore their imbalances. Gently, we found ways for them to bring their inner conflicts up to a conscious level. Once clients were able to see the imbalance, it changed and so did they. Many began to see how their femininity was not just a matter of how they dressed; it was about accessing that deep and enduring part of themselves they had been conditioned to ignore.

DISCOVERING MANY KINDS OF "MALE" WOMEN

Over a period of many years I noticed that not all "male" women were the same. In fact, they really had only their maleness in common. (Remember that when I speak about male women, I mean females who operate primarily from their masculine aspect rather than their feminine side.) For example, I observed that what I would come to call Andro women were hard working, as were their Good Doer sisters, but the Faux Fem and Cougar women were averse to holding a job. We will talk about these characteristics in greater detail, but I would like to point out that these original key distinctions enabled me to clearly separate these types of women from one another, so I could help the ones who truly wanted to transform their lives for the better.

As I became more adept at being able to see who these women truly were (their natural archetype), it became much easier to help them. Quite early on in the process, companies hired me to assist their senior female executives. Corporations were already starting to realize that there were significant problems developing between their female and male executives. Some of these women shared similar traits. They were ambitious, fearless in their desire for power, brusque, tough, and most of all, competitive. Since we usually associate these traits more with the traditional men in our society, I coined the term Andro Woman to describe this archetype. The women were seen as antagonistic, and sometimes they were, but they didn't realize it, and they were completely at a loss as to how to change their behavior.

Another difficult issue surfacing in business was that women were often highly competitive, unkind, and even downright subversive when it came to dealing with other women at work. This became a major issue as many talented but less assertive women suffered, which resulted in the inevitable loss of their talent to the company. Imagine a second kind of woman who is not as tough as the Andro. This second type is kinder and not nearly as ambitious. Power is not as important to her as a job well done and having the people around her happy. This second type of woman is still quite masculine, yet she genuinely cares about other people. In this way her feminine side is still in evidence. I named her the Good Doer, after a type of horse that thrives on very little feed or attention, who is willing to be worked by others but who does not seek reward for itself. In a business setting the Good Doer tries to avoid powerful positions, but they are often foisted on her because of her efficiency and willingness to work hard.

I liked the Good Doer, but I found myself worrying about her. Whenever a Good Doer came into my coaching practice exhausted from her busy day, I knew she needed serious help. So I devised a way to deal with her type of issues as they came to light, and the program worked beautifully! I found a way for these women to value their contributions and reap more rewards for themselves instead of always allowing their talents to elevate other people. One of the key benefits I saw as a result of coaching Good Doers was an improvement in their health.

FINDING MEN ON MY DOORSTEP

Although I started by coaching women, I soon found that men came looking for my help too. Women sent their partners, or a man they knew at work, to see me if they thought that man was brave enough to really look at what was happening in his life. Once again I found myself making interesting observations and noticing these men's similarities. Since I was coaching some very masculine women at the time, the first really noticeable thing was how feminine these first male clients were. It made sense that my masculine female clients tended to partner with men who exhibited the opposite internal polarity. Feminine men are naturally attracted to masculine women, and now these men were sitting in my office!

One day I got a lovely surprise when a man named Michael entered my office. Tall and mild mannered, he did not seem highly feminine. Hmmm, I thought, we must have another archetype here, a new one. Michael was the owner of a multinational business, a successful, warm, and clearly kind person. It turned out that Michael already had a pretty good understanding of life, but he just could not fathom women, especially the women he had working for him in his business. Michael and I went on to work together, embarking on an amazing yearlong journey of discovery.

Michael learned that his mother was a Good Doer, and because of this he was at a complete loss as to what to do with the strong Andro women he kept finding in his business life. We sorted it out, and he became very adept at recognizing and dealing with Andros. As I discovered more and more men like Michael, I was able to create a name for his archetype: the Sensitive Man. While Michael fully lived up to that description, he also had another significant quality: bravery. It is one of the keys to this archetype. I have found that if the element of bravery is missing, then men fall into one of two other categories: the Highly Feminine Man or the Pseudo Masculine Man.

So in total, my research highlights five main female archetypes and each of them is distinctly male oriented to different degrees. Then there are three broad male archetypes that exhibit feminine characteristics in varying ways. While a five-to-three ratio may seem a bit skewed, it is not. There are more female archetypes than male archetypes in this inner male-female paradigm because my focus is to present the full range of masculine-oriented women who operate in our modern world, and they most commonly fall into five categories based on their behavior and beliefs. The three male archetypes I present are these women's natural counterparts, and they naturally fall into one of three main types.

TAKING THIS PARADIGM TO A FORMAL LEVEL

It has taken time and patience to develop these new archetypes of men and women, and I have done so in an attempt to bring some kind of sense to what is happening in the world. Understanding each type of man and woman in this modern era became my mission and my joy. My curiosity was rekindled every day that I worked with the wonderful men and women in my practice.

Once you understand each archetype, you can draw your own conclusions as to how these insights relate to you, your friends, your colleagues, and your family. Understanding the ways in which we are more than just our physical bodies might be challenging at first, but I have no doubt that you will resonate with these simple truths in the same way hundreds of my clients have. I strongly believe that the time for this exploration is here and now. Relationships today are fraught with more angst and misunderstanding between the sexes than ever before in human history.

But before jumping full tilt onto this roller-coaster ride, let's see if we can get a better understanding of how we got here. We will look at influences that include the industrial revolution, World War II, the feminist movement, the New Age movement, economics, technology, and the Internet.

CHAPTER **3**

How Did We Get Here?

SHE SAYS: "LET'S GET MARRIED!"
HE SAYS: "NO, LET'S JUST LIVE TOGETHER."

HOW WOMEN BECAME SO MALE

We have been living through monumental change for the past sixty years. Inch by inch, men and women have shifted their outward behavior to accommodate the internal changes that have occurred to all of us as a result of world events. The way we have been affected individually has changed us all as a society, bringing out the evolution of the male woman and the female man. Over time, women have lost touch with the feminine aspect of their being and have overdeveloped their masculine aspect. This means that the masculine side has become dominant, leaving our society with large numbers of women who are predominantly male oriented. This has created a seesaw effect, with a corresponding movement by men to their female side. That's why men today are more oriented toward their feminine side than ever before. To understand this shift, it's helpful to trace its origins. So let's take a look at how we got here.

OUR ANCESTORS KNEW THEIR PLACE

For thousands of years stereotypical roles were required for our physical survival. We needed men to be brawny and assertive. It was their job to go out, hunt for food, make stone tools, and fight off predators. Theirs was a highly protective role, for without it women and children would have had great difficulty surviving. Gender roles were clearly defined out of necessity. Men were hunters and protectors. Women bore children, were the nurturers and peacemakers.

Until the twentieth century men had the advantage, since physical strength and logic were essential to survival. Feminine traits by comparison, especially the innate ones such as intuition and creativity, were not valued as highly. Since men had the physical power, they took control of political power as well. Women were denied a proper education for centuries, ensuring they remained vulnerable. We know there are cultures today that still seek to keep women down by denying them access to education. Nor has organized religion been a friend to women either. Many interpretations of religious teachings have disadvantaged women by discounting them. In the Christian church, for example, women were not allowed any meaningful standing. Without the respect that went with status bestowed by the church, women were further relegated to the role of second-class citizens.

So throughout history men maintained dominance over women and therefore over the feminine. Being feminine was likened to being weak and submissive. In reality, nothing could be further from the truth, as we will see in future chapters. But eventually things changed. We evolved. The industrial revolution transformed the world of work so that being bigger and stronger was no longer a requirement for most jobs. As higher education and technology became more accessible to both men and women in developed countries, the playing field leveled out quite a bit, creating both opportunities and challenges.

THE MYTH OF THE GOOD OLD DAYS

So if we were destined to be equal, and the world now accepts this, why do men and women still struggle to get along, and why do they not treat each other with the respect they deserve? You might wonder why we can't just go back to the good old days, but the fact is that our parents and grandparents did not have it easy, by any means. In the past couples had little choice but to stay together, thanks to economic, religious, and social pressures. Those old ties are not nearly as binding today, and they haven't been replaced by new ones. Besides, there are perfectly good reasons why the old social conventions that served our parents, grandparents, and great-grandparents no longer work for us. We are living a different reality from theirs. Much more is required of us, and ironically we are less prepared than ever to handle the demands being made on us.

Many old skills for managing relationships no longer apply to a world in which women have achieved a degree of freedom and success unimaginable just a few generations ago. We are desperately seeking balance without even being aware that we are doing so; we just want the emotional pain and feelings of loneliness to stop. Unfortunately, we are going to have to live with that pain and suffering until we can reorient our thinking in a way more appropriate to the men and women that we are today.

WARTIME REALITIES AND THE 1950S CHARADE

In the 1940s the Second World War caused women to enter the workforce in significant numbers for the first time. In the United States, for example, women were needed because men had been called to active duty in the armed services. Out of necessity women stepped out of their roles as homemakers and mothers to take on the added burden of occupations that up to that point had been exclusively male. They performed these jobs well, and many women enjoyed this first taste of freedom that came along with their new earning power.

The difficulty came when it was time to hand those jobs back to the men returning from the war. Women did turn the jobs back over, but their thinking was irrevocably changed. Women had become stronger and more comfortable with their own masculine energy. They knew now that they were capable of holding full-time jobs outside the home. The genie was out of the bottle and it would not go back in. And then along came the 1950s, a period of stagnation in which both men and women felt stifled by their stereotyped roles. Countries that had just been through the upheaval of a world war were dealing with deep emotional scars and feelings of insecurity. In response, society tried to reestablish social norms. If everyone complied with them, perhaps a sense of stability could be restored. Authenticity was not encouraged; everyone just wanted to be seen doing the right thing. Suddenly everyone was trying to "keep up with the Joneses," working to become part of a perfect little family themselves, complete with the tidiest lawn, the newest car, and the prettiest house in the suburbs.

What government and church did not take into consideration was that the world had changed forever and there was no going back. Men were frustrated in their attempts to reestablish themselves in their careers and women were frustrated by being forced back into the limited world of homemaker. When women couldn't figure out why they felt so fatigued and depressed they went to the doctor, who responded by prescribing new and wonderful mood-altering drugs. Alcohol was also a socially acceptable way for both men and women to numb themselves to their uneasiness, unhappiness, and anxiety.

THE "ME" GENERATION

By the 1960s a full-scale sexual revolution was on its way. With the arrival of the birth control pill and the first abortion clinics, women suddenly had choices regarding their reproductive health for the very first time in human history. They could choose when to have children and even not to have a family at all.

Divorce had been largely taboo until the mid-1960s and early 1970s, but once the stigma was gone it was not long before the dissolution of marriage became a common occurrence. And some began to ask, Why get married anyway? Before long, marriage came to be seen in some circles as an antiquated institution that had been used to keep women in their place. Young people were finding that living together was just as good and far less hassle. Once the stigma of living in sin was no longer an issue, men and women were free to live however they pleased and sleep with whomever they wanted. Life was grand.

Shedding the old angst set the stage for further social change. By the mid- to late 1960s the feminist movement was on the rise. Not just the feminist movement but also the New Age movement, hippie culture, and the advent of the self-help craze. If you didn't like your life, your career, or your spouse, you could change it all! Read a book, take a pill, drop in or drop out. It was totally up to you. Freedom—what a concept!

In the midst of all this social ferment, technology and computers were also entering all aspects of daily life, causing us to evolve in terms of work and play. This was either good or bad depending on how you looked at it, and the full effect technology will have on us as a species is a story still being written. The main point is that citizens of the developed world were ready to become whoever they really wanted to be. Men and women were no longer shackled by social conventions. As stereotypes went out the window, men were encouraged to embrace their feminine side; and with the emergence of the feminist movement, women wholeheartedly embraced their masculine side. Societal factors had caused a profound shift in our internal gender balance. We have been dealing with the ramifications ever since.

THE RISE OF THE FEMINIST MOVEMENT

The feminist movement was a powerful act of defiance with far-reaching consequences. Women had been on a quest for freedom from the shackles of patriarchy for centuries, and now that an opening had finally come, they found the feminine courage and masculine bravery to insist they be treated as men's equals. Those brave feminists of the 1960s and 1970s stood on the shoulders of giants: women who had fought early on for social equality, medical care, the right to vote, and other basic freedoms. It was an evolutionary process that came to a head in the 1960s as a revolution.

Like most revolutions, its ramifications could in no way be predicted in the height of battle. We have since seen generations of women who have no idea of the pain and suffering of the women who went before. One step at a time, they turned the tide and changed the world forever. For the most part, young women today have been born into a world where it's not politically correct to dwell on gender differences. In many ways this is a wonderful thing for them, but they also seem to be a generation bereft of any idea of how to interact with men in a loving, sustainable way.

DEALING WITH THE UNFORESEEN

For all that the feminist movement was inevitable and invaluable, it was not without some unexpected consequences. One of the most disturbing was the emergence of the male woman in our society. In their quest to achieve equality, women did it the only way they knew how: by competing with men on their terms. This meant forsaking their feminine aspect in favor of the masculine approach. Enter the Andro Woman.

Gender confusion aside, there are a number of downsides to achieving equality. In their desire for full equality, women ended up severely overworked. Too many women today are stretched to the limit managing a job as well as their families. Too many are single parents, forced to be both the major breadwinner and the primary caregiver. If women were worried that they were undervalued in the home before the feminist movement, now they find so much more on their plates that they are being undervalued yet again. While women work themselves to the edge of breakdown and beyond, they don't realize the kind of example they are setting for their children, especially their daughters. It's no wonder that many women today say they do not want their mothers' lives. Young women have witnessed firsthand how overcommitment affects everyone in the family.

Women may now have the sexual freedom to choose any partner they want, but promiscuity can be a double-edged sword, as we'll see. On the one hand, women do have the right to behave in a way equal to men, bedding any partner they like. But on the other hand, if they aren't careful to choose the right partner, they are at higher risk of being left with a baby to care for and no man to help support them. We see it every day. Men can waltz away from parenthood on a whim, and they do. As social stigmas weaken, so does cultural disapproval for the absentee father, who is so common today. Feminine men feel less strongly than masculine men the moral imperative to step up and provide for the children they helped create, and to support the child's mother. When men abandon their responsibilities, women can find themselves enslaved once again, this time by the chains of poverty.

Another unfortunate aspect of the emergence of highly masculine women is that some more militant types still feel a desire for vengeance in response to the mistreatment of women by men over the years. These women use their masculine power to suppress others. Strongly Andro women take advantage of any perceived weakness by grabbing power for themselves, whether through fair means or foul.

This being said, Andro women can change. I have worked with many who have been able to locate a sense of decency deep within themselves and tread more carefully when dealing with others. I have seen their ruthlessness soften somewhat as they become more considerate of those around them. When they learn that respect is the key to good relationships, they realize they don't need to bully their way through life anymore. They learn to soften their approach in a genuine way, and as they reconnect with their personal feminine they feel more at peace within themselves.

WHAT IS THE COST OF THIS LOSS?

So what happens when a woman's development of her masculine side goes too far? Who will provide the nurturing in our society? Who will be the agent of compassion and peace? Who will make sure that warmongering is kept to a minimum? The world will be infinitely poorer for the loss of the feminine in women. Who will love these women? Who will fulfill their emotional needs?

Many male women are faced with these dilemmas. They work hard; they are successful professionally, but they are not necessarily happy. They tend to have children later in life, if at all. Many have a feeling deep within themselves that they are unfulfilled. This dissatisfaction is due to the loss of their feminine side, the part of themselves that actually defines them as women. They feel incomplete until they reconnect with that powerful, nurturing, mysterious creative side that is their birthright. They just have to discover how to do so.

This brings us to yet another by-product of the emergence of male women. With their rise there has been a corresponding shift in the number of men with a strong feminine aspect. With male-oriented women doing more, their female-orientated partners are doing less. This has made too many men lazy, relegating the hard work to women. Women are becoming the initiators of relationships and almost everything related to everyday living. Men are in danger of becoming passengers in life, leaving women to be the engines. We cannot lose sight of the fact that it is the job of masculine energy to initiate and direct. Men seem to have unwittingly relinquished that job to the masculine within women.

LIVING YOUR OWN TRUTH

Please note that the scenarios I describe are not true of all men or all women. In describing these cases I'm turning to the extreme ends of the spectrum first, whereas we humans have different degrees of these archetypal forces within us. As women, for example, we access more of our feminine side at certain times and more of our masculine side at other times, which is part of the nature of being human.

Nonetheless, it's helpful to bear in mind that if we arrived on this earth in a female body, then the feminine should be our dominant experience, just as those of us born as men were intended to have their experience be dominantly male. As a whole, we are inextricably interconnected with each other as men and women. If there is a shift in men, it will translate to a shift in women, and vice versa. We are tethered to each other, forever destined to feel the effects of the changes that occur in our opposite poles.

Most worrisome about this fact is that you run the risk of becoming a fake if you are predominantly operating from the gender trait opposite to the one you were born into. If you are a man, it behooves you to behave as a man while still being conscious that you have access to your personal feminine any time you need it. The same is true if you are a woman. You can drop into your feminine knowing that you are safe because you can always become your own protector by accessing your masculine essence.

FINDING SOMEONE TO LOVE

Even though the world has undergone major shifts, we are still human. If you are a man you have to meet certain basic needs in order to feel fulfilled. For example, the need to make your female companion happy and the need to protect her are two fundamentals that contribute to your happiness as a male of our species. But let's consider what you are up against. As a man you want a partner to protect and make happy, but all you are finding are male women who can do those things for themselves; they no longer need a man in order to meet their survival needs. These women have lost touch with their feminine selves, and along with it the ability and desire to be receptive. They do not realize this to their detriment, as we will see. That leaves any man trying to satisfy his natural male desires with just a precious few feminine women.

On the flip side of the coin, we have male women who are becoming more and more emotionally desolate, with little understanding of why that is. They have become comfortable operating out of their male aspect and are self-sufficient to the extent that they do not have to rely on anyone for anything. Yet in order to feel fulfilled a woman has to be receptive, a fundamental feminine aspect that many women can no longer find in themselves. Unable to receive, they ache for something they can't identify. These male women assume it is a romantic connection they are missing, so they find a man they can control and dominate. Since opposite energies attract, they attract feminine men. Unfortunately, their choice often leads to more unhappiness. Since their energetic makeup is the opposite of what it should be, these women become less and less fulfilled as the years go by.

IS CHANGE EVEN POSSIBLE?

By now you are probably realizing that our natural traits and archetypes can be very deeply held and as such they might not be easy to change. That is true, but still they can be changed, and I encourage you to at least try some of the new behaviors I will propose, and see where they lead you. This process becomes less scary as you start to experience positive effects from small changes.

With awareness and intention, significant change is possible, but there is a caveat. If you are in any kind of stable social group, be it a family, partnership, friendship, or work group, any change you make is going to affect the group as a whole. This change may be seen as destabilizing; those close to you may not welcome it. When you make a change in yourself, you may highlight the need for your partner to change. You are a puzzle piece in their life, and if you change you may no longer fit into the space allotted you. The same is true of your friends, your family, and your co-workers. All these people know what to expect from the *old* you, but the new you is unknown to them and therefore threatening. The *new* you could be confrontational. People can be so resistant to change that they may even say they liked you better the way you were before.

Even a small change will be experienced everywhere throughout the continuum of your life, and will affect everyone in it. For example, I have seen Highly Feminine men develop their protective masculine side, which changes the type of women they attract. They no longer choose to be abused by male-oriented women, or to defer to other men. I have seen Good Doers finally realize they are worthy of a life in which they take their own needs into account. They remain caring people who find great satisfaction in serving others, but they learn to serve themselves first.

GIVE YOURSELF A BREAK

The material I explore in depth in these pages may not always be easy to process. It is my experience that sometimes anger or other strong emotions come up when people are exposed to these concepts for the first time. Most clients I have worked with in my coaching practice push back and get angry at some point in the process. I therefore urge you to read this content with compassion, both for yourself and for those whose archetypes you recognize. We all need to feel understood. Knowing this, we can move into a state of balance with others and ourselves.

It's quite natural to feel anger when one of your negative traits comes to light. In fact, if you find yourself becoming angry as you read this book, you can still be happy at some level. Something has stirred deep inside you that has led you to become conscious of a quality you weren't aware of. Don't be too hard on yourself. The negative side of what is occurring for men and women, the difficult unfulfilled lives we lead in relation to each other, is seated in residual anger and pain that has never been addressed. If we resolve this anger and hurt individually, within ourselves first, we will go a long way to achieving peace between the sexes.

Let's face the facts. It's wonderful that women and men are seen as completely equal in our modern world, but we are still in the middle of a sexual revolution and therefore mired in confusion. Often we don't know how to behave, simply because we are creating new paradigms in our relationships and how we relate to the world as a whole. We are sailing in uncharted waters. This journey can be exciting, but it can also bring up emotions such as fear or anger.

As we have seen, this is not all bad. It is what needs to happen as we evolve. The good thing about uncharted waters is that we get to create a new way to relate to others, a system that works for us as we are today. In the upcoming chapters we will look at numerous examples of how masculine and feminine energy functions within us. But first let me introduce the basic concepts and the language we will be using, so you can get the most from your experience of this book.

CHAPTER **4**

Speaking a New Language

SHE SAYS: "MY DAD'S TERRIFIED OF MY MOM."
HE SAYS: "REALLY? MY PARENTS NEVER ARGUED."

POLARITY COMES FROM YOUR FAMILY OF ORIGIN

Within our physical body we possess two energies, masculine and feminine. The flow of energy between these two essences forms our polarity. Where does this polarity come from? It has its origins in the family we grew up with. We were each born as unique and beautiful souls with our own dispositions, even before we meet the people who will be raising us. Each and every family is set so that everyone has their place, and it is there that our natural energetic polarity first begins to develop.

There was a pecking order in your family home, and rules of conduct. Most of the time this same order translates into your life later on. It is very difficult to escape the order of things you were exposed to as a child. You learned how to communicate within a family and how to relate to all its members. You saw how men and women related to each other, for better and for worse. When you spend time with the nuclear family you grew up with, you find it doesn't matter if you haven't seen them for a while, even a long time. Once everyone is back together under the same roof, something remarkable happens. They all fall back into their old roles and their original positions in the pecking order. This can be extremely frustrating if you have been on a personal journey of change. When you walk through that front door it's as if you haven't changed at all. The energy that binds your family together is woven so tightly that its members usually don't want anything to change.

If you are the odd person out, the one who is trying to change, your effort can be an affront to the status quo. You may be seen as a threat to the family's harmony, even if nothing is ever said about it. The rest of the group are used to their arrangement, no matter how dysfunctional it may be, and they will not welcome anyone shaking things up. The family and its traditions will be protected as sacrosanct, even if the members themselves are not aware of what they are doing. If you choose to change the way you live and relate to other people, odds are you won't be able to hold on to this new way of living if you move back into your childhood home. However, you can still enjoy the familiarity that comes with family get-togethers. Knowing how things work within this group, and exactly where you fit into it, can provide a deep sense of security, which is why so many people look forward to visiting with their families.

WHY BLENDED FAMILIES DON'T BLEND WELL

The rigidity of family structures can create havoc for blended families as two people move in together, bringing their children from previous relationships. Many blended families have great difficulty jelling. Each side of the family comes into the new home from a different place and with a different set of expectations. When you consider that you're bringing together two well-established family groups, it's no wonder that newly blended families struggle to find equilibrium and are so easily destabilized. And when parents are not on the same page in terms of how the new structure will function, it makes things even more difficult. Unaware of the forces at work, each family member is at a loss to know how to fit into the new family entity. Everyone has a vested interest in hanging on to their old construct. Even if it didn't work very well, there is still great security in knowing you have a place in an established family dynamic and how it will react to your energy.

WE ARE NOT SINGULAR BEINGS

Throughout this book I will refer to *masculine* and *feminine* as essences, energies, aspects, or principles. These energies lie at the core of our human experience. The degree to which we outwardly exhibit one or the other indicates our polarity. The most important point to understand here is that human beings have both an energetic body and a physical body. Perhaps the French philosopher and Jesuit priest Pierre Teilhard de Chardin put it best: "We are not human beings having a spiritual experience; we are spiritual beings having a human experience."

The belief that humans have this spark of spiritual energy at our core is present in traditional wisdom throughout the ages. This inner spark, recognized by virtually every known civilization, has been given many names depending on culture, religion, or philosophy. For example, traditional Chinese culture refers to *qi* (also called *chi*), which is frequently translated as "life energy" or 'energy flow." In the Hindu religion this same energy is known as *prana*; Hawaiian culture calls it *mana*; Tibetan Buddhism refers to it as *lung*; and in the Hebrew culture it is called *ruah*. In Western philosophy you will sometimes hear it referred to as *vital energy*. Other belief systems in the Western world refer to *élan vital* or *vitalism*.

The concept that two essences, masculine and feminine, reside within our energetic field also goes back to ancient times, and has been mentioned by many religions and cultural belief systems. One of the most commonly accepted interpretations in both the Eastern and Western worlds is *yin* and *yang*, symbols of the *Tao* ("the Way"); Taoism is an ancient Chinese philosophy. Yin and yang is one of the oldest cosmologies in all of human thinking. Archeological evidence has been found for the concept of yin and yang going back at least five thousand years, and references continue from that point to the present day. Yin-yang theory is based on the premise that all life emerges from a point of perfect balance. Yin and yang are dynamic forces constantly interacting with each other, distinct and individual, but also inseparable. Within every object in the universe, and within each living being, a constant dynamic interaction is taking place between these two polar opposites.

According to Taoist belief, the feminine is yin and the masculine is yang. Many other dualities—such as male and female, light and dark, high and low, hot and cold, water and fire, life and death—are seen as physical manifestations of the yin-yang concept. For our purposes then, we are analyzing human actions and desires from the point of view that we each have within us a feminine essence and a masculine essence, a yin-yang polarity, regardless of physical gender or sexual orientation.

MAKING PROGRESS THROUGH ENERGY WORK

The stereotypical belief that men are completely and only masculine and women are completely and only feminine is mistaken. This simplistic way of looking at things doesn't begin to tell the whole story. I have worked with these concepts for the better part of fourteen years, trying to help my clients find a balance between their two essences, masculine and feminine, and to sort out their internal polarity. In my coaching and healing work, I help people understand the dynamics of their energetic bodies and their internal polarity in the context of their day-to-day lives. I help them bring their two internal essences into balance.

I do this by teaching clients how to understand, accept, and work with the constant interplay of their two essences by paying attention to how those energies are manifesting daily in their physical lives. They can't see the essences themselves, but with training they can start to perceive how their thoughts and actions are affected by those energies. With practice, they learn how to conduct themselves in more balanced ways. You can learn this too.

Once my clients have managed to restore their internal balance, they start to experience beneficial changes in their physical lives. For example, people who enjoy a good internal balance attract more of what they want in their lives, whether it is intimacy, deeper friendships, career success, happiness, or a return to good health. Whatever they want, they are in a much better position to get it because they are settled and balanced within themselves.

In the previous chapter we saw that during the past sixty years women have become more male oriented due to a unique set of social circumstances. Men, in turn, have responded by becoming more feminine, and surrounded by male women there is little room for them to display their masculine essence. To make matters worse, when two people come together as a couple their polarity comes into play in a big way, further complicating what is already a complex state of affairs.

PUT ANY TWO PEOPLE IN A ROOM

Given the fact that we each have dual aspects, when any two people form an intimate relationship there are actually four essences at play in that dynamic. This holds true for heterosexual couples as well as gay, lesbian, and transgender couples. For a heterosexual couple there would be two essences within the woman (feminine and masculine) and two within the man (feminine and masculine). So that is a total of four essences that may each be expressed in different intensities at different times within that relationship. Lesbian couples would also have four essences: two within the first woman (feminine and masculine) and two within the second woman (feminine and masculine). In the case where two men form a gay couple, each man comes in with his own two essences so there is still a total of four.

Each person brings varying degrees of masculine and feminine energy to every relationship, and we do this without giving it any thought. It's just the way it is. You could proceed through life oblivious to this fact, but don't be surprised if you then run into relationship issues that drive you crazy. The more complex the dynamic, the more we benefit from understanding what is going on within men and women, and that is what we are talking about here. When you understand the interplay of these four energies, you'll see why you are attracted to certain people and not to others. And you will figure out the best way to keep your intimate relationships balanced and healthy.

The same can be said for the workplace. Any time two co-workers at any level in an organization interact, four gender aspects are at play in the room with them. Both persons bring their own natural inclination, their own archetype, which influences how much of their feminine and masculine essences they bring to the table. The degree to which they access each internal energy determines their archetype within this inner male-female paradigm. Some co-workers just get along better than others because their archetypes are compatible. On the other hand, you can sometimes get stuck in a work relationship that turns out to be a complete disaster, full of deceit, power struggles, and sabotage. There are certain archetypes to watch out for, given that they are more prone to causing this kind of chaos in the workplace. Not surprisingly, these archetypes are the ones you should run from in a social situation too. And forget sharing any pillow talk. These archetypes make even worse significant others!

SEEKING THE RIGHT BALANCE STARTS WITH YOURSELF

In order to create balanced interpersonal or intimate relationships in your life, you need to be balanced yourself. When you are tapping into and using both your essences in a healthy way, you will attract the kind of mate most compatible to you, allowing you to form a sustainable, healthy, and loving relationship. So what does it mean to have your feminine and masculine essences in balance? To fully understand this, we need to become aware of how these energies manifest in your life, what they look like, and how they work. That is the crux of this book. Once you learn to develop the ideal balance, your life will blossom in many new ways.

The difference between you and the people around you is based on the fact that each of you came into the world a unique being. You then found your place within your family and were influenced to a great degree by its dynamics as you were growing up. This means that your orientation, or archetype, today is a factor of your original unique self, your experiences in life, and your environment. For example, we can make a general assumption that if you are the daughter of a mother who was quite male in her orientation, you will probably find yourself behaving in similar ways (unless you've chosen to go to the opposite extreme).

HOW OUR TWO ESSENCES INTERACT WITHIN OURSELVES

To understand the differences between our masculine and feminine essences, it is important to understand how they interact with each other. Feminine energy has enormous depth, strength, and creativity; steeped in mystery, it is nurturing and receptive. It is the less visible part of your energy, but it defines who you are. And remember that this beautiful feminine energy can be found inside both men and women. This creative feminine energy is your internal decision maker. Whatever you process with your feminine energy will play out in your masculine energy. This is because the masculine side is overt: it is the part of us that takes action to make things happen in the physical world. Masculine energy is about doing and giving, whether it resides in a male or female body.

Our masculine aspect is the face of our feminine selves, so our feminine energy shows up in our external masculine behavior. A popular unattributed description of the Tao puts it beautifully: "As the sun moves across the sky, yin and yang gradually trade places with each other, revealing what was obscured and obscuring what was revealed." Given the complementary nature of the essences, nothing can be hidden, try as we might. We are transparent, whether we are aware of it or not. Since masculine energy is controlled by our feminine aspect, an enormous responsibility rests on that feminine aspect to maintain the integrity of the whole. Our masculine aspect is devoted to expressing ourselves in the larger world.

ACTIVATING YOUR INTERNAL ESSENCES

There are several more qualities that contribute to our masculine and feminine aspects, which I will elaborate on below, but the four primary ones are nurturing and receiving, doing and giving. Once we are aware that these traits are present within ourselves and we work to keep them in a good state of balance, we become happier. Try to imagine these four traits at work within you and how they play out in the course of your daily life. It might look something like this:

You are a kind and giving human being (giving is a masculine trait), while at the same time you have no difficulty receiving all the good and wonderful things that come to you throughout the day (receiving is a feminine trait). You are physically active, so you might go for a workout at the gym and then work at your office for several hours because you have a deadline to meet. Both of these are external activities, so they emanate from your masculine essence. Later that same day you might feel the urge to sit quietly and have a cup of tea, tapping into your feminine essence as you contemplate what you need to do next, or run through your mind your actions for the next day. Contemplation is generated by your feminine aspect. During this contemplative time you might make some big decisions about how you want to change your life (you're still thinking it through, which means you are still using your feminine aspect). So you take the steps necessary to carry out those decisions, perhaps by calling a friend about a new job that has opened up in their company. Making that call is a manifestation of your masculine energy.

As you can see from this example, whether you are male or female you have just tapped into both aspects of your energetic body; in fact, you are activating them and using them all the time. When the balance of these interactions gets out of whack, that's when your relationships and work life can spin out of control. To keep this from happening, let's take a closer look at how you can learn to recognize your two essences in the various ways they show up in your daily life.

EXAMINING THE BEAUTY OF THE FEMININE ESSENCE

To my mind, the feminine essence is like a dark lake. Its true depth is not visible from the shore; one would have to dive into its darkness to experience it profoundly. Herein lies the difficulty with the feminine, which can be large, unwieldy, and chaotic. While it is the source of great creativity, it does not stop to order things and take steps to bring them to fruition. That is the job of the masculine aspect. Our creativity lives in our feminine energy. The more available we make ourselves to that energy, whether we are born in a female body or a male one, the more prolific and inventive our creative life will be. Without connecting to the vast potential of the feminine, innovation is just not possible. The feminine aspect is the home of ideas plucked from somewhere beyond understanding.

If we allow our feminine essence free range, we are apt to bring to the world more brilliance than we can imagine. Creative people understand this process. They also know that it takes a disciplined masculine energy to bring those fantastic ideas into being; without it those ideas may remain mere fantasy. As you can see, the brilliant creative spark that arises from our feminine aspect is deeply reliant on the health of a well-disciplined masculine essence for its survival.

RECEPTIVITY, ACCEPTANCE AND JUST *BEING*

Another key element of the feminine is its ability to receive. The stronger and healthier your feminine essence, the greater your ability to draw to yourself what you need and want. Receptivity is a nuanced quality very much dependent on your overall health. Your feminine essence is the bedrock for your energetic health, so you want to keep it clear and bright; this advice is equally important for both men and women. The thoughts and dreams that reside in our feminine essence attract similar energies, both positive and negative. Therefore, keeping your feminine positive draws the positive range of your desires.

It is also important to remember that our feminine aspect is the underwriter of our decisions, good and bad. This driver is internal and powerful. When accessed fully, it gives women and men the ability to say no and mean it. When developed in a man or woman, this power keeps them from being abused in any situation. Paradoxically, acceptance is the feminine trait that can become the catalyst for the change we want to manifest. If we do not clearly see and accept our strengths and limitations, we close off any possibility for change. We turn instead to manipulating others in order to get what we want. Unfortunately, this problem is rampant in our society. In summary, the feminine essence is our place of being that provides a hearth for rest and regeneration. Here we can connect with our spirit, with a sense of peace. To take time to *be* is very different from doing nothing. Being is an internally active process.

Contemporary masculine women have far too much to accomplish in any given day to allow themselves to just *be*. But this is the first order of business for women in search of their feminine aspect: to allow themselves to have nothing to do and nowhere to go. Men who are also charged with too much doing fall into the same chaos, and would be well advised to tap into their feminine and give them-

selves time to recharge and think. To just be. In the state of just being, women and men can allow all their beautiful feminine traits to
emerge once again. Each of us can then give ourselves over to a quality that many men and women don't even realize they have access
to. Many women have lost the art of connecting to their intuitive
selves, and most men never knew it was possible.

ADDITIONAL ASPECTS OF THE MASCULINE ESSENCE

I've pointed out that the masculine aspect is about doing and giving,
but there are several other masculine qualities that play supportive
roles, including competitiveness, aggression, and protectiveness.
These are all very much part of the masculine principle, and the way
they are expressed tells us if this aspect is healthy or not. For example, men and women can manifest their masculine energy in healthy
competition, or they can choose the kind of competitive spirit that
gets what it wants or dies trying.

Competition without the wisdom of the feminine to temper it
and guide its course can become all consuming. Without balance,
the competitive spirit can also become addictive. On the positive
side, when the drive to compete is balanced by one's internal feminine aspect, it can become the impetus to raise the bar in ways that
inspire us to do our best.

Aggression is another element of male doing. Aggressive behavior
too is not always negative; you can pursue your goals aggressively to
achieve the outcome you desire. But if that aggressive behavior becomes exclusively directed against other people, then we see the ugly
side of the masculine aspect in play.

A third facet of masculine doing is the desire to provide protection.
When I ask women what they miss most about the old-fashioned
man, the most common answer by far is "protection." Protection can
be enjoyed by a woman who has enough feminine energy to allow a
man's masculine protective instincts to flow toward her without allowing them to control her. Unfortunately, many modern women will
never have this experience. And for their part, young men have not
learned the gallantry that allows a woman to relax into her feminine
aspect without fear of losing her independence.

For a number of decades now, women have developed their masculine protective abilities to the point of feeling they don't need, or want, protection from a man. The truth is that many women don't need it, but it would be a good experience to have if they wanted to establish balance with their feminine aspect. External masculine protection allows the feminine aspect to relax and reconnect with its source. Nothing nurtures a woman so effectively as the surety of masculine protection. If you can have this experience, you can allow yourself to relax your masculine aspect and move deeper into your feminine self. You can sink into a state of true contentment.

On the other side of the equation, a man's happiness is directly proportional to the happiness he is able to deliver to the woman in his life. If he is wise he will choose a woman with the ability to accept and receive his love and protection. Whether you are a woman or a man, the ability to protect carries within it the seeds of leadership. Sovereignty does not come without responsibility. This is particularly evident in these tumultuous times, when the vulnerable are at great risk because society does not take on enough collective responsibility for protecting them.

TAKING INITIATIVE AND PROVIDING DIRECTION

Yet another masculine trait is the ability to take initiative and be directive. In times gone by a woman would never call a man first or approach him for a date. There was a very good reason for this reticent behavior. Allowing a man to take the initiative was a simple way for the woman to test his directive abilities. This process also allowed the man to exercise his masculinity in relation to a woman. If a man cannot take that initiative, then you can rest assured he will lack direction in his own life and in your life together. I'm not suggesting that women take the role of passengers in a relationship. That's not balanced on any level. But what we do see today with internal gender role reversal is that men are now the passengers in many relationships.

If a woman is working outside the home, in order to be effective at her job she has to take initiative, and if she is managing other people, she has to be able to provide direction and demonstrate leadership. When the same process is applied to a man-woman relationship, however, a woman should be able to settle into her feminine essence and allow her partner to step into his masculine aspect. In a balanced relationship the woman will always have equal input into important decisions, but it has been my experience that women value initiative and direction from their men even if they don't always agree with the direction. Many women these days are tired of making all the decisions for their male passenger partners. Later we'll see how much the roles within relationships have reversed, often with unhappy results.

THE CRITICAL NEED TO GIVE AND RECEIVE

The next masculine trait that requires a bit of explanation is the ability to give. We've seen that the feminine aspect is receptive. For a person to be balanced, they need to be able to receive and give freely. This ability is fundamental to our being. When it is unopposed, it allows an easy natural flow between the feminine and the masculine. This process is a loop of energy flowing between the two genders like a figure eight lying on its side, a sign of our infinite potential.

Relationships work best when the feminine aspect in the woman is in receptive mode, encouraging the man to act from his masculine energy and take the initiative. However, when a woman takes the active role and asks a man out, say, this puts the man in a role that draws on his feminine energy. Men conditioned to lean on their feminine aspect are often reluctant to approach the woman. This is one more indication of just how far society has fallen into chaos where the masculine-feminine balance is concerned.

Pressures on women today require them to be far more active with their masculine energy, and this habitual doing is steadily eroding women's ability to be. As it becomes more and more rare for young women to have seen their mothers in a receptive state of being, how will they learn how to take it on themselves? Because of the way life has changed for the modern woman, we can already see several generations of women who have lost much of their feminine aspect. Unless it is stopped, this breakdown of the feminine will keep gathering momentum.

THE LAWS OF ATTRACTION BETWEEN THE SEXES

With four energy states actively at work in intimate relationships, attraction is not a simple matter. Attraction is caused by the principle of polarity, in a process that is exactly the same for same-sex couples as it is for couples of the opposite sex. For example, if you are a male-oriented woman, chances are good that you're going to be far more attracted to a feminine-oriented man than a highly male-oriented man. This is polarity at work. Conversely, a highly feminine man is not going to find a highly feminine woman attractive. The tug of polarity just won't be there. Fortunately, it's possible for polarity to shift within couples, allowing partners who have been together for a long time to still be strongly attracted to each other.

Another reason for a relationship veering off course is that one person within a couple can decide to pursue a path of personal growth while the other refuses to even consider changing. This can and often does spell disaster for the relationship. If one person in the couple changes dramatically, the balance of polarity shifts and the degree of attraction will shift accordingly.

Polarity is responsible for attraction and repulsion on an ongoing basis. We are effectively magnets, drawing to ourselves all the energetic forces and entities that turn up in our world. We also have the power to change and thereby alter what turns up in our energetic field. Thanks to changes in the world over the past six decades, new archetypes for both men and women have sprung into being. We will look at these archetypes and how they play out in terms of relationships.

Just like in a playground, there are always going to be those you would prefer to play with and those you try to avoid. We are naturally drawn to those whose energy is a good match for our own. Relationships are often seen through the lens of opposite attraction. We will see that what is actually at play is a couple's opposing internal energy.

EQUAL BUT DIFFERENT: A NECESSARY COMBINATION

As men and women we were clearly not destined to be the same. If we were, we would have been created as androgynous beings. As females and males our bodies operate in the same basic manner, but we are different. This difference allows us to create new life. In the face of our ability to co-create, it would be ludicrous to assume that we are not equal on every level. The time has come for us to embrace our equality with the full knowledge of who we are. Men and women are equal; we were born that way and we should proceed through life as equals. When we die, we die as equals. Any inequalities, real or perceived, that we have to deal with in our lives are not due to one sex being inferior in any way to the other. Those inequalities have to do with fear and control issues in our society and our upbringing. Whenever anyone uses our differences as an excuse to do harm, it tears at the fabric of society.

I believe that our work as women right now is to accept and believe in our hearts that we are equal to our opposite gender. Posturing and pretending to be men doesn't cut it. And depicting men as villains, or becoming as violent as they have been through the ages just perpetuates the inequality women have had to endure. Behaving as if we are not equal will only widen the chasm between men and women. If war between the sexes keeps escalating, there will be little peace for anyone. Instead, the time has come for women to own the fact that they are different but equal. As women respect themselves more, they gain respect from others. This is a healthy basis for the way forward that will lead to an unprecedented level of equality, allowing relations between the sexes to finally evolve.

PUTTING THIS NEW KNOWLEDGE TO GOOD USE

Having traveled through descriptions of the attributes of the internal masculine and feminine, we can see how these energies work in tandem; it is impossible for one to exist without the other. They are interdependent and interconnected; forming a spiral of energy, they intertwine themselves through men and women alike. The next section of this book gives examples of how these traits work in the real world. You will see how clients of mine have managed to find balance and improve their lives and relationships by embracing this new inner male-female paradigm. Once they created a better balance within their internal masculine and feminine, the change was made manifest in their external lives.

PART
TWO

CHAPTER 5

What's Your Archetype?

SHE SAYS: "WHO DO YOU THINK YOU ARE?"
HE SAYS: "I DON'T KNOW. WHY DON'T YOU TELL ME . . ."

SO JUST HOW MASCULINE OR FEMININE ARE YOU?

Time for a bit of fun before we launch into the specific archetypes! The following quiz will give you an idea of your general level of internal masculine and internal feminine to see which shows up more in your daily life. Please note that this quiz is purely for fun. In real terms, it takes careful thought and analysis to truly determine a person's archetype, and that assessment is best done by a third party who is well studied in each of the archetype personalities and knows how they manifest. It is also true that some people may have aspects of more than one archetype. But for the general reader, I have found that the following questions, when answered as truthfully as possible, will give a quick barometer reading of the extent to which you access your internal masculine and internal feminine essences in your day-to-day activities. The scoring chart follows. Have fun!

TEN QUIZ QUESTIONS

1. *Do you take regular time for relaxation and reflection?*
    A. I find time every day to reflect.
    B. I don't have time for quiet reflection.

C. I make it a point to sit quietly at least once a week to relax and reflect on my life.

D. I don't believe that any kind of meditation or reflection really helps.

2. *You have just heard that a friend has become ill. How do you respond?*

   A. I leave it to the doctors—they know what's best.

   B. I immediately ask if there is anything I can do to help.

   C. I call the friend in a couple of weeks to see if they're okay and feeling better.

   D. I offer to pick up the friend's children from school and deliver a casserole for dinner.

3. *You notice a colleague is being bullied at work; what would you do?*

   A. I do nothing and pretend I haven't noticed. It won't help to get involved.

   B. I take the person aside and offer support, like taking them out to lunch.

   C. I feel compassion for them but I leave them to handle the situation on their own.

   D. I do not hesitate to speak up on their behalf when an opportunity arises.

4. *You are out on a dinner date and the bill arrives. What do you do?*

   A. I pretend the bill hasn't arrived and wait to see what the other person does about it.

   B. I pick the bill up without hesitation and pay the full amount.

   C. I'm ready to pay my portion of the meal but I wait for the other person to take the lead.

   D. I pick the bill up and calculate the exact amount we each owe. I then ask my date for their portion.

5. *You have spotted an attractive person living in your building.*
   You find yourself interested in them. What do you do?
   A. I watch them from afar but never make a move to interact
      with them.
   B. I formulate a plan that allows me to bump into them
      repeatedly, to make them aware of me.
   C. I wait for them to notice me. When they do, I smile
      warmly.
   D. I walk up to them when the opportunity arises and
      introduce myself.

6. *You have been asked out on a date. You like this person, but the*
   person is slow to finalize the arrangements. What do you do?
   A. I don't do anything. I wait for them to call with the
      arrangements.
   B. I call them within a short space of time to clarify the final
      arrangements.
   C. I exercise patience. I don't need to know what, where, and
      when. If they call too late and I've made other plans, they'll
      have to organize another time for our date.
   D. I call the person on the pretext of having to speak to them
      on another matter and then at the last moment ask what
      the details for the date are.

7. *You have changed your hairstyle dramatically and suddenly you are*
   the focus of your social group. When people give you compliments on
   your new look, how do you respond?
   A. I receive the compliments with warm satisfaction.
   B. I say thank you but then immediately make an excuse, like
      "Oh, I just needed a change."
   C. I behave graciously toward anyone who delivers a
      compliment.
   D. I feel embarrassed that my new hairstyle is causing such a
      stir.

8. *Your partner tends to forget to do their chores around the house. What do you do?*

   A. I wait for them to find the time to do their share of the work.

   B. I do their chores, my chores, and anything else that needs to be done around the house.

   C. I leave the situation for a while and notice if they are preoccupied with other more important business. I then ask when I can expect them to do their chores.

   D. I stay on top of it and nag them until they do what they said.

9. *You find yourself being pursued by an unwanted admirer. What do you do?*

   A. I hide around corners whenever I see them coming.

   B. I glare at them aggressively to frighten them off.

   C. I give very clear verbal and nonverbal indications that I really have no interest in their advances.

   D. I tell them firmly and without any hesitation that I'm not interested in them.

10. *You are working too hard. You are fully aware that you're becoming really run down and exhausted. What do you do?*

    A. I start to take time for myself every day, even if it's only thirty minutes of solitude.

    B. I set time aside and book a holiday as soon as possible.

    C. I sign up for a yoga or meditation class.

    D. I just keep going in the hope that I will eventually get on top of my commitments.

HOW TO SCORE YOUR QUIZ ANSWERS

To tally up your score, add up the number of times you answered A or C. This combined score is called your F-Quotient. Then add up the number of times you answered B and or D. This combined number represents your M-Quotient.

If your F-Quotient is between 7 and 10, you tend to operate more from your feminine internal gender than your masculine. The higher this number, the higher your inner polarity is to the feminine; in other words, whether you were born into a male or female body, your natural instinct is to be primarily feminine in your reactions to daily life activities. We will see many examples within the archetype chapters coming up that will give you more insight into how your naturally feminine nature impacts on your daily life and relationships.

If your M-Quotient is between 7 and 10, you tend to operate more from your masculine internal gender than your inner feminine aspect. The higher your M-Quotient, the higher your inner polarity is to the masculine. In other words, your natural instinct is to be primarily masculine in your reactions to daily activities in your life. Remember, this is true whether you were born into a male or female body. How this result manifests within your life will be easier to understand once you delve into the upcoming chapters.

If you scored 4, 5, or 6 in either quotient, it means you have also scored very similarly on the opposite quotient, indicating that you are relatively well balanced with regard to your internal genders. In certain circumstances you will favor your internal feminine side; in other cases you will use your masculine aspect to deal with what life is presenting to you.

In general terms, the more balanced a person is with regard to how they use their two internal genders, the happier and more settled they will be in dealing with daily challenges and in trying to balance the two sets of polarity that come into play when an intimate or interpersonal relationship is formed. The complexity of the give-and-take between two people is very much the subject of this book, particularly how being out of balance affects our lives.

READY TO EXPLORE TODAY'S ARCHETYPES

Now that you have an idea of how masculine or feminine you are with regard to your internal genders, it is time to move into more in-depth discussions about each of the eight archetypes I have researched and documented. Each archetype chapter starts with a case study based on case files, but each personal story is written as a composite. I have combined different aspects and I have made a point to change names, jobs, and life circumstances in order to protect the privacy of these past clients and friends.

So now we know that once women were unleashed from the world of domesticity that had been their ball and chain for centuries, they were free at last. No longer tied to the home, they found themselves free to explore their maleness and participate in masculine pursuits. Not surprisingly, all kinds of women did just that!

Vast numbers of women embraced their new maleness in a way never before seen in human history. Many became fully male in every sense of the word except physically. They became highly male-oriented women who were ambitious, competitive, and even aggressive. Two archetypes are the most highly Andro: the Villainous Andro Woman and her sister, the Virtuous Andro. It is important to note that the other three female archetypes are also masculine oriented, but they are male to varying degrees and have different motivations.

At the same time as the world was changing, with women embracing their new masculinity, men began tapping into their feminine side. In fact, there are huge numbers of men today who are very comfortable with the feminine side of themselves. As mentioned, under my inner male-female paradigm these feminine-orientated men fall under three broad archetypes.

But as more and more men embraced their feminine side so wholeheartedly, the women in their lives found that they had to pick up the masculine slack being created or nothing would get done. So while the Andro sisters entered the male world by choice, the women who were partners of the newly feminized men were forced to enter the male world out of necessity!

The women who picked up the obligations left behind by all the increasingly feminine men found themselves suddenly in charge of keeping all the threads of family life together and working full time as well. I meet this kind of woman over and over in my practice: she is mother, housekeeper, and breadwinner all rolled into one super-slave. I call her the Good Doer. Her archetype is the first we will explore.

These three archetypes don't tell the whole story, however. There is another group of male women who have held on to the very powerful façade of being feminine. They are master manipulators of any man they set their sights on. They look like a woman, they walk like a woman, but unfortunately that is where the analogy ends. In this case you are not dealing with a full-blown feminine being. She is indeed so falsely feminine that I have named her the Faux Feminine Woman.

Then over the last few decades yet another curious female archetype has emerged. She preys on men very much younger than herself. Her motives are unclear; however, I surmise that they are partly revenge: to draw a young, defenseless, inexperienced male into her lair with her experience and charm. Society has named this woman the Cougar; it is the archetype name I have chosen as well.

Once we complete the five female archetypes, stay tuned for the three male archetypes, the first one being the Sensitive Man. He finds that protecting others comes quite naturally for him. He is able to care and feel deeply for others but can also take action when needed. His archetype is under attack, and Sensitive men are not always sure how to act in dating situations, given the amount of confusion between the sexes and the abuse heaped on them by highly masculine Andro women.

The other two male archetypes we will end with are the Highly Feminine Man and the Pseudo Masculine Man. Each one accesses his internal feminine gender in different ways to different ends. Once you understand how to tell one male archetype from another, the chances of finding the right match for a work associate, a friend, or an intimate partner will be much higher.

So just to be very clear: all our female categories have some degree of masculine orientation, and our male types tap into their feminine side to varying degrees. Polarity and the laws of attraction between the sexes bring them together, and any one of our masculine women could be attracted to any one of the feminine male archetypes.

The best way to understand these complexities is to peek into the lives of our various archetypes as they go about their daily lives. So let's jump into our first case study and see what the life of the Good Doer is like these days.

CHAPTER 6

The Good Doer

SHE SAYS: "I CAN TAKE CARE OF MYSELF, YOU KNOW."

HE SAYS: "GREAT. COULD YOU TAKE CARE OF ME TOO?"

MEETING DEBORAH: RUNNING ON EMPTY

When Deborah, an acclaimed restaurateur, stepped into my office she was noticeably harried, and I detected that she was running on empty. Her business was a success, but she was at the end of her tether after many years of sustained stress. At home she had two teenage daughters who were starting to push their boundaries to the limit. Yet Deborah did not realize she was under enormous stress. She seemed to think her lifestyle was normal.

I greeted her warmly the day we first met in my office. As I invited her in, I began as I usually do: "How can I help?" She sat down on the large sofa but remained perched on the end of the seat. "Please make yourself comfortable, Deborah. We have ninety minutes together and I want you to feel relaxed and at ease."

Reluctantly she settled deeper into the sofa and placed her handbag on the floor. As with so many clients, I noticed a change in her breathing. I knew she was becoming a little more settled. I turned on some very gentle meditation-type music and within moments, Deborah began to cry.

A TIME FOR TEARS

I let her cry as I sat and held the space for her to release whatever it was she needed to let go of in this way. She started apologizing, clearly embarrassed at her unexpected show of emotion. It was not unexpected for me; this was part and parcel of a normal day's work. I kept my eyes averted to avoid causing her any further discomfort and offered her a small cup of green tea. She took it gratefully and began to sip. She started to calm down.

"Well," she said, "I didn't come here to cry. I'm sure you don't want to be dealing with some kind of blubbering client, now do you?"

"Actually, I'm very happy for my clients to cry—we do that here all the time," I explained gently. "Many of my clients view my office as a sanctuary where they can do just that."

Again she was visibly taken aback and she offered me yet another apology. "I just feel it is most inappropriate for me to howl on our first meeting, quite unprofessional in fact."

These few interactions had already given me a clue to the type of woman I was dealing with that afternoon. It was clear that people went to Deborah to cry; she was definitely not used to being the one crying. Deborah did not realize how much she was telling me by her actions and her responses. She was quite probably a Good Doer.

When Deborah commented that she found the room quite peaceful, I explained that I tried to keep the space that way because clients seemed to really appreciate a safe and quiet place to unwind and sort out their thoughts. She accepted this, but I could tell she was not used to being nurtured.

Like so many Good Doers, Deborah was having a difficult time just stepping into the space and being at ease. She was struggling to take any time at all away from her working day to "talk about my-self" as she described it, and she confessed that she felt guilty at this self-indulgent behavior. None of her responses were new to me. I briefly outlined the benefits she could expect from the time she spent with me. I guaranteed her that the bottom line of her business would improve if she took the time to look after herself.

I had come well recommended to her, so she already seemed to have a good deal of trust in me. She settled into the session and we discussed her perceived goals. She became more content when we discussed the benefits for the business—that sold her—but she was still a bit reticent when she realized that to work successfully with me would mean being prepared to transform some parts of herself along the way.

THE GOOD DOER WILL ALWAYS GET IT DONE

True to form, Deborah turned out to be a trooper. I had no doubt she would be conscientious and follow through with her commitment to the process, because Good Doers do what they need to do. They are highly focused on how they affect the lives of others, and for Deborah that meant she always considered other people first: her business partners, staff members, clients, children, and now me.

As we spent the rest of the first session outlining her goals for her program, she kept them rather businesslike and I understood that she needed to feel this was not going to be a self-indulgent exercise. She did ask one personal question though, which surprised me for a first encounter with this type of woman. "Do you think this will help my exhaustion? I've been to the doctor and he ran a number of tests but he couldn't find anything wrong with me."

If I had had any doubt whatsoever of who this wonderful woman was, I knew now. "I'm confident that if you don't have any underlying medical conditions, we'll be able to get you and your life into balance," I assured her. "Once we have that, your exhaustion will dissipate." With that, Deborah had taken the first step of a journey we would share for the next eighteen months.

As I fully expected, Deborah returned the following week with her homework in hand. She followed her new ritual of making herself comfortable with a small cup of green tea, repeating this protocol readily after just one session.

"I was looking forward to the music," she said as she settled into the sofa. Once the music was on, her breathing relaxed. We lost no time; she was clearly ready for the change she hoped the program would bring.

Her eagerness to begin the second session was rewarding, to say the least. Deborah had lost her apprehension; somehow her guilt had lessened. Then I realized that because I had asked her to complete a significant amount of "homework," she felt assured that she was not being self-indulgent. Everything in her life took effort and she never shirked a responsibility. She was working toward something and it required effort; once there was effort involved, she was comfortable.

TAKING HOLD OF ONE'S TRANSFORMATION

Deborah had revisited her doctor as I had asked. He was happy to reassure her that he could find nothing wrong with her health. She was in fair shape and she was given the go-ahead to proceed with her program with me. Tick that box.

She had her homework completed. Tick that box.

Now she was able to concentrate because she had completed her allotted tasks and followed through with her responsibility to get them done. She had written at least twenty pages in her journal and covered all the topics I had requested. I had not seen such a diligent client in a very long time! Deborah was a machine. For a woman who was supposed to be exhausted, her zeal was nothing short of exceptional.

As part of the homework, I had asked her to give me a rundown of her activities and tasks for the past week. She had co-opted her diary to her journal and, between the two books, I was amazed at the schedule this woman undertook on a weekly and day-to-day basis. Besides the commitments to her children's school, their extracurricular activities, an extremely active business, and attending to demanding clients, Deborah also carefully watched over her aging parents. I thought to myself, This woman is the quintessential superwoman. I was worried but did not allow her to see my concern.

Instead I gently asked her, "Deborah, of all these commitments you have on a weekly basis, which ones can you dispense with?"

"None," she responded.

"Deborah, we have to clear your schedule. There are just too many commitments for you to keep, as well as your new commitment to yourself."

She quickly pointed out, "But I did all the homework you requested. I managed to fit it in along with all the other activities on my schedule."

"Yes, you're an extraordinary woman. I have not seen this kind of commitment in a long while. But the key phrase here is that you had *to fit yourself in*. Do you realize what you're saying? You have *to fit yourself into your own life!*"

I could see the disappointment on her face. I could sense that on some level she felt she had let me down, and of course she hadn't. This was her response to yet another task being loaded onto her already extended schedule. She would not say no to another commitment; she would simply reorganize her calendar to accommodate the extra task.

COMING TO TERMS WITH THE *DOING*

Deborah was definitely on the high end of the spectrum for a Good Doer. From an internal perspective she was out of control and out of balance, but she certainly had all her external duties, tasks, appointments, and commitments well and truly under control.

I thought to myself, Her levels of stress must surely be intolerable. But somehow Deborah's sense of duty, her compulsion to *do*, and her inability to ever say no to anyone were phenomenal. I realized I was going to have to be very sensitive and gentle with Deborah and slowly reveal to her the dangerous precipice she was on due to her extreme level of overcommitment.

"Deborah, you are going to have to clear a few of these commitments off your calendar for next week."

"Why?" she responded.

I explained that she needed to have the time to relax and do things she might have wanted to do but just never had the time for. "This is an exercise to wean you off the habit of the constant activity you appear to be so addicted to."

She was suddenly defensive. "I'm not addicted to doing all these things. It's just, if I don't do them, then who will?"

This was a common refrain I had heard many times from Good Doers, and I responded in my usual way. "I think you'll discover that if you pull out of these commitments, someone else will fill the vacuum you create. Someone else will step up to do those tasks, and hopefully they will enjoy doing them. How does that make you feel?"

"Redundant," she replied.

I nudged her a bit, asking how that would make her feel, having someone else fulfill her perceived obligations.

"Not good, frankly," she said. "I'll feel as if I'm slacking off. I'll more than likely feel guilty and useless."

So I put the request back into positive terms. "Then our job is to get you to clear things off your calendar and not feel as if you've let anyone down, or feel that you've given up your place in the world. The fact is that you're taking on a number of responsibilities that are not yours to take on. It is a type of arrogance to believe you're the only one who can perform all these tasks. In my opinion, it's a form of control."

With that, a deathly silence emanated from the sofa.

THE TRUTH REVEALED

We sat in silence for a while. This had clearly been a huge revelation for Deborah. She needed some space to digest what she had just realized: surely this was the basis of her exhaustion and fatigue. I offered her yet another small cup of tea, which she accepted gratefully. She sipped. We sat together like two companionable cats, in the comfort of silence, knowing that from this new realization would come the space for transformation.

The truth is that the Good Doer Woman can be a wonderfully kind person. She is also resourceful and can be an astute problem solver, but all these abilities often work against her when she ends up solving everyone else's problems on top of her own workload. She tends to have an amazing capacity for work but lacks the ability to say no. This leads her into areas that are not really her concern; she takes on things that should not be her responsibility.

This is a key issue that this type of woman must learn to master: leaving other people's responsibilities firmly with them. There is very good reason for this thinking. If you do not take care of yourself first, you end up with less industrious people making use of your good nature. Deborah's compulsion *to do* had to be brought to her attention so she could begin to take care of herself and slow the internal ever-spinning wheel that seemed to terrorize her into nonstop activity.

GETTING BACK IN TOUCH WITH THE BODY

Over the next few months Deborah started to see how she consistently overrode the wisdom of her body. Together we were able to stop the process that would most likely lead her down a path to illness or complete burnout. She finally began to realize that she had to change the way she was living her life. Before our program together, she had treated her body as if it were an enemy to be ignored or overridden if it complained. Over time Deborah learned to use her body as her barometer and began to relate to it as her friend. So now if she felt tired, she would change her shifts. If she felt overwhelmed, she divested herself of commitments that were not a priority.

In fact, she became a master of prioritizing. Deborah had come a very long way in nine months. She had lost weight, trimmed her commitments down to a manageable level, and learned to delegate housework and the many chores at home to her more than capable teenage daughters. Most importantly, she had learned that when she was prioritizing her week she had to put herself in the frame first. Then everything fell into line after her commitments to herself. I was very proud of her transformation. She even started going out socially with friends.

DIVING BACK INTO DATING

Now that Deborah had more space in her life, she was not prepared for the feelings of emptiness that emerged. "Before when I was so busy, I never had a moment to think," she told me. "Now that I have time to contemplate, to meditate, it's bringing up some really strange sensations."

"Like what?" I asked.

She said a little shyly, "I feel lonely for companionship and I haven't felt that way since John and I split up."

Divorced for ten years, Deborah had never felt she had the time or the inclination to pursue another relationship. During that time she felt that a relationship would just mean more work for her, another commitment for her to fit into her already crowded calendar. This was another breakthrough point, so I explored it with her. "Do you mind if I ask what manner of man John was?"

She bluntly answered, "Well, not a very nice one actually. I realize, now that I've become so much more focused on myself, that he didn't respect me at all during our marriage. He was just like everyone else. He loaded me up with responsibilities that were rightfully his to shoulder."

"Does he shoulder that responsibility with the girls now? Has he changed since your divorce?" I asked, but she said no, he hadn't. I sensed this could present an ongoing issue and repeat itself in a new relationship, so I explained my concerns to her.

"Deborah, as we've discussed previously, we need to stabilize you and make sure that your feminine self is solid enough to get back into dating. You need to be very clear about what you will and will not put up with from a future companion."

She nodded in agreement. "I don't want another relationship like the one I shared with John."

I continued my train of thought. "I know this might sound a bit clinical and not very romantic at all, but you're the type of woman who is vulnerable to men who would prefer not to work hard at things. That could mean working at the relationship or just being industrious in their daily activities."

She said she was aware of that now but she was still a bit worried. "How do I determine if I'm getting involved with the wrong type of man? I don't want to retrace my steps down my sad history in relationships. You know, I always seemed to end up doing all the work and taking all the responsibility."

HOW POLARITY POINTS US IN CERTAIN DIRECTIONS

I explained to Deborah that up to now she seemed to have a history of attracting Highly Feminine men or Pseudo Masculine men into her life, two of the male archetypes we will cover in subsequent chapters. You will learn all about them and how to recognize them, but for now picture these men as exhibiting more feminine traits than masculine; that was what she was drawing to her. I told Deborah that there was nothing really wrong with her, that through our energy we tend to attract people into our lives who are a perfect match to our own internal imbalances. Unless we are aware of who we are energetically, and work hard to keep our internal energy in balance, we will keep repeating the same pattern.

For most of her life Deborah was a *doer*, a masculine trait, so the men she attracted were just the opposite: they were feminine in their internal nature, more thinkers than doers. This is the law of polarity, the other concept that comes up and impacts us in our interpersonal and intimate relationships. Because of our work together over the past year, Deborah was starting to get it.

"I understand what I've been doing and I'm so much better at recognizing when I'm being taken advantage of now, but how will I know if the new men I'm meeting are sincere or not with their intentions?"

I said that the onus really fell on her to keep her eyes wide open and make those distinctions early in the relationship. She had more information now, and she was not the type of person to lose the ground she had just established for herself. "The litmus test for you, Deborah, will be if you're with a man and you start to feel the compulsion to do everything for him. Then you'll know you're getting back into trouble."

"Can that still happen?" she asked, kind of shocked.

"Oh yes, it can," I told her firmly. "We don't get rid of our natural predisposition to our predominant polarity that easily. You've been acting from your masculine for many years—overdoing things, overdoing for others. You'll have to be vigilant for a long while, particularly when you're entering a new relationship."

I explained that dating can be quite a vulnerable time. "When we're single, living by ourselves, we have a lot more control over our internal genders and therefore our polarity. We can change our behavior and that will ultimately change our polarity. We can manage our energy very well since it's only just ourselves: one single person. I find this is particularly true with women when they start to reconnect with their feminine after a long absence from that connection."

I reminded her that we are energy first. "So now imagine that a new man comes into your life. He brings with him his energy and his polarity. Think about how a magnet works: opposite poles have a strong attraction and like poles repel each other. Well, it's the same thing that happens between people in a relationship."

She nodded and fed back to me her understanding of all this. "So you're saying that when a man enters my life, his energy will affect my energy, and if I'm not conscious of what's happening I could fall into my old way of being? If he's really kind of feminine and I'm not careful, he can get me to fall back into using too much of my masculine energy all the time, and I'll get out of balance again. Oh, I really don't want that. That would be awful."

KEEPING ON A BALANCED COURSE

I assured her that this was not all bad news. I just felt that we needed to have this conversation because she was so much on the high end of the spectrum of *doing*, which had so strongly polarized her into using her masculine energy for so many years. Because of that strong natural polarization, she would still be vulnerable to feminine-oriented men if she was not careful.

Deborah was so typical of this kind of masculine woman. She would so willingly take on responsibilities that were not hers in the hope of alleviating the other person's load, or the perception that she was doing the right thing. The problem with this behavior was that she ended up living her life for other people.

So what happens to her unlived life? My experience shows that the Good Doer is so used to living only part of a life that she does not know how to take the first steps off the path. Her habit of rescuing others from both themselves and their responsibilities leaves her feeling burdened by guilt if she dares to put herself first. But to break the cycle, and for her own health, she must begin to shift her priorities.

FIRST STEPS TO RECONNECTING WITH YOUR FEMININE

If you identify yourself as a Good Doer and you would like to start to make changes in your life, you will need to become really present to yourself first. This might be an extremely alien concept for you, but that is the process.

With almost every task you undertake you are going to have to make a conscious evaluation of whether this is a priority for *you*, or if it's a priority for someone else and they have managed to engage you in their process. So whenever someone asks you to take on something new at home, at work, in your family, or your community ask yourself, What's my motivation for taking on this task? Is there anyone else who can do it? Do I think no one else is capable of doing what needs to be done? Am I rescuing this person for their good or my own need to feel valuable? When you answer these questions honestly you can determine if you are living your life for yourself first or for others first. You will come to understand that your value is intrinsic simply because you exist, and you will no longer feel so compelled to constantly be doing for others.

Be aware that you might encounter enormous resistance within yourself when you first start this practice. You might find belief systems emerging in your consciousness that you were not aware of before you started your transformation. This is not unusual. These beliefs could be yours or if you think about it, perhaps they came from your mother, or even a grandmother.

Within our family units, core beliefs can travel down to us in ways we don't realize and we unwittingly embrace them as our own. When you notice this happening, do not take the process lightly. These beliefs might constitute a whole system that forms part of your cultural heritage or it might just be a familial belief system that functions within your family. Be considerate of your past. It has brought you to where you are now. However, the person you are now is probably a very good person; and you live in a very different society, a more modern society, than your ancestors did. You have choices and you are more aware of the cost of ignoring yourself and your health.

DEALING WITH ANGER

The process of change in our modern times is a delicate one that requires patience and diligence. Many people in your life have gotten used to depositing their responsibilities on your doorstep and now it is time to return them. Anger will more than likely emerge within you as you start to divest yourself of many unnecessary tasks: things you did every day that were never your duty in the first place. It is natural to want to project that anger onto those who loaded you up with unnecessary responsibility but the question to ask is, Am I angry with them or with myself for not taking responsibility for my own life? Remember that they only did what you allowed them to do.

Don't be surprised if you realize that you are angrier with yourself than with anyone else. It is crucial that you are not too hard on yourself at this stage. You did not know any better and now you do. Celebrate your new knowledge and awareness and commit to a change for the better.

When anger does emerge, the time has come for the greatest healer of all: forgiveness. Forgiving yourself is one of the greatest gifts you could ever offer yourself for your personal healing. The truth is that Good Doers are incredibly hard on themselves. The high art of self-forgiveness will allow you to surrender to something beyond yourself. When you do this, you will find that the negative thoughts from your past and about yourself now have an opportunity to dissolve under grace.

TAKING TIME TO BREATHE

Because Good Doers do not stop doing, it is wise to have a practice that ensures you give yourself time to breathe and come to a quiet place within yourself. Your body needs an opportunity to come into this quietude. Breathing practices are very helpful for keeping in touch with the body. You could also join a yoga group and enjoy the peace and quiet of that practice. As your meditative practice grows and you try to take some personal time each day, your body will calm down and slowly you will become more and more aware of your body's wisdom.

If you continue a yoga practice, tai chi, meditation, or some kind of exercise that takes you inward on a regular basis, two great things will happen. First, your inner wisdom will start to emerge. Second, you and your body will start to work together for your greater good instead of letting your actions override your body and its warning signs. Before long you will arrive at a very nice partnership with yourself and find the balance that was lacking in your previously hectic life.

As a balanced person, using both your feminine and masculine aspects in right order, you can then attract a partner who is also balanced. Your feminine will be at a higher level, so that the man you meet can be more masculine. That way you will share the thinking and the doing, the giving and receiving, and together as a couple you will be better able to ride out the ebbs and flows that are a natural part of our day-to-day relationships.

As you have witnessed, the Good Doer is one of life's good people. She is well versed in the art of self-sacrifice. She does it effortlessly, but she still has to work hard to look after herself. She is the antithesis of the next woman we are about to meet.

CHAPTER 7

The Villainous Andro Woman

SHE SAYS: "YOU *MUST* DO WHAT I TELL YOU."
HE SAYS: "YES, SIR!"

CASE STUDY: ROXANNE

As I read through my presession notes on Roxanne, I found myself sighing. She had written introductory notes and sent them to me ahead of time so I could determine whether we were suited to each other, and if I could help her achieve what she wanted out of life. In the email she'd sent she said she had everything materially she wanted in life but that it was time she had a man, a home, and a baby. Concise writing, no messing around, as if she could just pick up these things at the local supermarket.

I caught myself wondering why I felt so sad. I had seen so many women like Roxanne in the past ten years. In fact, I have found it to be quite a common story of women in their late thirties or early forties who find themselves in crisis and don't understand the full impact of what that crisis could mean. I knew her situation could have a serious impact on the rest of her life if it was not handled with care. I realized that I was sighing because the issues she was describing were endemic and I knew that if Roxanne and I were to journey together through my coaching practice, we could be in for quite a bumpy ride.

Roxanne turned up for the appointment right on time and she brought the same no-nonsense attitude I had seen in her emails. She was a tall woman in a very smart suit and extremely high heels, a clear sign that she wanted to give the impression that she was in control of all situations in her life.

"Roxanne, it's very nice to meet you," I said as she entered. She put out her hand to shake mine. I was not expecting her to be anything other than highly male in her attitude and, true to form, she launched right in.

"Well, I was glad that you had a cancellation and I could see you earlier than you first said. You see, I'm on a mission now to get this thing sorted out."

I was not at all surprised at her stance. She wanted to resolve this matter as quickly as possible. She appeared to approach her personal life almost as if it were a file on her desk that had to be handled then put in the out box.

And Baby Makes Two!

"So, Roxanne, shall we get started?" This was all I had to say. Roxanne did not hesitate.

"Well, I'm thirty-eight years old and I've achieved what I want to achieve, mostly. There's always more, of course, but I've come to realize that if I don't have a baby quite soon, I could be in danger of having a very lonely old age." Just like that. Her rationale was on the table.

I responded in the same direct way. "Okay, Roxanne. First then, I'd like to clarify your motivations for wanting to have a baby. You say that you're facing a lonely old age. Is that a good enough reason for wanting a child? The reason for my question is that I think it's important to establish sound reasons for asking for what you want. Aren't children precious in our lives for their own sake and not just as an alternative purpose of the parent? It's just a thought that I would like to put out there."

She saw my point and knew her answer. "I have thought about that but I want a child. If I don't have a father for the child, then I'm willing to have one on my own. I'm financially secure and I don't care if there isn't a father."

I was starting to get a little exasperated with this rhetoric because I had heard it many times before. "Roxanne, forgive me, but I'm going to pose another question for clarification. Is it in the interests of the child to arrive into the world without knowledge of his or her father? Don't you think that it might be important for the child to believe it's loved by both a mother and a father?"

This brought a very quick retort from Roxanne: "No, I don't. I think that's very old-fashioned. Everyone's resorting to this way of conceiving now if there aren't any men around."

"Everyone?" I asked. "Don't you think that's quite a leap?"

She moved on with the relentlessness of a bulldozer. "I don't care. Anyway, I'm used to getting what I want and now I want a baby."

I could see that she was single-minded in her pursuit, so I changed directions slightly. "I hear you, Roxanne, but before we get to the baby, let's back up and discuss a relationship. I'm going to make an assumption here that all things being equal, you would prefer to have a father for your future child."

"Yes, of course," she agreed. "It's just that I'm having a lot of difficulty finding a man I want."

What Lies Beneath the Sadness

My questions were designed to get to the bottom of this high Andro Woman's motivations. So far they were tracking the way I would expect them to. Roxanne was particularly direct and without any guile at all. She was also quite impatient, as if she expected me to give her everything she wanted in our first session. From my end, I was not even clear that I wanted to proceed with a program for her. If it weren't for the underlying sadness and desperation I heard in her voice, I would have told her we were not suited to each other.

But I was pretty sure that beneath her tough Andro exterior there was a small lost girl who was so lonely and so desolate that she just wanted something or someone to fill the void. She had little capacity or understanding to help herself. I decided that compassion was the road to travel, so I continued. I wanted to help Roxanne find a purpose for herself first rather than looking for it outside herself. Extreme loneliness seemed to be motivating her to *do* something, and that something was manifesting itself as a desire for a child. But before moving ahead, I needed to know more about the woman behind this tough, almost rough, exterior.

"Roxanne, just talk to me about yourself. Start anywhere and don't hold back. Whatever comes into your mind, just let it out."

She did not hesitate. "Well, you might as well know that I'm an alpha female. My mother and her mother were too, and so that's who I am. I like the way I am because I take no prisoners and I'm used to getting what I want. I'm a lawyer and have risen up the ranks of my firm and I'm now a partner. I've achieved almost everything I've ever set out to achieve in my life."

She hesitated for a moment and I took the opportunity to interject. "Would it be fair to say, Roxanne, that you've achieved everything materially and careerwise but not necessarily in your emotional life?"

She responded in a mildly irritated fashion. "I guess you could say that, but I think I've just been unlucky in love. I'm not sure I even believe in love, so that's why I want a baby more than anything. I want a baby more than I want a partner."

I don't think Roxanne realized how blunt she was in delivering this information. Nor do I think she realized how callous she was when she referred to relationships and the possibility of having a child. I let it go and allowed her to continue her story about herself.

Climbing the Ladder of Success

There had been twists and turns throughout her career. Bosses she had had liaisons with and colleagues who had been removed because they were in her way. She meandered through the maze of her rise to the top of the legal profession without so much as the blink of an eye. All of her corporate assassinations were laid bare; she did not appear to have any regrets whatsoever about her career path and what I thought was a rather dubious rise to the top.

None of the tactics she described were unusual or surprising to me. I had heard and experienced them all before. The rise to the top of her profession for an Andro Woman is apt to leave bodies by the side of the road. Roxanne continued regaling me with her achievements. She owned a wonderful home, enjoyed exotic holidays, and drove an expensive car that she believed was befitting of her station within a prestigious law firm.

Roxanne had strong opinions about most things and was very forthright as she announced one of those opinions. It felt like a direct order that had to be obeyed or else there would be consequences; I felt quite sure I would be the one feeling those consequences.

"I want an alpha male. I'm an alpha female and as such I deserve an alpha male partner. I don't want anything less. You have to tell me how to get one of those men."

This pronouncement was almost too much. "Roxanne, I think we need to clarify a few things before we continue," I told her firmly. "I don't help you 'get' anyone. I only work with you. I'm not a matchmaking agency and I'm only interested in your reaching the potential you want to reach. I would never involve you or myself in any actions that would trespass on another person's rights."

I wanted this next point to be crystal clear to her, so I spoke a bit more strongly. "What that means is that we do not manipulate anything or anyone so you can achieve what you wish to achieve. Please understand that this is a critical condition of what I do. We need to be clear that you're on board with that process. This process is all about *you* and only you."

I let this sink in and we had a few moments of silence. Then the analytical Roxanne was back. "Well, that's interesting. How do you do that? Frankly, I would not have a clue. I'm used to moving people around so that I get the outcomes I want."

"Well, that's not the way I work. Shall we continue?" I asked.

All of a sudden, she appeared to be quite enthusiastic and hopeful. She wanted to know how we could work so that she could attract a different kind of life. I think the concept was so intriguing to Roxanne because her entire life and the successes she'd enjoyed had all involved getting what she wanted at the expense of someone else. I don't think that before this point Roxanne had ever given those other people another thought. In fact, it became obvious to me that she had no notion that one could achieve one's goals without hurting other people. That was not the kind of thinking she was familiar with and it was not part of her experience at all. She had no understanding whatsoever of what life could be like without the element of manipulation. Manipulation had always been the major tool in her toolkit. I saw it that first day and it was revealed to me over and over again as we worked together over the next few months.

Is This All There Is?

The truth was that on paper Roxanne had a good life. She had a life of achievement and outward material success. But inside she felt empty and desolate, and she was looking down the barrel of a life as barren as the Sahara Desert as she aged. She was astute enough to realize that if she did not change her course, and change it quickly, her advancing years and the ticking of her biological clock would bring only more of the acute loneliness she was beginning to feel. The possibility of a melancholy lonely old age was looming and had every probability of becoming a reality.

I had assumed correctly when I read her first notes that if she could not find a man to be with her, then she would want a child to guarantee someone in her life as she aged. This is a very sad reality that faces many an Andro Woman because they spend so much time on their careers, flexing their masculine muscles with little regard to their emotional lives. Andro women could find solace through their feminine aspect, but they are so severely imbalanced that they don't know where to begin. Their internal imbalance almost guarantees desolation and loneliness as Andro women get older.

"Roxanne, let's take a look at the possibility of your attracting an appropriate partner into your life. I gather from what you've told me that the men in your past were not suitable. I'm sure you have some ideas why those relationships did not work out?"

Sure enough, she had a litany of reasons. "Oh yes, one unsuitable man after another," she began. "I got sick and tired of even considering another relationship. I did have a very long-term affair with a colleague, but of course he was married and he never did leave his wife. Typical. He was the managing partner of our firm. He was, however, very helpful with my success at the firm. But now I'm thirty-eight and I need a child."

I took no notice of her constant reference to her desire for a child and plowed on with my questioning. I thought I would return to another concept she had mentioned earlier.

"Roxanne, why do you use the terms *alpha female* and *alpha male?* I find it intriguing. I know it's popular terminology, but I think it's important to get clear on what they actually mean in terms of the work I do. This kind of jargon often starts on the Internet and then takes on a life of its own. A lot of these expressions aren't even accurate or helpful, and sometimes they serve to set a person up for disappointment. I wonder if maybe your thinking on this matter is why you haven't found the right partner."

She looked at me a little quizzically and explained her point of view. "Well I'm a go-getter and I get what I want. I don't like wimpy people and I certainly don't hang out with 'girly-girls.' I want a man who's alpha because I deserve that kind of man."

Getting Stuck on the Terminology

I could see that we were going to be there for a while as I explained another way of partnering to Roxanne. This explanation was going to be a long way out of her comfort zone and I would not have been at all surprised if she walked out of my office, never to return.

"Roxanne, in my opinion, the term alpha male doesn't really apply to modern-day couples. If we look at the animal kingdom, where the term originates, a pride of lions has an alpha male as the head of the pride. No other lion within that pride would have the temerity to disrespect the alpha male.

"The alpha male will choose an alpha female to be his partner," I continued. "She is chosen because she is strong and can support him in his job of looking after the pride. He is the protector and the lion that gives direction to the pride. These are core masculine traits and they are valid for human beings as well as the animal kingdom."

At this point I took the example back to her life. "My question to you is, Are you prepared to be the support person in a relationship?

Are you prepared to support your alpha male in his quest of protecting and giving direction to the pride?"

She looked at me as if I had taken leave of my senses and quickly set me straight. "No, I'm not. That's crazy talk. I'm used to being top dog in my world and I'm not about to be somebody else's helpmate."

I had clarity. I had the answer I was looking for. She had delivered it to me in no uncertain terms.

Polarity Doesn't Lie

"Well, indulge me and let me explain the very simple process of polarity." I went to the white board and proceeded to draw the four energies at play within the two people in any given relationship. I chose to use Roxanne's polarity as the example for the woman in the drawing. I drew a little gingerbread woman with a line down the center of her body.

At the top of the image I put a large *M* for masculine and small *f* for feminine. "That's what you look like from an energetic perspective, Roxanne. If you could actually see your energy, that's what it would look like."

She wasn't sure she understood: "You mean I'm more masculine than feminine? How can that be? I'm a woman, after all."

"You might be a woman but you're dominating out of your masculine energy," I explained. "You're also a very dominant personality. Do you think a true alpha male would be attracted to you with the high-level masculine energy you're carrying at this time? Answer off the top of your head, Roxanne—don't think about it."

"I guess not," she said sullenly.

I went back to the white board and next to the gingerbread woman I drew a gingerbread man with a line down his center. At the top I put a large *F* for feminine and a small *m* for masculine and informed Roxanne that this was the partner she was actually destined to attract. It simply could not work any other way. That's how polarity works: you attract the opposite of your dominant pole. Polarity never lies.

We talked about this concept for quite some time, because it was so new to her. Roxanne had developed her masculine energy to such high level that the only man who would have any interest in her would be one with a highly feminine orientation. Attraction follows the rules, whether we are aware of them or not, and whether we like it or not. So Roxanne's dream of mating with a highly masculine alpha male was just that: a dream. There could be no attraction of masculine to masculine and that is just the way it was.

An Alternative Type of Relationship

Roxanne was devastated by this news. She seemed pretty sure she was entitled to an alpha male, but she had never taken into account what an alpha male might want in his choice of partner. She was arrogant and stubborn on this matter, seeing it only from her own perspective. It was abundantly clear to me that she had little ability to take another person's desires, wants, and views into account. She was so self-centered that another's needs just didn't factor into the picture she imagined for herself.

Without her realizing it, this was yet another key indicator that Roxanne would be much happier with a man who would do her bidding at all times and not present her with any opposition. I could see that a more feminine man might be a wonderful partner for her. He would enjoy the fact that she would take the lion's share of responsibility for their lives while he assumed only a small portion of it. Roxanne could call the shots and he could follow up with whatever she required. In other words, he would not have to take the initiative or the lead. She would issue the directions and he could be her helper and second in command. When I pointed out this possible relationship to Roxanne, she was shocked, dismayed, and a little confused.

She sat silently on the sofa, not saying a word for a couple of moments. I had delivered an unexpected blow. The reality was that her inability to find a successful relationship was the result of looking in all the wrong places. She thought she wanted a so-called alpha male and she had found that very man on quite a few occasions, but he had always tired of her. Not to mention that she soon found him far too domineering for her own tastes.

From what she told me, those relationships ended by mutual agreement each time. She had never understood why these men had tired of her or why they had become so vexing to her, particularly after she had gotten what she wanted from them. And she had gotten many different things from these powerful men whom she had dated: promotions to the next level, seats on this or that prestigious board, access to private clubs. Her desires for things that would help her in her upward trajectory were quite numerous. But in the end, each relationship petered out without any viable explanation. I could see her mind ticking along, putting what I said in perspective.

"So in a nutshell, what you're saying to me is that I'm the alpha male in a female body and I actually need an alpha female in a male body?"

I smiled with delight that she had found a sense of humor about this rather bad news. "Roxanne, that is so insightful, and it's true. Your preferred partner would be an alpha female housed in a masculine body."

Rethinking What Is Possible

She might have been right but she didn't like it one bit. "I thought it would be the simplest thing in the world to get the man of my dreams. I thought it had not materialized for me because I hadn't focused on it properly and hadn't given the process more attention, that's all. Now I have what sounds like the answer. It certainly explains the lack of success I've had in love." She fell silent once again.

The penny had dropped and she knew now that she was responsible for the state of her emotional life. If she wanted a different outcome, she was going to have to be prepared to either change herself dramatically or accept herself wholeheartedly and be happy with a more feminine type of man than she had envisaged for herself.

My feeling was that Roxanne's masculine traits were so deeply entrenched that it would be asking an awful lot of her to make the complete switch required for her to attract her dream version of the alpha male. Her best course of action was to accept herself, and maybe softening some rough edges would enable her to move closer to her feminine pole without forsaking all the strong masculine traits she was so heavily invested in. If Roxanne could achieve even a small shift toward her internal feminine aspect, then the man that she would eventually partner with would be able to occupy at least some of the masculine space within the relationship.

I took a chance and posed the next logical question. "Would an alpha feminine male partner be so bad? He would probably be an exceptional man, and if you're prepared to make certain changes to your own masculine ways, perhaps a small internal shift, then it could be a very good partnership. I think the key here, Roxanne, is that you're going to have to give a little to gain a workable and balanced relationship."

I invited her to stay a while longer and we ended the session enjoying some tea together. She was clearly in a state of realization. She was starting to see her life very differently, and the new information we had just shared was clearly altering her awareness. As we sipped our tea I could see the stress visibly disappearing from her face. She looked quite different compared to the tension-ridden woman who had shown up a couple of hours earlier.

Agreeing to Start the Process of Change

Introspection and contemplation were new processes for Roxanne; she was, after all, a person of action. I wasn't sure what she would decide to do. She said that although our first session had been more revealing than she expected, she was somewhat relieved that she could rethink her situation from a different perspective. I was really surprised when she announced that she would like to continue the program. We discussed that no matter what the outcome of her program, there could be no guarantee that she would find the man she envisioned or indeed even have a child. But she made an astonishing observation.

"I need this program. I can see that I've been living a life well and truly out of balance. What saddens me is that I don't even think it was the life I wanted or that I would've chosen for myself. I was trained and molded into being a lawyer without realizing what was happening. This is my chance to review my life, and I think I really need to do that from a new point of view."

My instincts at the beginning of our session had been correct and I was so glad that I had not dismissed Roxanne as a high end of the spectrum male woman for whom there was little hope.

Fear of Discovery

The program I set up for Roxanne focused on her finding her feminine self, and as she progressed she became much more introspective. She even developed a new habit of questioning her motives for almost all her actions, which I felt was incredibly courageous on her part. I found her bravery at implementing new ways quite heartening. She didn't complain and she developed a sense of humor when she looked back over many of her former traits. Roxanne began to discover a part of herself she was not aware she had, and she was finding the path of discovery quite exciting, even exhilarating at times.

As our weeks together progressed, Roxanne generously allowed cracks to appear in her otherwise perfect but brittle exterior. She started to *feel* herself and face her emotions rather than hiding behind the mask she had so expertly crafted over the years. It was so well crafted that it had in effect taken her over, and in the process she had lost a very vital connection with herself, particularly her feminine self. She never strayed from the task at hand as we went along, and I believe that was her masculine training at work. It stood her in good stead for the process of rediscovering her feminine self. Whenever she had a new process to tackle she did it without complaint. She was uncomfortable a lot of the time and she disliked me on more occasions than I care to mention. I stayed the course because I knew she was worth the effort.

As she tackled the task of unmasking herself, she made some amazing discoveries and she was brave enough to discuss them. At first there was a strong sense of wanting to deny she was the way she was and make excuses for her past choices. However, slowly but ever so surely she realized if she wanted a different life she could no longer hide from the truth. Surprisingly, one day Roxanne came out with a revealing disclosure. I was aware of what was going on but had left this process with her. It needed to be her personal realization and it was so wonderful that it worked out that way.

Roxanne flounced down onto the sofa. "Well, I've had a hideous week. It was extremely uncomfortable, not to mention sad. I've realized that one of the major reasons for my denying what I do is that I'm so desperately afraid of being discovered!"

Fear of discovery. I had encountered this one so many times with male women.

I asked her what she meant by that and her answer was direct as an arrow. "What if *they* find out that I'm not as good as I make out I am?"

"Does it matter?" I asked her. "After all, you're good—your success in court proves that."

She shared a little more and I found her candor quite refreshing. "I know, but what I've discovered about myself is that it's my fear that drives me to win and sometimes it causes me to stoop a little low, and now I'm not proud of that behavior."

Confession Is Good for the Soul

I could see that Roxanne was now becoming quite courageous, but she was not finished with her confession. "The other thing I've found out about myself is that at the bottom of all my bravado, I'm desperately afraid. Now I understand why I get so bitchy and why I'm such a driver at work, and even worse—why I'm the driver in relationships and then wonder why they don't work out. The reality is that I'm the one who's actually being driven! I'm being driven by my own fear! Fear is my master and my slave driver."

Roxanne continued with her story of discovery, realization, and growth. She knew she was not a popular woman in her work environment, and even though she pretended not to care, she was starting to feel the effects of the whispers, especially about how she had arrived at her partnership position. In the past she would have driven everyone under her authority harder and harder until she got the results she wanted. That would also have kept them quiet and deathly afraid of her. She would not have put up with any challenges to her authority.

She'd also had difficulty keeping her staff, and the other partners had brought it to her attention. They had made it clear that staff changes were costing the firm a lot of extra money and wanted her to be more mindful of her management style. They had also indicated that she *needed* to change so that staffing levels could be maintained with minimum disruption. She confessed to me that her fear of being dismissed was yet another reason for her initial visit to my office. She just could not bring herself to admit it to me at the time. As it turned out, she was killing two birds with one stone with regard to the program we were working on.

Roxanne had never been given the option of failure. She wanted to succeed and she had employed all the means at her disposal to make herself successful. Now she was beginning to experience another level of success, and that was discovery of herself. She was discovering the part of herself that until now she had not had the pleasure of meeting: her feminine self. In the absence of her feminine, she had become quite heartless in the management of her staff, the way she conducted court battles, and last but definitely not least, the way she treated the men with whom she'd had relationships. She was tough in every sense of the word. But she was also desperately out of balance in terms of her internal genders.

Accessing the Feminine Aspect

With regard to overcoming her fears and also finding better ways to relate to her staff and clients, Roxanne found that meditation classes helped enormously. She also took up a yoga class, so for two nights of the week she had time to herself for contemplation. These activities definitely allowed her to access more and more of her feminine self; they were a mechanism that put her into a receptive state of *allowance*. Most of all, the combination of these new practices allowed her to *let go* and stop believing that she had to do everything herself. Her control issues before her program had been severe. But she was letting go more and more, and as a result she was becoming kinder and a lot more forgiving of those around her.

She continued to dedicate time to her personal development and because of her discipline, she succeeded in bringing her fear levels to a place where she could manage them well. She stopped driving people in the workplace as if they were her slaves. And she also stopped being so manipulative that every move she made served only to get what she wanted. One day she came in and told me that the longer her program with me continued, the less she seemed to want! She even announced that she was achieving a strange feeling of contentment, something she had never experienced before.

This was fascinating to me and I could not resist asking her, "Roxanne, what does that contentment actually feel like from your point of view?"

"Well, it's quite difficult to describe," she began. "I just don't have this desperate need for a man or a baby anymore. I don't grab every new file coming into the firm either. Other people can get a chance at first pick. I'm okay with doing well, but not having to be the best all the time. That would have never happened in my old life."

"What about your need to have all the attention? Do you remember we discussed this a while back at the beginning of your program? Do you remember? Even when you were out with friends, it always had to be all about you."

She responded thoughtfully. "Now I sit quietly for a while, each time before I go out. I put myself into my feminine before I step out the door. I see myself in a receptive mode, so I listen to others' point of view and I ask them about themselves. I allow them to share their stories before I dive in and make it about me. I'm so ashamed that I always made everything about me. I don't know why people even invited me out to join them for dinner."

Recognizing Transformation

In the past Roxanne never knew why she was so sad or lonely or fearful, but now she found answers in the time that she took for quiet contemplation. So much was revealed to her.

"When I was finally in the space that could allow those dreaded feelings to surface, I discovered yet another awful truth. I felt as if I was carrying the burdensome fear of not being good enough." Roxanne took a deep breath and continued in quite a quiet voice. "It was not until I reconnected with my feminine self that I could see all these things. Before then, all I did was drive myself to work and to *do*—and demanded to be the center of attention until it all came crashing down on me."

Roxanne finished her program and I heard from her about a year later. She was happy to tell me that she had married another lawyer and had retired from the law. And miraculously for Roxanne, who had turned forty the previous month, she was now expecting her first child! I believe that Roxanne's ending was a happy one because she committed to making a personal change at a very deep level, and she stuck with it. She allowed her mind to be open to the possibility of a more fulfilling life beyond material success. She took the courageous steps needed to visit her internal unbalanced self, recognize the true issues, and make the changes needed to balance her two energies: the masculine with the feminine.

BEWARE OF THE VILLAINOUS ANDRO WOMAN

Roxanne's example proves that change is possible, but many Andro women don't have the slightest desire to change. Many of them are not even aware of how ruinous their behavior is to both their professional and personal lives. Many are too young to have any notion of the women's history that has gone before them, and they don't care anyway. They want power and they are going to do whatever they need to do to obtain it.

The Villainous Andro is a skilled and masterful politician when she has a big endgame in view. The larger the endgame, the larger her ego is going to have to be to carry her forward and through the rough terrain that lies ahead. She is very confident. Her confidence is matched only by her innate knowledge of how to use cunning and manipulation to her best advantage. She has practiced ingratiating ways that make her the dark side of a networker. Networking for business is part of business; it is a good honest action of connecting with people you can help and who can help you. But the Villainous Andro Woman is a networking trickster. She inveigles her way into the circles she sees as most advantageous to her and embeds herself like a virus. Once embedded, getting rid of her is like trying to get rid of penicillin-resistant bacteria.

The Villainous Andro Woman is astute at assessing which are the very best coattails to ride. She makes that decision quite early and then carefully maps out her steps to the top. There is little exchange in her interactions with others in her group, simply because she has little to offer in return and no interest in anyone else's success. This woman uses men because she can, coming on to them in order to gain advantage, perks, or anything else she wants; she then quickly tires of the relationships. She also either uses women or quickly disables them if they are of no use. For women who are not Andro, watch out for the Villainous Andro. She is not your friend and you would be well advised not to delude yourself into thinking she ever will be. Her motivation will be to use you, and when you cease to be of use you will cease to be in her world.

Anyone who has ever worked for a Villainous Andro Woman will tell you how she likes to micromanage and control all aspects of the work environment. When it comes to the Andro Woman's intimate life, the same scenario applies. Everything must be under her control. She will choose the man, and please note that *she* does the choosing. It will be someone who will neither contradict her nor confront her on any level. Her internal masculine essence is so predominant that she can only partner with a man with a high feminine essence. In her attempts to find a mate, the Villainous Andro borrows a number of tactics from her Faux Feminine sisters (described in chapter 9), only the Andro is not quite as polished as they are in the execution of those wily ways. Like her Faux sisters, the Andro will dress well; on the outside she will be everything she believes the feminine to be: impeccably groomed and in style.

But none of this external façade matters at the end of the day, because the laws of attraction and polarity dictate that she will end up with a man she can dominate. Our external processes might satisfy our egos and our beliefs about who we are, but it's our internal energy that determines whom we end up with in an intimate relationship. The Andro Woman may end up as part of a Split Couple, and that kind of match can sometimes be a lasting one, when both partners agree to make it work. An example of the dynamic between the Split Couple is described in chapter 15.

MOVING THROUGH THE PROCESS INTO PEACE

When it comes to the early version of Roxanne and her sisterhood of Villainous Andro women, they have lots of company. Huge numbers of Andro women operate in our world; you find them everywhere. But too many of them are finding themselves materially secure yet desperately unfulfilled, unhappy, and yearning for something more. Very seldom can they put their finger on what that something more is.

How are they to know that what they miss is the lost connection with their feminine selves? Most will just not find this answer, or if they do they won't be willing to put in the hours and introspection required to fix it. But those women who have the courage to look inside, the way Roxanne did, can learn to reconnect to the powerful mysterious feminine energy that lies dormant within them.

Without the ability to access their feminine essence, Andros will continue on the well-trodden path of their sisters, which can involve numbing the emptiness with alcohol, drugs, or more power and money. But those are not lasting solutions. Women and men must come into internal balance if they are to achieve peace and fulfillment in their lives. The feminine need not be lost. As Roxanne showed us, there is a clear path to finding it.

So now we have seen an example of the path the Villainous Andro Woman takes. She is ambitious, manipulative, and power hungry. The key distinction between her and her Virtuous Andro sister is that the Villainous Andro never has anyone else's welfare at heart. That said, it is time now to meet the Virtuous Andro, a woman who is also primarily out for herself but who does have the capacity to care about others.

CHAPTER 8

The Virtuous Andro Woman

SHE SAYS: "I WANT TO CONQUER THE WORLD."
HE SAYS: "SHOULD I PACK YOUR BAG?"

CASE STUDY: CATHERINE

Catherine had been the CEO of a prominent nonprofit organization for ten years. Prior to that she'd had a very successful corporate career, but once she found her true passion she sought out a group that shared her views. She found a great match, and when she was offered the position of CEO she felt as if she had come home. The position and the organization, the value system and the people it supported were a perfect fit for her ambitions. Catherine loved the idea of working for a cause, and the fact that this was a cause that could be furthered under her leadership was an extremely attractive proposition for her. For eight years she had done a stellar job of turning the organization around financially. As a result it was now able to extend its services into many more third-world countries than when she had started.

Andrea, a close colleague of hers recommended my coaching practice to her because it seemed that during the last two years the board had noticed a slight but perceptible change in Catherine's management style. The board members were concerned that all the good work that had been achieved was in danger of being sabotaged by Catherine's overreaching, which was not only happening within the head office but also in the foreign countries where the organization operated. The last thing the board wanted was an incident in a foreign country.

The organization never wanted to give the impression that it was impinging its views on the customs or the people of those countries in any way. It just wanted to go in and help the sector it had an interest in and do the best possible job for the people there. The idea of subtly *colonizing* was strictly against the organization's ethics. The board members feared that Catherine was beginning to lose sight of this essential operating principle; they found themselves caught in a dilemma between the ethical standpoint of the agency and Catherine's very good work up until recently. But they had taken a vote and it was decided that she must comply with the ethical standpoint of the organization or they would have to let her go.

Getting to Know Catherine

From the preconsultation notes Catherine had sent me, I found that she was married to a retired fashion designer, Andrew, and they were a childfree couple. They lived in the inner city with their little Maltese terrier, Missy.

"Catherine, very nice to meet you. Please have a seat," I said welcoming her into my office. Catherine sat down tentatively, which was a little odd for such a strong and clearly confident woman.

Her first words to me set the stage. "I must say that I find this whole process a little strange. I don't know what to make of it. I'm still trying to fathom why Andrea wanted me to see you."

So by this I knew that the board had not actually laid everything out for Catherine. They seemed to be counting on me to bring certain things to her attention. I gave her a brief introduction to my practice. "Andrea thought we would be a good match and I might be a kind of sounding board for you." She fell silent, and when she responded she seemed pleased to finally have a place where she could explore some of the events she had experienced in recent months.

"Well, it's nice to have someone to talk to," she began, gaining back her confidence. "It certainly is true that it's lonely at the top.

I'll just get to the point. I've felt a little restricted by the board of late. They don't seem to agree with the direction I want to take with the organization. But my feeling is that if we don't do something different and proactive, then we could very well lose out to other organizations that are operating alongside us in those areas."

I suggested that perhaps it was a question of how she intended to move forward and that the board members needed to feel confident that her new direction and process were within the bounds of their operating statutes.

She was very quick to offer her opinion on that. "Well, they have all been on the board a little too long in my opinion, and they've gotten stale. They don't realize how the game has changed on the ground," she explained. "We need to be really proactive now and if that means we have to *impinge* on people just a little, then so be it. As long as we get the job done and beat our opponents to the post, then we have achieved something bigger and better."

I sought to clarify her point. "So you believe the end justifies the means?"

She nodded. "Yes, exactly right. We can't be too precious in these environments, and if we don't bend our approach just a little, then we're in danger of not achieving our goals in those areas."

Morality Can Become Muddled

"I suppose therein lies the dilemma, Catherine, and from what you're saying it doesn't look like the board agrees with you. Obviously they have enormous respect for you and your achievements, but they're having a lot of difficulty morally reconciling the means you've been employing for the past eighteen months to obtain your results."

She stood her ground. "Well, I think they need to be a little more trusting of me. The area has been in a rather mercurial state in the past two years, and since I've been the primary person on the ground over there, that should be enough for them."

By this time in our discussion, it was clear to me that Catherine was what I call a Virtuous Andro Woman. She exhibited the male characteristics of being a doer and a leader; she was full of good intentions, a woman with a clear mission and a cause that she could hang her hat on. But like many of her Virtuous Andro sisters, she had to watch out not to overstep the mark in her desire for power.

Catherine was used to being the ultimate authority in the organization and now she was clearly resenting any kind of demand for accountability. She believed she was accountable only to herself. I had seen this happen before quite a few times with this kind of woman. She starts to believe she is the ultimate authority, which is tantamount to being a dictator. Virtuous Andro women start out with good intentions, but over time their desire for power and control has the tendency to overtake them. The more power they have, the more they want to control everything.

Now that I had a handle on things, I saw that it was time to move the discussion along so I said, "Catherine, can we speak plainly?"

She replied quickly, "Yes please, absolutely no point beating about the bush and I'm so glad to be able to air this problem. Frankly, I'm at a loss to see what their problem is. After all, I get results."

I explained that the board was not having a problem with her getting results, but rather that they didn't like *how* she was getting those results. I asked her, "Could that be it?"

"I think you could be right, but what am I to do now?" she replied. "I have commitments from people and I've made certain agreements. If I go back on my word, it will make my tenure with the organization impossible."

I said I understood her dilemma but that I didn't think she had a choice. I put it firmly, but as gently as I could. "Ultimately you work for the organization and not for the people in the countries where you operate. Without the organization, you would not be there to help them. So you're ethically bound to operate within the guidelines of the organization first. I don't see what else you can do."

Arriving at a Point of Decision

Catherine was faced with a choice that was not easy for her either way. She was a brave woman but now she needed to draw on her inner courage to do the right thing by everyone. She had overstepped the mark with the board and they would accept nothing less than the retraction of her recent actions or she would be forced to resign. I wondered if she would have the humility to admit she had acted in a way that her organization considered wrong.

What had happened was that over time, the power of being part of successful projects fueled Catherine's passion for what she was doing. But it also fueled the part of her archetype hungry for power. She was a Virtuous Andro Woman engaged in questionable behavior without even realizing it, and as a result her actions were starting to negatively impact not only on her colleagues but also on the very people she was so committed to helping. The more Catherine tried to control her environment and everything in it, the more she set herself up for failure on a grand scale. She did not realize just how controlling she had become over the past two years; she was desperate for complete autonomy in her role.

Our session had come to its end and we said our goodbyes. Catherine wanted to stay in touch, which I said was fine. Sure enough, she called me three weeks after our session. "Just thought I would let you know," she said. "The board has accepted my resignation. The good news is that I have another position in the very same country where I was last working. I'll be running my own organization for the government there, so I think it's a great result. I'm so happy to start something so new and exciting. I'll stay in touch."

I told her I was happy for her. Catherine had clearly reached a place in her career where she no longer wanted to be accountable to a board of directors. The only thing that would make her happy was complete autonomy.

THE CHARACTERISTICS OF THE VIRTUOUS ANDRO WOMAN

As we saw with Catherine, the Virtuous Andro Woman dominates out of her male aspect almost to the exclusion of her internal feminine essence. She has a strong social conscience and understands unequivocally that to lead she will have to serve, which in fact is her desire. She usually has a cause that inspires powerful convictions within her and spurs her into action. It is very often a cause dedicated to advancing the good of others. This woman may choose to become political in order to advance her very strongly held passions, or she may be thrust into power by the circumstances of her birth. There is a strong element of the warrior in the heart of the Virtuous Andro Woman; she understands and feels her purpose strongly. We can believe in her because she demonstrates through her own life that she has the courage of her convictions and the bravery to carry them out into the world. She is an unusual person and a rare one.

THE MODERN VIRTUOUS ANDRO WOMAN

We are all familiar with examples of prominent women of this type who have been active leaders in our modern world. When I think of Virtuous Andro women of principle and strength, I immediately think of Golda Meir, the fourth prime minister of Israel, and Dame Margaret Thatcher of Great Britain. While serving as British prime minister, Dame Thatcher was often referred to as "the Iron Lady," probably because she had a will of iron and got things done. An uncompromising leader, Thatcher did not mince words and had the ability to follow through on what she said—a distinctly masculine trait. My favorite line that is so commonly attributed to Thatcher is, "If you want something *said*, ask a man. If you want something *done*, ask a woman."

What strikes me so strongly is that Thatcher understood the power of the masculine within women. She also knew how weak and effeminate men could be and she did not spare them in her parliament. Some would say that she went too far, overstepping her authority at different times, or indeed many times, in her zeal to improve the society and economy of Great Britain. This is the slippery slope that Virtuous Andros walk. Not everyone agrees with their methods, but these women feel the way Catherine did: the ends justify the means.

Another famous Andro warrior woman is Aung San Suu Kyi, the Burmese opposition leader who lived under house arrest for fifteen years. She won the Nobel Peace Prize but was only able to collect it twenty years after it was awarded. Born into a political family, Aung San Suu Kyi was fortunate to observe examples of power used well when she was growing up. This Virtuous Andro works tirelessly for her people. Aung San Suu Kyi is a woman of small stature but has the courage of a lion. She is determined that democracy will return to Burma and has never waivered from that vision. I am always inspired by her because she is such a self-sacrificing, pragmatic, and stoic individual. Her masculine aspect is fueled by the determination to see the right thing done by her people. What an extraordinary example of committed leadership by a woman!

Virtuous Andro women understand the responsibility that comes with the choices they make and the sacrifices to their freedom or personal life they might have to be make in the name of their cause. This breed of woman is comfortable with power and comfortable with the ramifications of that power. As long as they do not step beyond the society's laws or mores in pursuit of their passion, the Virtuous Andros of this world are capable of bringing about monumental changes for the better.

COMPARING THE VIRTUOUS AND VILLAINOUS SISTERS

Catherine is typical of most Virtuous Andro women, who are usually passionately engaged in a cause. The Virtuous Andro Woman remains Andro in her internal makeup: highly masculine in her orientation and as such not well balanced internally. Her intent tends to be slightly different from the Villainous Andro's, but when everything is boiled down this woman is still very fond of power. She will seek it out just like her Villainous sister does. There are some key differences between her and the Villainous Andro, however. The Virtuous Andro does not usually ride the coattails of men the way the Villainous Andro does. As I said earlier, she is not likely to put up with reflected power; she wants power in its purest form and she wants to be the one who possesses it. These women will usually partner with a man who is on the high end of the feminine spectrum. In marrying Andrew, Catherine partnered with a mild-mannered man who was clearly feminine. He was highly nurturing of her and their little dog. It could not be any other way. She would not brook challenges from anyone and, again, like her Villainous sister, strongly masculine men would not likely be attracted to her anyway.

The Virtuous Andro has far more courage than her Villainous sister and she also tends to have the capacity to systematically think through strategy. This comes from the highly logical masculine energy that she uses to its fullest capacity. She will take action and she will follow through. Women like this have been with us throughout history, from Deborah in the Old Testament to Boudicca, queen of the Britons, to Joan of Arc who put Charles VII on the French throne in 1429. Throughout centuries the Virtuous Andro Woman has consciously forsaken her feminine energy for the purpose of becoming a warrior. Her internal imbalance is the same as any masculine-oriented woman's. She just has a better and more visible cause to which she dedicates her high internal masculine energy.

CHOOSING A CAREER PATH WITH POWER

Virtuous Andro women inhabit a broad spectrum, from the top echelons of government, like Dame Margaret Thatcher, all the way to the hard-working Virtuous Andro Woman who might be running a small not-for-profit organization in your hometown. Virtuous Andros are genuinely more compassionate than their Villainous sisters, and in the right circumstances they can be empathetic to those whom they seek to help. So from time to time, the Virtuous Andro will make small connections with her feminine self. But she has little interest in homemaking or other more feminine pursuits because she is fulfilled by her cause or her business.

Catherine was cut from this cloth and she was not willing to shift. She never asked me what she could do to change. I took it that she did not want to change. She had everything she wanted, and when she managed to procure an even better career opportunity overseas it was obvious that was the option she wanted: more power, more autonomy, and less interference. She set her life up to suit her needs and wants. Catherine attracted a highly feminine husband who would not challenge her. In fact, Andrew was happy to travel with her to her new overseas position. He took care of her daily needs and made sure they had a balanced home life. She also made a clear-cut decision that she did not want children. She was an honest Virtuous Andro in that she did not delude herself into believing she wanted to be a mother. She had a little dog, Missy, who satisfied any need for nurturing and unconditional love she might have.

Catherine is a good example of the Virtuous Andro; her masculine energy was strong and she used it to benefit others even though she was clearly focused on gathering power for herself at the same time. Her commitment to others is one of the key differences between the Virtuous Andro and her Faux Feminine sister, whom we will meet in the next chapter.

C H A P T E R 9

The Faux Feminine Woman

CAN ALL CLIENTS BE HELPED?

When deciding to take on a new client I sometimes tread a fine line. Can I genuinely help them or do they just want information to further the way they're living their life? Either could be considered help, but in a few cases furthering the way they live may mean they gain some deep and insightful information to aid and abet a less than honest lifestyle. When I suspect a client is meeting with me to advance a hidden agenda, I tend to rationalize this by telling myself that karma is a wonderful leveler. On the other hand, I also feel a responsibility to allow no harm to come to either my client or the people they are close to.

Fortunately this is not a dilemma that occurs frequently. Even so, every so often I get a knot in my gut that screams "Not this one!" I have learned to listen and politely decline clients if I get a strong negative feeling from them. But in the early days of my practice I was a bit more naïve and not as discerning with regard to the archetypes I describe in this book. In the beginning I thought everyone had good somewhere deep within the recesses of their being; that they intrinsically wanted to be better if they could. That is to say, I tended to believe that in general each of us strives throughout life to become a better man or woman, and to make a positive impact (or less of a negative impact) on the people around us and the environment. That's why in my early days of coaching I was occasionally faced with unusual clients who were well masked. They sneaked in under my radar.

BEHIND THE MASK: DELILAH

I will never forget the day Delilah flounced into my office, overly confident, quite loud, and really amusing. She greeted me as if we were old friends and made herself comfortable even before she was invited to do so. This was truly unusual in my office. People tended to be a little reticent until they were comfortable with me and my approach; once they knew what is going on they leveled out their behavior back to their normal confident selves. In this case though, alarm bells were ringing, but because Delilah was so entertaining I disregarded my intuition for a few minutes.

Delilah looked innocuous. She behaved in a very welcoming fashion, but I soon realized it was all part of carefully constructed behavior meant to put me at ease while she evaluated me. Her overly cheerful demeanor gave her the time and opportunity to see how far she could push me to get what she wanted. I was calmly alert and allowed her the time to play out whatever she needed to play out in order to feel settled.

Eventually the inevitable question arose. "Delilah, how can I help you?"

Bright and bubbly, she began, "Well, I'm not sure actually. My friend Alice hasn't stopped talking about you and I wanted to come and see you for myself."

"So this is a fishing expedition?" I responded with a wry smile.

"You could say that," she responded. "I was interested because you have her doing all sorts of homework and I couldn't understand why she'd want to do all of that extra work when she's such a good person already."

"Well, I can't talk about Alice, but I can tell you what we do here, if you're interested," I offered. "This is an assessment session, so you're not obligated to ever return if we decide we're not right for each other."

"Oh, well played," was her response.

I kept quiet and waited to see if she would reveal what was troubling her. Not for one moment did I believe she had just come to see what it was all about. She had to believe there could be something of value in the visit, or she would not have bothered to come.

Not a Usual Client Interaction

Sure enough, Delilah had a problem, but it was one I'd never encountered. "Well if I'm truthful . . ." she began, and then hesitated slightly.

I encouraged her by saying, "Yes, I would prefer it if you were truthful. We don't deal in lies and subterfuge here, Delilah."

"Well, I'm having an affair with my husband's best friend," she blurted out. Talk about dropping a bombshell! I remained composed, expressing no surprise.

She barreled on. "I don't know what to do. I don't want to leave my husband and I don't want to give up my lover. You could say I want it all my own way. I can't tell anyone because I'm friendly with his wife. We have quite a large social circle, everyone is connected, and it's all a little difficult, rather complicated."

I was pretty sure I recognized this type of woman. Delilah seemed to be on the high end of the spectrum for the Faux Feminine Woman. She had the ability to lie without any appearance of a conscience. She was capable of living with the layered subterfuge that comes with devious plotting and planning. Her unmitigated sense of entitlement was coupled with her belief that she should be able to have it all, with little regard for the other people in a situation. These were very clear indicators of her Faux status.

"Delilah, you have to understand—I can't help you," I told her firmly. "I deal with business issues and psychospiritual concerns. You need a psychologist or psychiatrist who can take care of you and help you figure out how you should proceed. There appear to be a number of people involved in your situation and all of them could be badly damaged and hurt."

Delilah was not easily put off, having decided she wanted to get my attention, and in her mind she was a perfectly good client. "Well, if it's a business angle you need," she offered with a giggle, "the boys work together."

Her comment might lead you to believe she was a little silly, but not for one moment was my vision obscured by that smokescreen. "No, no, I don't need an angle, and that's certainly not the kind of business problem I have expertise in," I said.

Many Players Hurt in the Crossfire

Since we still had another thirty minutes of the session left, Delilah proceeded with her tale of woe even though I had no intention of taking her on as a client. She revealed that she had met her husband at work, that he was her boss, and that it did not take her long to get him divorced and married to her. They had two little girls and a good life, but she was bored. All in a neat little nutshell, she revealed her current life.

Delilah appeared to have little regard for the damage she was wreaking on others' lives. She felt vaguely guilty about the adultery with her husband's best friend, but had little empathy for her lover's wife. She reasoned that his wife had "let herself go" after her children were born and was now more concerned with her kids' homework than her marriage! In this way Delilah sought to excuse herself from any wrongdoing and instead laid the blame firmly at the doorstep of the other woman for the misfortune of having been betrayed by both her husband and her friend. To hear Delilah tell it, the other woman had brought her husband's adultery upon herself!

Well, that was all a little too convenient for my liking. I did bring her betrayal of her husband up while she was telling her story, but she dismissed my concerns quite easily: her behavior was justified because once they were married he started neglecting her in favor of his work. She simply did not have any concept of what it meant to be a responsible adult. Taking responsibility for her behavior seemed like a very new concept to her.

Distressed, but It's Not Her Fault

In fairness to Delilah, she did appear a little distressed. However, I sensed that her distress had more to do with the possibility of her disloyal behavior being discovered than doing the wrong thing. This is often the case with Faux Feminine women, who are in the habit of getting what they want through deceit, distraction, and manipulation. Highly practiced at lying and being devious, Fauxs are so good at the art of manipulation that they no longer have to think about the next step. They flow from one dishonest sentence to the next without so much as the blink of an eye. They believe they are in the right, which makes them convincing liars. When you add up the Faux's silver tongue and probable good looks, if you are a man you are not going to stand too much of a chance. If you are a woman, particularly a Good Doer or an unsuspecting feminine woman, you might also find yourself being naïvely taken in by her tall tales, and it may well be your husband or boyfriend who is next on her menu. While I have not had many Faux Feminine women as clients, I have observed them in the workplace many times and through friends of friends. It took me quite a while to realize what they were capable of in terms of the extent of their ability to betray those closest to them.

No doubt about it: Delilah was a predator. She chased her future husband and took him away from his wife. She pursued his best friend, who became her lover, and she used all her Faux Feminine wiles to get what she wanted out of life. Her femininity was not real; it was a caricature of what she believed a real feminine woman was. She was merely a caricature living a pretend life and manipulating everyone and every situation to her own advantage. I had no choice but to say goodbye to Delilah after that one shocking session. I wished her well knowing that I would not see her again. And I did not. She had no desire to change, and since she was not able to manipulate me to her own ends, she moved on to easier prey.

CHARACTERISTICS TO WATCH OUT FOR

Perhaps you have noticed that Delilah was a shameless flirt; she even confessed to me that she could not help herself. This is classic Faux behavior. Flirting is like breathing for a Faux. If there is a man around, she will flirt with him. She has to have all available male attention focused on her. She goes after this attention and in so doing, she declares her masculinity. A truly feminine woman does not need to chase attention; she simply stands in her femininity ready to receive the attention that is rightfully hers.

You will know her when you meet a Faux Feminine Woman, because she puts herself at the top of her own list and ensures she is on the top of everyone else's list. You will find her lazy in terms of work although she can suddenly be quite industrious when she has a project that meets her own ends. A Faux tends to be good looking and well groomed, seeking the spotlight in all situations. She dresses fashionably and expensively and is often surrounded by people, but she is not a good friend. That is because, as we saw with Delilah, the Faux is totally untrustworthy concerning other people's emotions and cares only for herself.

You may find her serving on committees and involved in all kinds of busyness that ensure her days pass with the color and movement she needs for distraction. She also likes to have an active social life with her partner since those times provide an opportunity to socialize more with men and practice her womanly wiles. Being out socially gives her a wonderful way to keep her husband on his toes as it were, by having him recognize how attractive she is to other men. He usually falls for this ploy.

The Faux is firmly in her male aspect most of the time because she must be incessantly *doing* things. She fritters her days away in coffee shops and lunching with friends. There are endless hairdressing appointments and visits to the beauty shop, not to mention tennis parties and golf dates. She will do anything to keep from being alone, with having only herself for company. She does not want to have to go within and examine her life. That would mean tapping into her feminine aspect, something that is alien to her.

THE FAUX FEMININE WOMAN IS ALIVE AND WELL

This type of woman has been with us since the beginning of time, and she will probably always be with us. Some even believe it is the innate nature of a woman to be completely and utterly dishonest in the way the Faux Fem is, but I don't believe that. In the past when men were highly masculine and controlled the world, they often factored dishonesty into the process when dealing with women, expecting that every woman they met was out to manipulate at all times. In those days when a woman was after power she might well exchange sexual favors and use feminine wiles, since those were her only currency. They were the only nets she could cast to ensnare power.

But fast-forward to today. The lines between men and women are not as clear-cut. Things have changed quite dramatically because now women can have power in their own right. In developed countries, women have the legal rights, the ability, the education, and the support to become whoever they want to be. On the face of it then, if there is no need for the Faux Feminine type of behavior to exist in our current times, why is it still so prevalent? The truth is that no matter how far we seem to evolve socially, we remain fundamentally human. Unless we address our ever-present human frailties, our real evolution remains seemingly slow and painstaking.

So then since human frailty is at play here, we find that within the Faux Fem is a woman who has a strong desire for power but wants it without having to work for it; therefore she is happy to enjoy reflected power from her partner. The Faux has no desire to be ordinary; she wants to live in an elevated position in society and to enjoy the trappings of power but without having to roll up her sleeves and put her shoulder to the wheel to earn it. Seeking power without working is the key distinction between the Faux and her fellow sisters, namely the Andro Woman and the Good Doer. These other women are willing to work and are quite happy to do so for any power they enjoy.

NO PUNISHMENT FOR HER CRIMES

In the past the Faux Feminine Woman was restricted by the social norms of her time. That meant that men, who occupied pretty well all the masculine space within society, made sure that if a woman stepped out of line and sought power on her own (thus breaking with tradition), she could be punished for it, sometimes punished to death! Remember the stoning of so-called adulterous women? Well, the Faux is still routinely adulterous in our times, but since the threat of severe punishment has been removed she can freely prey on men and behave aggressively while pretending to be a highly feminine woman.

Many feminine men today are attracted to this type of woman, yet they don't understand why they are so bedazzled by her. They don't realize that her lovely feminine exterior is a sham, a masquerade; that underneath it she is all male in her actions and desires. The men the Faux Fem attracts don't see her as dangerous to their masculinity because they themselves are highly feminine; they don't really act from their masculine aspect on a daily basis. Because the Faux so strongly and consistently attracts feminine men, we know it is proof positive that she is operating out of her masculine aspect and merely hiding behind the high heels, the perfect lipstick, and the beautifully manicured nails. So just to review, in the past women learned calculating ways to overcome the suppression of the patriarchy. As time went on it became acceptable female behavior to be wily, and if a woman mastered the manipulation of men her chances for a better life improved exponentially.

Today we still have this type of woman. It is quite likely that her early parental influences played a large role in how she operates in the world. If her mother was a manipulator, then she learned at the feet of a master and odds are that she followed in her mother's dishonest footsteps. Or she might have been conditioned by the example of other women in her family. If they thought it was okay to be an opportunist, perhaps we can forgive her for merely carrying on a family tradition; she might never have known another way of being. Or she might have inherited an innate need for revenge against men that she acts out unconsciously by entrapping and then destroying them, not unlike the praying mantis or the black widow spider.

DISCOVERING WHAT IS UNDER THAT DRESS

To the trained eye the Faux Fem looks ridiculous. Everything she does is only an attempt at being feminine. Because she is unmistakably disconnected from her true feminine aspect, she runs the risk of looking like Delilah, the caricature I mentioned above.

The famous designer Coco Chanel was a woman with a highly developed masculine side, however, she believed that it took a true woman in her feminine to wear a dress effectively. If the woman was not in her feminine, the dress could not make her feminine. Coco Chanel worked hard to become a leader in the fashion industry, building a legacy that survives today. She was probably more of an Andro Woman, but she never lost the priceless connection with her feminine aspect. By tapping into the power of her true feminine, she understood women and what they needed to be elegant, classy, stylish—and most of all, comfortable. Coco Chanel had the ability to graciously move between her feminine and masculine aspects. Her astute approach to fashion could only have come from someone who understood the importance of being authentic to the feminine self. If you are a woman then you must be true to who you are. Regretfully, the Faux Feminine Woman has lost that connection; it is her disconnection from her feminine aspect that renders her absent from the "dress."

The Faux Feminine Woman's manipulative ways are aided and abetted by the feminine man's reticence to step into his own masculinity and therefore the masculine space that is his birthright. This has created a dishonorable axis between the weak effeminate man and the malevolent masculine woman. The axis exists between all our archetypes and forms the cornerstone to the corrupt power of the male woman. Understanding the process and workings of this axis is crucial to the reversal of the unhappiness and desolation that exists between men and women in the ever-widening chasm of discontent in which we find ourselves.

THE FAUX IS A MASTER GOLD DIGGER

So if the rules of polarity have created this chasm between men and women, let the buyer beware. Let the men of this world be on the watch for this shameless gold digger. The new and improved masculinized version of the Faux Feminine Woman goes brazenly forth to claim what she wants; she feels so entitled that she does not hide her shame. She may be subtle depending on how classy she is or completely brazen, but either way she heartlessly helps herself to any unsuspecting man's wealth and power. In fact, she is without conscience and will often punish the man she is stealing from. There are many cases of abuse from the overtly masculine Faux Feminine gold digger. She can enslave an unsuspecting feminine man and drive him into debt just to keep her happy. He does not realize that satisfying her is an impossible task.

When we look at it, the Faux Feminine Woman is the seasoned mistress of the past. She has no qualms about being the "other woman." Rather, she wears her duplicity like a badge of honor. Like Delilah, she does not hesitate to steal her best friend's husband, boyfriend, or significant other. She wants what she wants and many times, this woman is so spiteful that she may go after a friend's husband just to see if she can steal him away This is predatory masculine behavior at its extreme and most dark. This woman is not a candidate for the new sisterhood of women. She is not a friend and should never be trusted. She cannot trust herself because she does not know who she is. She is capable of unplumbed levels of deceit.

PROTECT THE CHILDREN FROM THIS WICKED WOMAN

The Faux Feminine Woman does not make a very good mother. Her high levels of deceit permeate her being and they will automatically be passed on to her children. Children absorb the behaviors of their parents as if by osmosis. The bottom line is that the Faux has no access to her heart center and therefore very little access to her feminine self. The feminine demands that you travel deep into your heart to find the compassion needed to understand and nurture yourself and others. This is not a quality that can be manufactured or faked.

Heartfelt feelings are at the very foundation of the feminine. If as a woman you are not genuine in your feelings for others and cannot find empathy toward your fellow human beings, then you are in grave danger of becoming deeply male and fully disconnected from your very precious feminine aspect. No amount of fake artistry will substitute for the genuine feelings of the feminine heart. Your heart center is where it all begins and ends. After her children, the person most at risk from this woman is her partner or husband. He will be the target of her vengeance because as a person in masculine form he has the ability to trigger the worst of her ways. The Faux, whose feminine side is paralyzed, has a strange disdain for men ironically coupled with a strong need for their attention and approval. This creates a bizarre dichotomy within her that results in unpredictable actions that create confusion for both herself and her male partner. If you have ever lived with a Faux, you have seen this dynamic in action, and it is not pretty.

DATING A FAUX IS COURTING DISASTER

When a Faux sets her sights on a man it is as easy for her to ensnare him as it is to take candy from a baby. She is particularly attracted to our Pseudo Masculine Man because they are two of a kind. These two can be very attracted to each other, and they initially find each other's exploits very exciting. She is attracted to his feminine side and he is drawn to her to highly masculine side. (The Pseudo Masculine Man is described in chapter 12.)

On the surface, they both think that they are attracted to the opposite pole. He might think she is very feminine because of the way she looks, and she might think he is very masculine because of his macho activities. But in reality neither is what they appear to be. Still, they are well matched for the opposite reason: they are both quite far out of internal integrity, so they seem to be suited, and they understand each other. But their bliss can be short-lived and usually is. Both the Faux Feminine Woman and the Pseudo Masculine Man are social climbers who want someone to support their desired lifestyle. In reality, though, someone has to hold the ladder while the other partner is climbing, and in this union neither one wants to hold the ladder. Neither one wants to do any work, so this coupling will usually end unpleasantly with disappointment all around.

The Faux is not likely to be attracted to the Highly Feminine Man since he is a little too passive and boring for her. If she does develop an attraction to him, it will depend largely on what he has to offer her. If the tradeoff is reasonable, anything is possible. The coup for her is to land herself a Sensitive Man because he is successful in business and in life. She will often mistake his sensitivity for stupidity, a common problem for people carrying high sensitivity. The Faux will see his sensitivity as an opportunity to take gross advantage of his kindness. This man carries the feminine traits devoid in her own personality, so they could make a viable Split Couple (explained in chapter 15). In short, the more successful the Sensitive Man is, the more attractive he will be to the Faux, which turns out to be a great match for her but not so much for him.

Lacking a connection to her heart center, the Faux Feminine Woman has very little ability to be genuine. This leads her behavior to be superficial and manipulative. She will flirt and flutter around, all part of an attempt to gather more and more attention for herself. She believes this attention will elevate her not only in the eyes of others but more importantly, in her own eyes. The reality is that the Faux Feminine Woman is a bottomless pit. Her need for attention and position is insatiable. Firmly occupied with herself, she has little generosity of spirit or empathy for anyone else. Whether you are a man or a woman, if you find someone with these characteristics, run don't walk, to the nearest exit.

Without doubt, Delilah showed us the wily ways of a well-developed Faux Feminine Woman. The Faux Fem has a cousin with many of the same manipulative ways, but she is probably a little older in years. Read on to discover what makes the Cougar tick.

CHAPTER 10

The Cougar

SHE SAYS: "THAT SOUNDS LIKE THE BEE GEES."

HE SAYS: "WHO?"

THE MAKINGS OF A COUGAR'S LIFE

Kate came to see me on the recommendation of her good friend Mary. Kate was clear on the telephone that she needed a friendly ear and some practical advice because she was facing some life-changing situations in her personal life. Although Kate was not really the kind of woman I would normally work with, I thought that if she was Mary's friend, then I would do my best to be a sounding board for her at this time in her life. When Kate arrived for her appointment, I was a little taken aback. She had sounded very businesslike on the telephone, so I was not prepared for the petite, beautiful, immaculately dressed woman in front of me. Like her Faux Feminine sisters, this woman was designer clad from head to toe. She settled onto the sofa, placing her very designer handbag at her feet.

"Kate, it's so very nice to meet you. Mary let me know that you're facing a few challenges at the moment," I began in order to break the ice.

"Yes, you could say that," Kate said in a tired voice. "I feel that they're more than challenges. They're more like hurdles and they keep being placed in front of me. I seem to race from one disaster to another. There just doesn't seem to be any rest."

I expressed sympathy for her situation and asked, "So Kate, how can I help?"

Unexpectedly, she leapt into her story without any preamble. "The fact is that my husband of thirty years left me three years ago, for— would you believe it—his assistant. Isn't that a little clichéd in this day and age?" she said bitterly.

"I suppose it is, Kate, but all we can do when faced with these kinds of things is to look after ourselves and our own health first. The rest is out of our control," I offered gently.

Adding Insult to Injury

With that she launched back in with more bad news. "You see, that brings me to my next challenge. I've just heard that his new wife is having a baby!" Kate's indignation at her former spouse's behavior was palpable. Her anger was obvious and her confusion about the situation even more so. "He's a father of twenty-five-year-old twins, for heaven's sake. What's the matter with him?"

I suggested that this was not such an unusual situation, but my main question to her was why was she still so angry three years after the divorce. "Your notes here say that you've been seeing a therapist. Surely you must have worked through most of the emotions by now?"

She replied bluntly, "Well, I haven't. That's why I want some kind of new strategies and a different perspective. I have something else too. My boyfriend of the past three years has just informed me that he's ending our relationship. Wait for it—he's going off with some young thing he met in a nightclub."

At this point I was a little confused. She had been divorced for three years but she had had a permanent relationship of three years? And it was ending. "Kate, this does seem like a double blow. I'm very sorry to hear this. It must be distressing for you."

"Distressing!" she yelled. "You have no idea the anger I feel welled up inside of me. I can't tell that starched-up therapist of mine. She just doesn't understand me."

Frankly, I wasn't feeling that I understood Kate either, but I thought that if we kept talking we might get to some root causes, particularly for the anger. I asked her to tell me about her boyfriend, since the breakup seemed to be the source of her most recent upset.

The Charms and Challenges of the Younger Man

"Pete is wonderful, kind, incredibly good looking, and younger than me—he's twenty-eight."

I tried not to show my dismay. I figured Kate must be in her early fifties or so. I kept quiet, hoping she would pick up the ball and elaborate on her distress.

"He told me he wanted a family, and although he loves me—he does, you know—he wants a family more, and I don't need to tell you that is the one thing I can't give him."

Again I remained silent. Kate was not the first woman I had encountered who'd found solace in the arms of a very young man after a divorce. It was quite fashionable within my client base.

"Why does everyone leave me?" she continued. "And they all leave me for younger women, and they want families. This is crazy. I'm attractive, aren't I?"

I assured her that she was and that I thought the situation was not caused by her looks.

"What do you think it is then?" she went on. "It must be that I'm losing my looks. Why else would they run off with these simpering young things when they could have me?"

I decided to wade in with some observations and see where we would go. "Kate, surely you realized that at some stage your twenty-eight-year-old beau was going to want a family of his own. Even though he was probably very happy with you, you were at very different stages in your lives. That was bound to have an impact at some point, and in your case it happened sooner rather than later."

"But I love him so much. I gave him everything he needed. I remade him, restyled him—new car, new clothes, everything," she replied, still bereft and unable to understand what was going on.

I went back to my point. "I think you would have to agree, Kate, that this isn't just about material things. This young man wants a life and he wants something you can't give him. That part of your life is past."

She spat back at me, "So you're saying I'm over the hill."

"No, Kate, on the contrary. I'm saying that perhaps it's time for you to embrace the next stage of your life."

But that was not in her plans. "No, no, I just want you to tell me how to get him back," she insisted. "Mary told me you had really different ways of helping people and I want you to help me get him back."

Finding a Way to Let It Go

At this point I had to be firm. "Kate, I would never enter into that kind of manipulation. This young man has made a decision and I think that as a caring person you need to respect his decision. You came together at a time in your life when you needed solace. He helped you prove to yourself that you're a very attractive woman. Why not leave it at that and feel comfort in the knowledge that he'll go on to be happy. That will give you the freedom to find your own more permanent state of happiness."

She returned to her blunt tone, not pulling any punches. "I have to tell you that I'm not enjoying this conversation, and I don't want him to be happy!"

I said I was sorry, but that I didn't do strategies and scheming; I encouraged her once again to let him go.

"But why should I let him go? He owes me."

So there. That was it. I explained that he did not owe her anything, that they were two adults who had entered into a relationship for a time and now it was at an end, whether she wanted it to be or not.

"Kate, all I can do is explain how I work and what I would recommend to help you. My next step with you would be to explore what your journey was in that relationship and what your next step is for your inner growth."

She looked at me a bit confused, so I continued. "Kate, Pete came into your life for a reason and now he has to leave. Did you learn anything from the relationship with him?"

She thought about that. "Well, I enjoyed having him on my arm and everyone could see that I still had *it*. I wasn't over the hill just because my husband left me."

I nodded. "So really it was about how he made you feel, that he made you feel attractive and wanted when you were feeling discarded?"

She agreed, "Yes, absolutely."

So I asked her next, "Is that enough to sustain a lasting adult relationship? What do you think was in it for Pete?"

That was easier for her to answer. "Well, you know how connected I am in this town. He liked that. It made his career prospects a lot easier because I offered him connections he could never get on his own. I created a new, sophisticated Pete and he liked the new man he had become. Plus we had an amazing physical relationship."

This all made sense to me but I wanted Kate to see it too. "So would it be fair to say that it was a mutually beneficial relationship for a time?"

She nodded, and she seemed ready to argue her case once again, but I continued on.

"Kate, the reality is that when one person in a relationship decides it's at an end, then it's finished. The only thing the other person can do is accept that fact in a healthy way and move on."

Dissecting the Cougar and Cub Dynamic
By this time I felt I could comfortably dig into this issue with her, so I did. "Kate, from my perspective you've sacrificed your ability to be truly feminine in this relationship. You took the lead and provided all the direction for this young man. You actually did all the work and he went along for the ride and the benefits. Now we might wonder, how was that right or fair to you? The problem is you encouraged this behavior on his part by not expecting him to be the *man*. He could play at being the man when in actual fact he was just a boy in a man's body."

"A very sexy boy in a man's body!" she pointed out with a smile.

"That might well be true," I said, "but you took the fundamental essence of his manhood away from him. He could never spread his wings to become a fully fledged man with a healthy masculine essence as long as he was with you. He might have had everything he could want materially, but he arrived at a place that demanded he ask more of himself.

"I believe that Pete wants to be the man in a relationship, so he has chosen a younger woman who will allow him to be just that. Fatherhood will be good for him. He'll have to step up and take responsibility for another human being. By giving him everything, you denied him the opportunity to flex his inner masculine muscles and step fully into his manhood."

It was beginning to finally dawn on her. "So you can't help me get him back?"

"No, Kate, but I would love to help you move on to the next stage of your life. It's actually a really exciting phase: a time of wisdom and reflection."

She said I was making it sound like she was ready for the nursing home.

"No, Kate, you misunderstand me. I'm just suggesting that you haven't given the next stage of your life a chance. You haven't investigated the satisfaction you could have from living a life that's in its proper sequence for you, and therefore in right order."

Kate sat silent for a moment, and I let the silence fall around us like a comforting blanket as she started to process the full implications of her young lover leaving her forever. We'd been sitting like that for a couple of minutes when she abruptly announced that she had to leave and would be in touch. I did not think I would hear from Kate again. An inward journey did not seem to be in the cards for her at this time in her life and she was the only one who could decide when, if ever, she might be ready.

Returning with More Heartbreak and More Questions
Kate did come back to see me, but it was two years later. She had embarked on yet another Cougar-type relationship that had just ended in tears. When she returned to my office she was in a different state of acceptance. We ended up going on a short journey together for a few months that seemed to give her some peace of mind and

closure on that chapter of her life. One of the exercises I went through with Kate was particularly effective. I asked her to sit quietly and meditate on the issue of being in a relationship with a much younger man. I asked her what was coming up for her. Was she blissfully happy? Did she want the relationship to continue given that the odds were stacked against its longevity? I asked her to contemplate whether this kind of relationship would still be viable for the young man if she were an older woman *without* financial security.

Eventually she was able to open up and we discussed at length why she was not embracing the next natural stage of her life. Together we explored what that could look like, what would it feel like. I encouraged her to reconnect with her internal feminine aspect, suggesting many of the same techniques I found so helpful for male-oriented women of all kinds. She finally opened up and faced her fears about being seen as old and unattractive, past the point of being able to seduce a man. She realized she had been using a younger man as a panacea for a number of deep-seated internal worries, but once she began to realize that her life was far from over she was open to giving up chasing cubs. She came to terms with her life and her age, and I was proud to see her gracefully move into her own better space with confidence, courage, and pride in herself and her accomplishments.

CHARACTERISTICS OF THE COUGAR ARCHETYPE

The term *Cougar* is not one I coined; it is a word that has been in the popular media for years to describe an older woman who chooses much younger men for her intimate relationships. Within my inner male-female paradigm, *Cougar* works well, which is why I use it. The Cougar archetype described here is a composite of the Faux Feminine Woman and the Andro Woman.

The Cougar is a mature woman, probably divorced, and if she is also a Faux Feminine Woman she quite likely has a mammoth divorce settlement under her belt that makes her financially independent; she doesn't need a man in any way for financial security. If she is an Andro Woman she might or might not be working, but she is probably financially independent as well. If you combine the traits of these masculine-oriented female archetypes into a Cougar you get a powerful cat with a lot of life experience behind her, along with well-honed masculine traits. If she sets her sights on you as a young man you will not have too many valid defenses against her advances.

Like her Faux Feminine and Andro sisters, the Cougar is automatically the predator, the chaser, the one in complete control of the situation. She has financial and worldly wealth, connections, her own home, time to travel, and many other achievements of the mature woman. The Cougar is emotionally experienced, with a well-constructed feminine exterior and a strong male interior. You will find her active on the dating scene, keeping her eyes out for young sensitive feminine-oriented men. These young men are her prey—prey who will not escape the claws of this experienced cat.

BEING DRAWN INTO THE LIFE OF A CUB

If you are a young man, the truth is you may not want to escape. You may like all the attention, the gifts, the connections, and the fine things in life. But as a younger man you also need to be aware of the possible devastating ramifications you could experience in your emotional life with her. You may be drawn to her, but since she occupies all the masculine energy in the relationship there is nowhere for you to go with regard to flexing your internal masculine aspect. If you spend too much time being a kept man you may never find a healthy internal balance between your own masculine and feminine energy.

Think about it. Why would an older, attractive, and financially stable woman desire a younger man so ardently were it not for the fact that she could have full control over the relationship? Many people do not see anything wrong with these kinds of relationships, figuring it is not that much different from an older man going after a much younger woman. At a glance there does not appear to be a difference, but both are out of natural order and frankly ridiculous, you could argue, and I would agree with you wholeheartedly.

The problem is that the argument does not stack up energetically because men and women although definitely equal are not constructed in the same way, for good reason and purpose. Otherwise we could all be one gender and be done with it: no more warring

between the sexes. We would all get along in our androgynous existence. But let's face it, if that were the case we would all be bored to
tears. So if we look at the differences, this is the way I see it. The
cougar is a predatory cat—no ifs, ands, or buts about it. She is a
slinky cat on the prowl and that automatically puts her into her male
essence. She predominates from her male side because she was probably set up that way since she was a little girl.

AGING GRACEFULLY IS NOT EASY

The Cougar is very concerned with her physical appearance and she
will go to great lengths to appear feminine and young. The Faux
Feminine Woman does this as well, but as she ages it is not something new she has to learn; it is an extension of a beauty regime that
now has to cope with an aging body. The Cougar is really an old *girl*
with well-developed muscles that can make her a formidable male
predator in a woman's body, a woman with no concept of how to age
gracefully. She does not want to age at all, and by continuing to
choose a much younger male partner she finds she can feel younger
and more vibrant. Some people say this is a bit like an older man
dating a much younger woman in order to feel virile once again, but
this older man and the Cougar are not the same. The biggest difference is that the Cougar is a woman! By definition this means she is
meant to be predominantly feminine, not predominantly masculine.
Her internal balance should be to her feminine essence first and
then her masculine essence.

Turning to the older man who might still be chasing young skirts,
this older man would need to find a strong connection to his masculine aspect first and then balance his feminine side accordingly.
The male essence is outgoing and by its very nature predatory. The
male essence hunts and protects so while it may seem a bit unfair or
unequal, the older man is probably more in line with his nature
when chasing a woman of any age. Not for a minute am I saying
that he is in right order to go after someone half his age. All I am
saying is that he is probably acting out the natural process for a man
and any variables in this scenario are between the individuals and
their personal needs and desires.

Now back to the older woman. If she were in right balance and operating mostly from her feminine essence, she would not be hitting on such younger men or indeed on anyone for that matter. As an older and more mature woman, she would move gracefully into her advancing years, acting appropriately for a woman of her age. Being in right balance and having a healthy receptivity, she might well find a Sensitive Man closer to her own age and stage in life who could be her partner and equal. Younger men in their twenties and thirties would hold no interest for her. They would simply not turn her head because she would be a well-balanced, mature, and interesting person in her own right, with no need for youth to prop up her aging beauty. This older woman would create her own balance, which would demand that she turn inward with a focus on her feminine side as she reached her mature years, radiating the well-earned peace, wisdom, life experience, and confidence that come with a life well lived.

We have now explored each of the masculine-oriented female archetypes within this inner male-female paradigm. It is time to turn to their masculine counterparts: men who are far more in touch with their feminine aspect than men in centuries past. The first is the Sensitive Man. Let's meet him now.

CHAPTER 11

The Sensitive Man

SHE SAYS: "I'M SO TIRED OF BEING HOME ALL THE TIME."
HE SAYS: "WHAT DO YOU MEAN? I THOUGHT YOU WERE HAPPY."

EVEN THE SENSITIVE MAN HAS HIS CHALLENGES

I met Ryan at dinner party hosted by a friend of mine. He was in his mid- to late forties with an engaging smile and the clearest blue eyes I had ever seen. We started our conversation over drinks, and I quickly figured out just by the way he spoke about his business and his employees that he was a man with a fair level of sensitivity. He knew who I was in the social circle and announced he would like to sit next to me at dinner if that would be all right. "I want to pick your brain," he said.

We sat down, and after a few pleasantries about our families I asked the dreaded question, "Where's your wife tonight, Ryan?"

He replied with a smile, "Well, that's the perfect opener. No wife currently. It's kind of a long story. What I really wanted to ask you is if I could come and see you at your practice."

I still did not have an answer to my question but at least I knew what was on top of his mind. "Of course, Ryan, you're Amelia's good friend, so please give me a call."

As the party went on that evening we carried on our conversation, talking about his children and various general topics. Eventually he said, "Can you tell me, Jen, where have all the good women gone?"

117

I laughed and told him that was the million-dollar question. "I don't think they've gone anywhere. I just think they've morphed into something else," I offered. "And the traditional good woman has become extinct. I don't think she had much of a choice."

Ryan looked relieved. "So it's not just me then? You see, Maria and I divorced three years ago and I've dated some really crazy mixed-up women since the breakup. The whole experience has caused me to rethink finding a new partner at all."

In the Company of Men

I assured Ryan that he was definitely not the only man thinking that way. "I have many men whom I see who've had the very same experience," I explained. "It's important not to rush the process. If I were you I'd take the time to reassess everything in your life. The worst possible action you could take is to fall blindly into a relationship without giving yourself the proper time to evaluate how you fit with the person who's shown up in your life."

He stopped me as I was about to proceed further into explanation. "Are you sure you don't mind discussing this outside of your office?" he asked respectfully.

I assured him that I love to talk about this topic; since it's my passion, anytime is a good time. "I would say, just based on our chat this evening, that you're quite likely what I would term a Sensitive Man."

He looked at me and said, "I thought I kept that part of myself well hidden."

"Well, from my perspective, I think you should be proud that you carry that level of sensitivity. Sensitivity is something to be extremely appreciative of. Imagine a world filled with nonsensitives? It would be a very harsh place."

I continued on. "Stop me if I'm wrong, but I expect you have no problem making the hard decisions, nor do you have a problem carrying them out. You have sensitive moments and you're also sensitive to other people's feelings. I would guess that your intuition is probably in good shape, but you probably don't think of it as intuition. Instead, you just figure it's best to rely on your own judgment or your hunches, since those are right most of the time. You're also probably quite good at taking advice. Am I on the money thus far?"

"You're making me sound like a hero," he said with a smile. "But yes, I'd say you've read me like a book. How can you do that?"

Recognizing Championship Behavior
I smiled back and continued my train of thought. "Ryan, in my world, we call you a champion. You look kind of surprised and humbled, but then that's the typical reaction from a champion. Men like you are fast becoming extinct, just as are the traditional good women you mentioned earlier," I said.

"It might seem somewhat hopeless, your quest for the woman who's right for you, but I would highly encourage you to maintain the good fight of being a decent man. I can tell you that women need many more good solid men like you to serve as an example to the younger men of this next generation. Otherwise, what will happen to our daughters and our granddaughters?"

He was pensive for a brief moment. "I have to say, I don't feel like much of a champion," he admitted. "A lot of the time I feel like I'm losing the ability to be a man at all."

"It only feels that way because very often your masculinity is under threat, and since you're not even aware of what's happening you just feel very uncomfortable. Is that correct?"

He lowered his shoulders in relief and let out a sigh. "You've hit the nail right on the head," he said. "What's going on? I was out of the dating world for twenty years and I have to tell you, I'm mightily confused."

I smiled again, knowing how he felt. I had heard this complaint more times than I could count. "Ryan, take heart," I said. "Yours is not a difficult issue to correct. It just takes a little understanding of what's happening in your *unseen* world as opposed as to what's happening in your *concrete* world. If you're open to that conversation then we can certainly explore a whole host of opportunities for you in the future."

He liked the sound of that: that I thought there was hope for him. He shared a bit more of his frustration. "Amelia told me a little bit about how you work," he said. "I'm open to anything that will explain this terrible desolation and confusion that I'm feeling regarding the opposite sex. How things change when you aren't looking."

"Change is really the only constant we have in this life, at least that's my experience," I said. "The trick is not to be afraid to embrace our changing world. Don't get left behind. That's where the confusion lies, in my opinion. The whole world, as we used to know it, has changed."

"So then what's happening for me with these women?" he asked. "They seem to range from mildly overbearing to outright mean."

It was my turn to smile again, knowing exactly the kind of women who were out there. I said I thought he had been meeting examples along the spectrum I term the *male woman*.

He elaborated on his discomfort with these male women. "Well, I don't like the way I felt with them and frankly, I felt the same odd way with Maria toward the end of our marriage, and that's why I had to get out."

Why a Marriage Might Not Make It

I decided to change gears slightly, since I was wondering about his work and his ex-wife's background. "Amelia told me you've taken over a number of companies in the last five years, Ryan. You've expanded internationally to China and Europe and you've been very, very busy—is that right?"

"Yes, absolutely correct, it's been just manic," he said. "I've hardly had a moment to myself, often traveling overseas for months at time. However, those acquisitions are now settling down and the outside companies are well integrated into our corporate culture. My people are doing a great job."

"The reason I asked about your work, Ryan, is that I figured your masculine side has been tested over the last few years," I explained. "Your career caused you to really live more and more from your masculine side. You're lucky. Sensitive men like you can get things done when they need to and that's a very good thing.

"But I bring it up because your career and its pace would've had an effect on Maria too. You were away from home for months at a time, and she was left to deal with the children and all the other things you would normally have taken care of. She was probably quite a masculine woman to start with, and your circumstances drove her further into that side of herself without either of you realizing it was happening. When you returned home, you'd lost polarity with her. You were both very strong in your masculine sides at that time, out of necessity, and since masculine to masculine doesn't attract, your intimate relationship was in jeopardy."

"You are so right," said Ryan. "I never thought of it that way, but when we were young we often did bump heads when she working as a lawyer. She could be quite imperious at times and I didn't like the *feeling* then either. I had no idea what I was feeling. I just knew I didn't like it. Was my own masculinity rebelling at her masculine behavior then too?"

"Ryan, that's very insightful and, yes, that's quite likely what was going on," I said.

"Then as soon as the children arrived she seemed to settle down. She loved being home with them and working just part time. There were all kinds of things I could help her with, so many activities and house things to do. It was a good time for all of us."

He sighed again before continuing. "But then once the kids were grown up and she was working full time again, we ended up losing touch with each other, pretty quickly it seemed, only this time we couldn't to get any connection back at all. It didn't help that my work was just so hectic and that I was still traveling so much."

"So as you found out, Ryan, when both people in a relationship are out conquering the world, it's on both of them," I told him. "In a way, you were lucky that you had enough desire to hold on to your masculine self and not relinquish it all to Maria or these other women you've been dating."

Being a Man without Apology or Compromise

He continued telling me his side of things. "I just can't do that. It feels wrong inside of me not to be the doer and fixer at home," he said. "I couldn't just ride along, even though I did feel for Maria. She took the breakup very badly. But then she was always sort of resentful of my business life because she felt she had given up her career when the children arrived. I thought we had agreed I would be the bread-winner while the children were growing up, and I was perfectly happy to do that: to provide for all of us. But that part of my life is over and I'm wondering what to do now," Ryan said.

I was happy to offer some suggestions. "I think you'd be best suited to a woman who's very much in touch with her feminine self. I can see you being very happy with someone as capable as you are of balancing both her masculine and feminine energies, but who is safely housed within her feminine self.

"A woman who's comfortable with her femininity will be happy you have the masculine traits that did not allow you to be a passenger in your relationship with Maria. A feminine woman, unlike Maria, won't be competitive with you. She'll be happy to be your equal in every sense of the word without emasculating you. That means her levels of receptivity will be high. She'll be able to receive your protec-tion. She'll understand that you're not trying to disempower her by looking after her. That would also mean she'd be able to reciprocate by being happy and engaged in your well-being as well."

Ryan looked thoughtful as he answered. "I know you're right with this, I always felt a level of competition between Maria and me even when we were in a good place. I never understood why that made me feel so uncomfortable until now."

I confirmed his realization. "There can be no ease between a cou-ple when competition is present. When a woman's receptivity is in good shape there's no competition. If she's comfortable with her femininity, she will receive and happily give. When receptivity is ab-sent and competition is present, another odious element creeps into the relationship. Instead of the ease of receiving, there will be taking. Receiving and taking are closely aligned but the distinction between them is determined by intent. When there is incorrect intent you will almost always feel a sense of entitlement emanating from the other person."

Ryan looked at me soulfully and I detected a misty look in his eyes; I felt he was still grieving the loss of his marriage. I sensed that he was in a deeply receptive state and ready for more information.

In fact, he was hungry for answers to the perplexing questions regarding his recent experience with women, so I continued.

"Ryan, a man like you has to be very, very aware that you would be high on the list of women who are less than honest and who are on the prowl for a good man. Don't be taken in by women who might appear to have your best interests at heart. My advice is to test those intentions and make sure your goodwill is going to be well reciprocated and not taken advantage of."

The Sensitive Man is always at risk of being polarized into his feminine side by masculine women, so I let him know that if he allowed that to occur he would be back in the same position he'd found himself with Maria. I reiterated why the best match for him would be a woman who was, like him, also quite fluid through her masculine and feminine but who would be primarily at home within her feminine energy.

"With a woman like that, you'd be able to be in your masculine energy without having it constantly threatened by your partner. That can become an exhausting process for a man who's comfortable being masculine. It's wonderful to see that you haven't apologized for being a man. I think that's key to our future as a healthy society: having more and more men become true owners of their masculinity."

We were so engrossed in our chat that I hardly noticed the other party guests were starting to get their coats and edge toward the door. The night had flown by and I'd enjoyed meeting Ryan very much; such a breath of fresh air. We both stood up to get ready to leave and he expressed thanks for my candor and indicated that he would very much like to come and see me.

"I have some other business issues and relationships at work that I bet you could help with. May I give your office a call?" he said in closing.

"I hope you do, Ryan," I said. "I look forward to hearing from you."

CHARACTERISTICS OF THE SENSITIVE MAN

The Sensitive Man is different from his more feminine male counterparts because his masculine aspect is in good condition and it is fully activated. If we look at his feminine traits, we can see how they are tied up with his sensitivity. He tends to be a kind, compassionate, and considerate person, having little trouble nurturing either his family or his colleagues. He might not always choose to be the nurturer in the work environment but he is the kind of man whose right actions afford a sense of protection.

Ordinarily sensitivity is regarded as a feminine trait, and it is. But remember that women are not the sole owners of the feminine aspect; within each of us there are both masculine and feminine essences. We need to understand the true nature of sensitivity in order to wrap our heads around the Sensitive Man archetype. Some people think that when someone is described as *sensitive* it means they are submissive or weak, but that is not the meaning I use. Within this inner male-female paradigm, someone who is sensitive is kind, empathetic, and courageous. Men who are in touch with their feminine side but who still keep their masculine aspect in good working condition are the new modern-day warriors, the champions.

By honoring his feminine aspect, the Sensitive Man automatically honors his sensitivity and in so doing he has constant access to his creativity. His creativity is fundamental to his ability to innovate and that gives him the ability to make decisions that are a little outside of the normal linear, rational decision-making process. The way he honors his feminine process releases him to his masculine power in ways not previously recognized.

A MAN OF ACTION AND PROTECTION

So let's take a closer look at this man's masculine persona. He is a man of action, and it is usually right action. He does not accumulate knowledge through observation and then leave it sitting in a safe place; he follows through and does what needs to be done. He is reasonable, logical, and able to implement processes. He is naturally a good leader. He is secure within himself, which frees him to be collaborative and to lead by example.

Depending on what he does for a living or how successful he is, he will often wisely find individuals with a good masculine aspect to implement what he needs done on his behalf. He draws to himself good people in the workplace. The level of confidence with which he lives his life allows him to trust the abilities of those around him. People enjoy working for him because of his creativity, his wise masculine decision-making ability, the protection he offers, and his fairness—all good qualities for an employer to have.

The Sensitive Man is brave so he will take risks, but not unreasonable risks; he considers things appropriately and takes risks accordingly. His courage engenders trustworthiness and this makes him a powerful person in his own sphere of influence. Nor is the Sensitive Man the world's greatest talker. He is not the one telling stories and jokes at the bar because he has no need to be the center of attention. He does have a good sense of humor, just not the kind that ridicules others. He sees the funny side of things and he can be quite quirky. He speaks when he has something significant to say.

SENSITIVE MEN AMONG US

The Sensitive Man is wonderfully developed when it comes to his ability to protect both his own feminine aspect and the vulnerability of others. A modern-day warrior, he protects the vulnerable among us whether they be animals, the poor, the mentally ill, the very young, or the very old; basically anyone in need of assistance. He is brave and stands in the path of those who would not hesitate to brutalize the innocent.

An example of this type of man is Paul Watson, captain of the *Sea Shepherd*, founder of the Sea Shepherd Conservation Society, and an early member of Greenpeace. Feeling a deep empathy and compassion for the animals subjected to cruel methods of culling, Watson left Greenpeace when it had a change of leadership and the incoming leader decided the organization would no longer take direct action to halt the callous activities it once opposed so valiantly. Therein lies the ability to discern. In the case of saving whales, if direct action was not taken it could be argued that whales would be almost extinct. On this matter, Watson would not be swayed. His is the story of a true modern-day warrior.

Another good example of this modern-day warrior is the well-known British chef Jamie Oliver. Oliver decided to use his celebrity to help the severely overweight. His Ministry of Food attempts to bring nutrition education to those in underprivileged, undernourished, and severely overweight communities, helping people by actively promoting the fact that you must make your food choices consciously in order to live a long, healthy, and active life. This has not been an easy journey for him. He was not met with open arms, especially when he took his ideas to America where he was actively scorned by powerful food companies and their advocates who opposed the changes he was so passionate about. Had he not carried the modern-day warrior actively within him he could easily have given up. Jamie continues his work through his programs for teenagers at risk by giving them apprenticeships in his specialty restaurants around the world and through his television shows.

WE NEED MORE MODERN-DAY WARRIORS

The men mentioned above are just two examples of this new style of Sensitive Man our millennium is calling for. Modern-day warriors can come from any background; they do not need to be captains of industry but many of them are because that is a role in which they feel very comfortable. The days of the dishonest, selfish, and power hungry tyrants within organizations are coming to an end. We require so much more from our leaders in corporate life right now: that they be balanced, fair-minded, and right thinking.

Fortunately, we have the possibility of a new day and a new way of conducting corporate life. If this new type of warrior leader, the Sensitive Man, can continue to move business along the track of *right* rather than the track of *greed*, then anything is possible. Waxing lyrical about this man's virtues might be a little irritating, since by comparison we have judged our other archetypes rather harshly. But the truth is that this man is the best of all of us; he just happens to be housed in a masculine body.

As this man is erring slightly more on the feminine side of the spectrum, probably through environmental reasons, he will probably be attracted to one of our male-oriented women. The Good Doer would be the best partner for him. She is still very much in touch with her feminine aspect and they would probably share a similar outlook on life. However, depending on his upbringing, his values and lessons already learned, he can be vulnerable to any of the male-oriented women. At times he may find himself confused and a little bewildered by the manipulations of the Andro and Faux Feminine women, but unlike his much more feminine-oriented brothers, this man has enough strength to take action when he does recognize what is going on, and handle the situation.

It is important to note that the masculine aspect of a man needs to be recharged. The Sensitive Man regularly energizes his masculine polarity through healthy relationships with good male friends who, like him, are solid and dependable. They might dine together after work, play golf, or bond over fixing things or working some pet project that needs to get done. Generally when men gather, their activities are less about talking and more about doing, as compared to women who are quite happy to simply engage in conversation.

One of the most endearing qualities of the Sensitive Man is that he is genuine. He is not a person who pretends or poses in order to seek attention. It is these very traits that distinguish him from our next archetype, the Pseudo Masculine Man.

CHAPTER 12

The Pseudo Masculine Man

SHE SAYS: "LUCK WON'T FIND YOU A JOB."
HE SAYS: "I THOUGHT *YOU* WERE MY LUCK."

CASE STUDY: OSCAR AND ABIGAIL

When Oscar entered my office I was a little taken aback. I was not expecting this robust, fit, attractive-looking man. The referral was from his wife, Abigail. I had coached her on a transformational program and she had responded very well to her newly discovered talents. She really wanted her husband to join her on her exciting journey, thus my meeting with Oscar had been arranged.

The truth of the matter was that Abigail was a driven woman who had goals and dreams for her family. She was concerned that Oscar's attitude was a little listless and she wanted me to inspire him toward more meaningful work. Well, that's not quite right. What she said was *any* work would be good. She had been supporting the family by herself since their first child was born, and now that they had their ideal family of two she was anxious for some tangible support from her husband. When she set the scene for me about all this she had been polite, but I detected that she was at the end of her tether. She was adamant that the time had come for Oscar to step up and take his place as the breadwinner of the family.

There seemed to be absolutely no reason why he shouldn't. After all, he was a qualified civil engineer. Abigail had found the name of a headhunter for engineers and she had even seen several positions advertised in the newspaper. She strategically placed these leads on the breakfast table a couple of mornings in a row, but when she returned from work at the end of a long day, she discovered they had not been touched. In fact, no mention was ever made of them. When Oscar chose to ignore these leads it made Abigail feel subtly ignored. No matter what Abigail said or did, Oscar showed no serious interest in returning to the workforce.

Abigail's Point of View

Abigail had poured her heart out to me on this topic prior to my meeting Oscar, and in my role as coach I helped her understand the dynamics of what was going on. When she first opened up about her marriage and her disappointment with Oscar, she became both emotional and subdued. I got the impression that she felt that if she whispered, none of the nightmare she was experiencing would be real.

Abigail felt I could be the same catalyst to Oscar that I had been for her in our coaching sessions. "What he needs is motivation and you can do that, Jen. I know because you managed to inspire me to be far more than I ever thought I was capable of," she said.

Her words were touching, but I was a little concerned. "Abigail, you were so easy to inspire because you were motivated," I said. "You just needed more belief in yourself and a clear pathway to achieve what you wanted. You were a dream client. You had everything in place, so there wasn't much that I needed to do except be there for you as you plotted your course. And you did just that."

But then I needed to explain to her why it might not be as easy for me to inspire Oscar toward a change in himself. "What you need to understand is that in my experience, I can only inspire someone who has energy, motivation, and drive. Plus they need to have the *will* to overcome their inertia. They might not know what their next steps are, and that's okay, but they need to be hungry for those steps.

"So what I mean is that Oscar will have to have the personal *will* to want to put in the effort it will take to achieve his goals. Do you know what he personally wants to achieve?" I asked.

At this point she became even more exasperated. "You know what, I have no idea. You'll have to ask him because I can no longer speak to him about this subject without it ending in World War III. That's exactly why I want you to talk to him!"

Oscar's Point of View

Oscar was a large handsome man with a ready smile and a charming manner. He could have been accepted into any job on any given day of the week: he was qualified, personable, and had impeccable manners. As he sat down and made himself comfortable, I told him that I'd had a wonderful journey with Abigail and that she thought I might be of some assistance with his next steps.

His reply was rather blunt. "I want to be frank with you. I'm only here because Abigail almost threatened me with a divorce if I didn't make an appointment to see you."

I met his candor. "Sorry to hear that, Oscar. I prefer my clients to be willing participants, not sacrificial lambs. So which is it to be?" This caught him a bit off guard, but with a little nervous laugh he said, "Of course I'm a willing client."

Those were the first signs of what I was pretty sure would prove to be my next encounter with the Pseudo Masculine Man. It was clear to me, despite his words, that Oscar was not a willing participant; he did not want to be in my office at all. He wanted to be at home doing whatever it was that he did all day while his wife was at work. I began by asking about his career.

"Well, I had a bit of bad luck," he began. "I was laid off from my job almost two years ago now, and there just hasn't been anything suitable in my field since then."

When I expressed surprise that there were no jobs at all for engineers in his industry he did admit, "Oh, there were some things, but nothing that I was interested in or wanted to be involved in."

I pointed out that that it is usually easier to get a job when you have a job, any job. Work is honorable and it tends to send a better message to employers if you are working. They usually understand that you might not be working at the job of your dreams, but they will almost always give you credit for getting out there and doing what needs to be done.

He listened to me but was quick to clarify his own point of view. "But you don't understand. Nothing needs to be done. Abigail has a fantastic job and she earns more than enough to support all of us."

By now if I'd had any doubts at all about what type of man I was dealing with, they were instantly dispelled. It was clear: Oscar was a Pseudo Masculine Man in the fullest sense of the term.

ABDICATING THE ROLE OF HUSBAND, FATHER, AND PROTECTOR

I sat quietly for a moment. The first thought running through my mind was, What a waste. This man had the makings of a champion. He had a wonderful masculine physique, a good brain, and a personable nature. When I encountered this type of man it was always a mystery to me why he was so reticent to step into the true masculine role. Of course, I understood from my practice, research, and analysis over the years that Abigail had unwittingly disempowered him with her own competence and success. But why was he so lackluster that he could not step up to the plate and support his talented wife in her endeavors? Well, obviously, he just could not. But the question for me always remains, Why is this happening and what can be done? In this case, I had a pretty good idea on both these counts.

Abigail was not responsible for his listless attitude to work and manhood. She was merely the masculine-oriented woman whom he had been seeking, probably for most of his adult life. Their affinity would have been palpable; they had the perfect polarity to form an attraction: her masculine energy was high and strong and his feminine energy was high and strong. They made a perfect match energetically, but that did not mean it would be a fully successful match when it played out in the physical world.

The majority of women I encounter who are attached to these kinds of men tend to make excuses for them. Abigail did not. She had spent time with me and she knew that she had every right to pursue her own career. She did not have to carry a passenger in the process. It was maddening for her. She had a husband who was fit and able-bodied, with a good deal of intelligence, and they could have happily enjoyed their reversed polarity. It would have worked if Oscar was prepared to carry his fair share of the load. They could have had a happy interdependent life raising their children and being strongly supportive of each other. Instead Oscar abdicated his responsibilities, being quite satisfied to have her support his easygoing lifestyle at home.

When I think about it, the Pseudo Masculine Man is very much like the Highly Feminine Man, whom we will talk about in the next chapter. But the difference is that the Pseudo Masculine Man likes to give the impression of being *the man*. When you become aware of what he is doing, it can prove quite irritating, especially when he thinks he is fooling you with his little ruse. But make no mistake, the Pseudo Masculine Man is no man. He is a passenger in life. He wants to avail himself of the benefits life has to offer, and those benefits can be quite substantial; all he has to do is come across as the man. In Oscar's case, he had it made because he was good looking and intelligent. When you look at this combination of attributes along with his male form, he could fool almost anybody.

Pseudo Masculine Motivations

By this time I already had a lot of information from the first part of our session. I was fully comfortable with the type of man I was dealing with and I knew he would reveal himself even more to me as we worked through our next hour together. I was determined to see if I could help him, so I continued with my open-ended questioning.

"Oscar, what do you like to do in your spare time?"

He giggled at this simple question, and I found his laugh strangely disconcerting for such a big man. "I have quite a lot of free time these days, so I've taken up golf," he gushed. "I love being at the club. Do you play?"

"No I don't, Oscar. I haven't really ever found the time," I answered politely but I made a mental note of how skillful he was at including me in his conversation, drawing me in, or so he hoped, into his web. This is part of the charming Pseudo Man I had glimpsed before.

I asked if he had regular golfing group. "Oh yes, I have a number of friends that I partner with on a weekly basis. It could be good for business too. You know that most business is done on the golf course?"

I did of course know that, but I wondered what actual work Oscar would be talking about on the links since he had not worked in almost two years. When I asked if he had any other interests, he told me he liked to skydive and work out at the gym. As I mentally totaled up the hours involved in all these activities I thought to myself, Of course you don't want to go to work. There's clearly too much fun to be had with all the leisure time you have at your disposal.

These were all worrying signs. I was now afraid that Abigail would never have a husband to help her and would never be able to work fewer hours. Working a shorter week was one of her goals because she so desperately wanted to have more time with her children while they were growing up. In fact, it was her key motivation in having me speak with Oscar. She reasoned that if he found gainful employment and started bringing home a paycheck again, she could have more precious time with her little ones.

The Roots of the Pseudo Masculine Man

There are many different ways men become Pseudo Masculine, and I wondered what Oscar's influences were. So I asked him to tell me about his side of the family and whether they lived nearby.

"Oh, I come from a wonderful family," he said. "They don't live close to Abigail and me. They actually live on the other side of the country. I moved away when I went to college."

I inquired further. "Do you sometimes feel you'd like to live close to them again now that you have a family of your own?"

When he said no, it did not surprise me at all. This was common in the Pseudo Masculine men I had interviewed before. I had observed over the years that this type of man often moves away from a dominant authority figure. And sure enough, his next remarks were very telling.

"My father was a military man," Oscar continued. "He was pretty strict with us when we were growing up. We also moved around quite a bit. So I feel comfortable not being physically close to the family."

I pushed just a bit further. "Was your father well ranked in the military?"

"Oh yes, he was right up there, but I'm not really here to talk about him, am I?" Oscar said, letting me know he'd had enough of this line of questioning.

It was clear to me that his father was a powerful figure in his life, but I felt he was a figure of fear. Oscar seemed to want his approval and his attention, he even might have wanted to emulate him, but he did not want to be in proximity to him. Oscar was happy to drop the subject, so I moved on.

My next strategy was to steer our discussion back to Oscar finding employment. "Oscar, what do you think you might do in the future?" By now I was getting really tired of the pace of the conversation; it was like pulling teeth from a toothless man!

"Oh, I didn't tell Abigail, but I have an interview tomorrow. It looks good. I could tell on the phone the woman I spoke to was keen on me and she gave me some really good indications that I was right for the job." On the surface this sounded like terrific news, but underneath it I saw the arrogant swagger that is almost always present with the Pseudo Man.

"Well, that's terrific, Oscar. It might have been nice for you to share that news with Abigail first rather than me though."

In typical Pseudo man fashion, he replied, "Oh no, I don't want to get her hopes up. I might not like the job. If it isn't right, I don't care if they offer it to me or if the money's good. I won't take it."

Living in Arrogance and Illusion

I knew that this man was highly unlikely to become a long-term client of mine, so it was no loss to me that he did not want to change.

But with that thought, I felt sad and defeated on Abigail's behalf. Oscar was so utterly self-centered that his wife and her well-being were not even on his radar. The only thing in his sights was his own sense of entitlement to the life he wanted and had now grown accustomed to thanks to Abigail's hard work. It was clear that Oscar was not overly concerned about the care of his young family either. If he had been a man whose masculine energy was in good shape, he would have reverted to his protective instincts the moment he was laid off from his job. He would have done what a decent father does to ensure the safety of his family, which is to secure steady employment, whatever that might be at the time of the crisis. While it is true that the masculine-oriented man no longer has to drag the "kill" home to feed his family, he still has the same obligations for the protection of those in his care. This means taking a job or finding some gainful employment that will ensure the financial security of his loved ones.

Regretfully, many feminine-oriented men today have abdicated their male role to the masculine women in their lives. Those women could be their mothers, wives, or sisters. These men seem to have taken the path of least resistance because women are now able to "hunt" and provide. It has become acceptable for women to bring home the kill and feed the family because they are quite capable of earning a good salary and benefits. However, what these men do not realize is that in their arrogance and laziness they are easing themselves out of society. They hold little importance in the equation if they do not participate in the protection of their families. Women's equality has somehow given them the go-ahead to release their manhood into the care of the women in their lives, and it is wreaking havoc.

Surrounded by Pipe Dreams and Puffery

But Oscar was not done. It seemed he was looking for redemption as he explained, "I'm thinking of going into business for myself."

I smiled and inquired further. "I think it's terrific to be self-employed, Oscar, but have you thought it through? It takes quite a bit of discipline and wherewithal to find a solid stream of clients, enough to get the business started and viable. Then it will likely be a good three years before the business really gets going."

"Yes, I think you're right," he said. "But that's okay because Abigail has a really secure job that she likes, so I'm sure she wouldn't mind being the major earner while I get the business on its feet." When I asked if his wife was aware that he planned to launch this new business idea, he covered himself quickly. "Goodness no, I haven't told her. I'm still thinking about it. No use talking about it before I'm ready to do it."

Well, not much use for me to talk about anything else with Oscar at this point. I had a clear picture of him. He was a dreamer. He had pipe dreams that would eventually cost Abigail dearly if she did not take the situation in hand. She would need to use all her masculine energy to steer herself and her family in the direction she wanted them to go. Clearly, her husband had very little masculine direction or motivation and no *will* to do a job that might not suit him. In fact, there would be only a few jobs he would even want to do. I came to the conclusion that Oscar simply did not have working as a priority in his future.

As we wrapped up the session I invited him to call me if he needed any advice for his upcoming interviews. We both knew he would never call. He had done what Abigail asked and now he could relax back into his old ways. We said polite goodbyes knowing we would never meet again.

RELATIONSHIP REALITY CHECK

To understand what had happened in Abigail and Oscar's marriage we have to go back to before the birth of their babies. Abigail was a highly successful and accomplished businesswoman. Oscar was employed but had already shown signs of not being overly enamored with corporate life. He was sometimes arrogant at work and had missed a few project deadlines. When layoffs were on the horizon, he knew his name might be on the list but nothing had been decided. Besides, this was before the children came so it did not concern Abigail at all. She was hopelessly in love with her good-looking man-about-town.

And Oscar adored Abigail too. She was everything he wanted, the woman of his dreams. He loved her competence, her no-nonsense attitude to life, and most of all he loved the fact that she was a go-getter. They were hopelessly in love and in a state of high attraction to each other. So you can only imagine how confusing and disconcerting it was for Abigail when she discovered after the birth of her first baby that there were cracks appearing in their relationship. Oscar was suddenly unemployed, she was more exhausted than she thought possible, and they were squabbling every day. But she pushed her feelings away thinking she was just tired and not coping with her newborn as well as she would have hoped.

However, as the baby grew, her feelings of dissatisfaction with Oscar did not abate. She was mildly concerned that she would not get the attraction back for Oscar she'd once had. Again she told herself that she was the problem and it was just that she was adjusting to being a new mother. When Oscar seemed to have more evenings out with his friends and began playing more and more golf, she grew more concerned but wasn't sure what to do. Then it was time for another baby. Abigail once again immersed herself in baby world and continued to make excuses for Oscar, usually finding some way to quietly blame herself. Maybe he did not find her new motherly figure attractive. Maybe her hormones were still out of whack. She fabricated any number of potential reasons for the problems in the marriage, but she really had no clear proof that what she was thinking was actually what was happening for Oscar.

POLARITY CAN BE BLISSFUL OR A BURDEN

In terms of this inner male-female paradigm, what had actually happened was that with the arrival of each baby, Abigail's polarity had shifted. Abigail was on the high end of the spectrum of her masculine when she met Oscar and he was on the high end of his feminine essence. That was the reason for their high level of attraction when they first met and set up their home; the strong polarity in the relationship contributed to the bliss. However, with the birth of each baby, Abigail moved more into her own natural feminine aspect, causing her internal essence to shift closer to the feminine and further away from her high masculine. She discovered that she liked motherhood, and shifted yet again.

At this point what would have been ideal in this situation was for Oscar to step up and fill the masculine space in the relationship that Abigail had vacated with the birth of her children. But he did not. He stayed steadfastly rooted in his feminine and that started to cause major issues in their relationship. With the polarity between them sliding off balance, Abigail was losing her attraction for Oscar. The more feminine she became in her role as a nurturing mother, the more Oscar's attraction toward her waned. Feminine to feminine causes a lack of attraction so the more feminine Abigail became, the less polarity there was between them. The rules of polarity had allowed them to have a perfect and blissful attraction in the beginning, but those same rules were now creating a burden. They did not realize what the shift would cost them. As per the undeniable rules of polarity, the attraction they had originally felt for each other had dwindled to almost nothing.

LIVING THE LESSONS OF POLARITY

When life-changing events come along, both members of a couple need to be flexible in order to adjust and find equilibrium. If Oscar had embraced the fact that all relationships are dynamic and constantly shifting, and been willing to shift himself as needed, the two of them could have maintained a better and healthier relationship. And they could have found their way to a new equilibrium with regard to the polarity between them. As it was, however, Oscar's fixed stance in the relationship left them with little room to maneuver, and they were unable to improve the situation they found themselves in as new parents. Instead of stepping up to a more masculine role in the relationship, Oscar chose to exploit the situation subtly (and sometimes not so subtly) to his advantage. And at the same time he was sending a clear message to Abigail that he had no intention of changing.

So if they argued about how much golf he played, he would say how stressed out he was and that he needed the relief. If she asked him to give her more help with the children, he said he was too busy with his networking and his job search. If they squabbled about money, he would say there were just no jobs; that he was trying his hardest. In the next breath Oscar would subtly suggest that since money was so tight, maybe Abigail could cut her maternity leave short and maybe ask for a raise, since she was so valuable to her company. Oscar's behavior was designed as a clear indicator to her that he was very displeased with the way things had turned out for them and most importantly, how they turned out for *him*. Abigail felt she was being punished for being a mother and causing their perfect life to change.

The bottom line was that Oscar was not up for the responsibility being a father demands. He needed to step into the natural masculine role of being the champion, the defender and protector of his family. Stepping into his masculine aspect would have solved two major problems in their relationship. First, if Oscar took a job, even it was not ideal, he would relieve his wife of the full financial burden she was buckling under. Second, being a provider once again would help him access more of his internal masculine essence. That would fill in the missing masculinity in their relationship, putting the polarity between them back into a positive state. The newly balanced polarity would restore the intimate attraction to each other every couple needs in order to be happy and for a marriage to be sustainable. Regretfully, Oscar did not want anything to change; he stubbornly wanted to hold on to his old life.

MORE SIGNS OF THE PSEUDO MASCULINE MAN

The Pseudo Man, like our Faux Fem Woman, is not likely to recognize himself in these case studies. It has been my observation that this man is so busy being somebody other than who he actually is that he is left with little room for introspection.

The Pseudo Man is always ready to blame someone else but very, very rarely will he shine the spotlight on his own shortcomings. In a relationship with him you could find yourself being the person who is readily blamed, and you will often find yourself accused of being unsupportive. This approach is designed to cause you to question yourself: Am I being too harsh? You could also find yourself feeling guilty. Once the guilt settles in, he has you exactly where he wants you. But remember, whenever there are two adults in a relationship, it means each person has to take responsibility. One does not get to carry the entire load; that is the rule in all levels of the relationship.

I have seen many women completely heartbroken by this type of man who is always full of promise but delivers very little. The woman tricks herself with the optimistic view that he will "do better next month." Or "The right job is around the corner for him. I just have to be supportive and patient." And the one statement that will allow a woman to trick herself more than any other is "But I love him." Yes, love is great. But if you forsake yourself and decide to go down that path, then you have to take complete responsibility for your actions and stop complaining about him. Remember, you are not responsible for him anyway. He is an adult and he needs to behave as such. I cannot stress this enough—it is *not* about you.

If you find yourself going up and down with this man's moods and promises, then know you are on a roller-coaster ride that will have no end. You have to make the decision to get off a ride that is taking you nowhere. He needs to step up and claim his manhood, and if he says he loves you, then remind him that love equals work and true support. Love requires demonstrations of good intention. Intentions without action remain just that: hollow.

You might wonder how I know this with such certainty? It's because I've been there. I consider myself an intelligent and successful person, but I have been fooled and heartbroken by the Pseudo Masculine Man more than once. My biggest heartbreaks, the most horrible times, came about after falling under the spell of the Pseudo Man. In all honesty, when I look back now, the signs were there. Very early in each of those relationships, I saw indicators that those men had no intention of stepping up into their masculine role. But each time, I foolishly gave the guy the benefit of the doubt because he was so charming. And somehow I seemed to find a way to blame myself, which is typical of what women do, even those of us who should know better.

I don't make excuses anymore and I advise women today to keep both eyes open in the dating world. All adults, men and women, need to be aware of the type of person we are attracting. Another example of one to watch out for is the Highly Feminine Man, our next archetype. He's not a heartbreaker, but his behavior and characteristics can still cause issues for the women and men he encounters daily. Let me introduce you now.

CHAPTER 13

The Highly Feminine Man

SHE SAYS: "YOU'RE PAINFULLY SENSITIVE."
HE SAYS: "I THOUGHT I WAS JUST SENSITIVE TO PAIN."

CASE STUDY: LIAM

Liam came to see me on the recommendation of his good friend Max. Max and I had had a wonderful journey together and Max was eager for me to shed some light on his friend's plight. The relationship between Max and Liam seemed to be in transition. "Jen, I just can't be there for Liam anymore," Max had confided to me. "He's a great buddy of mine, but the issues he's having now are becoming a little too large for me to deal with. Frankly, I can't hear about them anymore. Besides, I just don't know what to tell the guy. I feel for him, but I'm at a loss as to what to say." I told Max that it would be my pleasure to assist his friend and be a sounding board for him. "Thanks, this guy needs a 'girlfriend.' I just can't be that for him," he said with a smile as he left my office.

Liam arrived for his appointment the following week. He was an immaculately dressed man. When I say immaculate, I mean not a hair out of place, shoes so shiny you could see your reflection in them. His suit was stylishly cut and obviously very expensive; cufflinks on his beautifully tailored shirt. I had not seen a man so elegantly dressed in a very long time. And when he greeted me Liam's level of innate politeness made me feel like I had stepped into an

142

age gone by. It was quite soothing in a strange sort of way. This man was so respectful that I could imagine there would be many instances in today's world where he might feel a little out of place.

"Good morning, Liam, so very nice to meet you." As I extended my hand to shake his, I almost felt as if he were going to kiss mine. The impression I got was that this man would never step out of line. I thought to myself, How unusual for our times, and how fascinating.

He sat rigidly upright on the sofa so I encouraged him to relax in whatever way he needed to. "I want you to feel at home here, that you can let go of any formality that might get in your way." With that, I moved away, turning my back to him briefly as I turned on some music and got a pot of green tea. When I turned to face him again, Liam looked only marginally more comfortable, and I resigned myself to the fact that it would take a while for him to feel at ease in these surroundings.

Overwhelmed at the Office

"Liam, how can I help you? Max mentioned that you were feeling a little overwhelmed with some of your employees and there were also a few things going on at home. Is that correct?"

"Right on the money," he responded. "Max has been a wonderful friend, but my issues have become so pressing that I feel I might have worn out our friendship. He said you have a unique way at looking at problems and I feel another set of eyes on these issues might be helpful."

He seemed ready to open up so I invited him to go on. "Why don't you give me an overall view of what's going on and then we can break it down and see what we can do?"

"Right, well, first up, my wife is threatening to leave me and frankly I don't know what I'd do if she did. And secondly, I have a few employees who seem to be pushing me and I honestly don't understand what they want from me." Liam further explained that he was the CEO of a medium-size architectural company. He had forty employees and five senior architects who worked directly under him. He still did some of the architectural work himself.

"So, Liam, would it be fair to say that you find yourself sandwiched between your work life and your home life? That neither area seems to be working well for you at this time?"

His response was immediate. "That's putting it mildly! It's just awful. We have so many deadlines to meet and there's just so much going on that doesn't have anything to do with work."

I glanced at Liam over the top of my glasses and noticed the pain etched on this very gentle man's face. From the information Max had given me I already had a good idea of whom I would be dealing with before his appointment. I watched Liam's discomfort at having to share his problems. I could see that he was a deeply internal man, sensitive and introverted; he was not the type of person who was happy talking to strangers about what was troubling him.

I dropped my voice and spoke quietly, hoping Liam would feel my empathy, because I felt for him. Looking down the barrel of a divorce was horrific, and when that was combined with problems at the office any normal person would be distressed. For someone like Liam, who had all the characteristics of what I call a Highly Feminine Man, this was an intolerable situation.

Sorting Out All the Issues
I decided to use my usual approach of breaking things down to see what the most pressing issues really were. "Why don't we deal with one situation at a time and then we can have a look at how one impacts the other in terms of how you might want to deal with them," I offered.

"Right. Okay, well my wife thinks she no longer loves me and wants to leave," he said sadly. "She feels I don't value her enough and she's tired of my 'gutless' behavior. I'm not much company when I get home from work. She has many, many girlfriends and they seem to have a very big influence on the way she thinks these days."

I asked Liam if that made him feel isolated from her and he nodded.

"That's exactly right and frankly I don't have the energy to deal with her obtuse conversations about these women when I get home after a very long day," he said.

"Yes, I understand," I said. "But you still want the relationship?"

"Yes, of course I do," he confirmed. "She's behaving strangely right now, but she's a fantastic organizer. She runs our home with military precision and she's an amazing cook. Last but certainly not least, I love her." Liam looked so sad at this point, I thought he might cry.

"Liam, do you have a good personal assistant at the office?" He responded with a wry smile. "Oh yes, I have Samantha, who is amazing. I call her my 'office wife.' We all love her. If she decided to work anywhere else, I think that could be as bad as my wife leaving me." Liam dropped his smile and suddenly looked very worried; it had just dawned on him that maybe Samantha might leave him too.

The situation was clear to me now. Liam was indeed a Highly Feminine Man and he needed these highly efficient male women to run his life. He probably was not conscious of this when he married his wife Christine, or when he hired Samantha. I allowed him to sit and contemplate this little lightbulb moment he was experiencing. There is nothing like quiet reflection to bring home news of this kind.

As he sat, I continued making my own observations. Liam had been married to Christine for fifteen years and they had two children. He loved his children but did not enjoy the noise or the mess they created. He had a great business with good people working for him but suddenly the wheels were coming off in both his private and business worlds.

The Andro in the Room

My next question was directed toward his business life. "Liam, what's going on in the office?"

An audible sigh escaped from this exasperated man as he responded. "I just can't fathom it. I have a senior architect, a woman, who seems to be driving everyone crazy. Then I have three other seniors coming to me on a daily basis complaining about her and frankly I don't know what they expect me do."

I had already figured out from the way he was talking that the woman would be an Andro Woman and the seniors probably had a healthy masculine energy as well. Liam, on the other hand, was the feminine element in his office. "Liam, could we drill down a little further with this problem? What are the three senior architects complaining about?"

He seemed a bit embarrassed but he answered honestly. "Well, from what I can tell, Ruth is apparently taking liberties with her time, turning up late and not getting jobs done on time, which throws the timeframes out for the junior architects. One of the seniors even alluded to the fact that she might have a substance abuse problem."

I was alarmed and said to Liam that this sounded rather serious. I thought we should deal with this problem right away but I needed to know a bit more about Ruth. "Liam, have you noticed anything strange about Ruth yourself?" I asked.

"Not really," he responded, "but then I don't actually have much to do with anyone directly. I spend a lot of time in my office. The way I look at it, everyone in the office is an adult, so they can manage themselves, don't you think?"

I chose not to respond to that question, but this was certainly another clue. Liam's high femininity was causing him to hide in his office rather than being front and center in his own business. So I asked another question. "What else are people saying about Ruth? It seems to me like it might be a much bigger problem than you realize."

"Well, apparently Ruth is saying they can do what they like but that her job is rock solid because she is so connected to me," Liam responded.

I posed my next question with an air of caution, not sure of what I was about to discover. "Liam, is that true?"

He hesitated before he answered, which wasn't a good sign, but I felt he trusted me enough to be fully honest. "The truth is that we had a fling at university. I do regard her as family now and it would be hard for me to let her go."

Drilling through the Denial

I decided to risk everything now and ask Liam a deeply personal question. "Liam, does this have anything to do with your wife threatening to leave you?"

Again he took a moment before he answered. "Yes, it does. Christine feels that Ruth takes liberties and she is also acutely aware of my indiscretion with Ruth all those years ago."

I continued to tread carefully as I asked if Ruth was maybe talking about their past relationship at the office and maybe that was how it had gotten back to his wife.

"Exactly," was Liam's response. "But how did you know?"

"Well, it just seemed coincidental that you had home and office problems at the same time. When that happens, things are often related," I responded.

Liam now seemed ready to offer more information; it was as if he was so relieved to have voiced the issue out loud that he wanted to purge himself of everything to do with the problem. "My senior architects are all threatening to leave and set up in opposition to me if I don't do something about this problem."

This was an extremely serious situation and Liam was without doubt a Highly Feminine Man. This archetype very often will not take action even when the issue is quite blatant yet has a rather simple solution. I had to tread lightly with this gentle, sensitive man because he was not the type to cope well with any perceived judgment on my part. I set about putting my case to him so he could see the facts for himself more clearly and then arrive at his own conclusion. Liam seemed to be a decent person who did not want to confront the truth because he just did not know how to take matters in hand. The problem was staring him squarely in the face but he was incapable of taking action.

"Liam, are you quite sure of the facts? Is Ruth taking liberties with the company's time?"

Liam was now quick to respond. "Oh yes, we have a time sheet system and she has apparently being doctoring the time sheets. She was caught out by one of the seniors who confronted her and then came tattling to me about it. Unfortunately, she also involved one of the junior staff members in this little scheme."

I was now clearly dismayed. "Liam, Ruth is effectively altering the culture of your office and setting an extremely bad example for junior members of your staff. This can have serious ramifications for your business and your bottom line."

He knew this was true and nodded sadly.

Facing the Emotional Upheaval

"Liam, would it be fair to say your bottom line has already been affected by Ruth's indiscretions?" I actually saw Liam's eyes well up with tears. I averted my eyes, not wishing to cause him any further embarrassment.

When he regained his composure, he responded. "Yes. Yesterday we lost a project that we spent six months preparing to present and quote on. That project would have secured two years' work for our company."

I thought I would push on with my questions. "Why did you lose the tender?"

He shook his head, looking rather mortified, and admitted that Ruth had had a liaison with the developer and the man's wife found out.

"Oh, and then—let me guess—your wife also found out?" I said. I could barely hear his answer.

"Yes," he whispered.

At this point I asked Liam if he could spare another half an hour on our session because I felt the issues were pressing and there was a lot at stake. He responded eagerly that I could take as long as I needed. He said he was feeling relieved and reassured me that he was prepared to look at the issues no matter how difficult they were for him to face.

I noticed that Liam was a lot more relaxed now even though he had just told me his distressing story. So I decided to be very direct with him. I felt he would be able to hear what I was saying even if it appeared a little harsh at first. I warned him that the paradigm I worked with could be a little jarring when one first confronts oneself with these new truths. He assured me that he was ready for whatever I had in my toolbox because he was a desperate man. Apparently Max had warned him to bring as much courage as possible to this session, and I could see that Liam had done so.

"Liam, your entire life is actually at risk, so we need to take a few steps that can alleviate that risk quickly. Are you okay with that?" I asked.

"Yes, let's get to it," he said. "I'll be so grateful if I can at least get some understanding of what's going on with me."

How the Paradigm Plays Out

With that, I had his permission to launch in, so I did. "I work on a number of levels at any given time," I explained, "but there is no use dealing with all those esoteric processes if we don't deal with the reality of the situation first. So I'll give you an overview of what I see and what your part in the process is.

"Please don't be offended if I appear direct, as sometimes things can look a little less than complimentary. But if you're willing to confront and understand them, then things can change rapidly. Ordinarily I would work with a client for many sessions over an issue this big, but we don't have the time. Time is of the essence for you." Liam was smiling slightly now and I began my diagnosis gently.

"Liam, you're what I would describe as a Highly Feminine Man. As such, you have some challenges when managing people and relating to those close to you like your wife and your employees," I explained. "You're highly intelligent and creative and that's very good for your business. Your feminine aspect is the part of you that dominates and this is what allows you to be so creative and innovative. I have seen some of your buildings and they are nothing short of beautiful."

I took a moment's pause and continued. "What's not so good is the fact that you have a lot of difficulty confronting people, especially those who need to be reprimanded for their bad behavior, such as Ruth. When you don't confront situations like that, you lose the respect of your colleagues and your employees. And the most important person you've affected is your wife. She appears to be so exasperated that she has one foot out the door."

I explained that his behavior showed a lack of visible strength compared to what is usually needed in business management, but that this was not unusual for a Highly Feminine Man. "The difficulty with your high feminine aspect is that your masculine forms your secondary energy," I went on. "But you do need to learn to use your masculine energy more often because that is your *doing* side, the one that's outgoing in the physical world. By accessing your masculine energy, you can then confront the people who feel free to play fast and reckless with your business and your personal life."

My words hung between us for a bit and I waited for Liam to absorb this explanation and the process I was describing. He did not seem shocked in any way, so apparently he had already heard about some of parts of my inner male-female paradigm from his friend Max.

Using One's Masculine Essence for Protection

When Liam responded, he appeared to be coming out of very deep thought. "This has been a problem for me my whole life," he said. I could see that pennies were dropping all over the place for him, so I stayed silent a little while longer.

When I continued, I went on to explain that another key element of our internal masculine energy is the ability to protect. This energy has to first protect one's own feminine energy, whether we are male or female on this earth. Our masculine essence then needs to expand out and protect everything around us that we consider precious and important. I could see that this aspect of our conversation was getting a bit confusing for Liam.

"I do want to ask you something," he said. "The word *protection*; it just sounds so archaic. We live in the twenty-first century. We're not in actual danger. What am I supposed to be protecting myself and my loved ones *from*?"

I had heard this one before so I was ready with my answer. "We might live in modern times but our internal construction has never changed in all the time we've been on the earth," I explained. "So let's make our protection relevant to current times. For instance, it's your role as the male element of your partnership to protect your wife from the possible scandal that could emerge from your indiscretion with Ruth all those years ago. Perhaps it wasn't a wise move to hire Ruth, when you look at it in hindsight. What do you think?"

I could see that Liam was visibly shocked and uncomfortable. But he did respond. "It was impossible not to hire her. To be honest, she bullied me into it and once she was there, I couldn't get rid of her."

This was a point I could not let slide. "So in other words, your wife has had to put up with your working with Ruth every day for the past ten years?"

He nodded.

Again I chose to stay silent, allowing him to process the enormity of what had just been revealed to him. Then I restated it so there could be no turning back in Liam's mind. "Ruth has endangered your company and she has definitely endangered your relationship with your wife, therefore your family is now in danger."

In a Duel for Attention

What had really happened was that Liam had been sandwiched between these two male women for a good many years and he had just accepted the situation as a fact. He did not realize that his wife might be suffering with the knowledge that Ruth still held a torch for her husband. Effectively what Liam had done was to leave these two male women to duel over him. I pointed out these implications to him. "You do realize, Liam, that you're effectively the female part of this duel?" He looked away sheepishly.

I knew he wanted an ultimate solution to this so I did not let him off the hook. "Liam, what I'm trying to get you to see is that your lack of protection of your own internal feminine energy has endangered your company. Because you didn't protect your feminine and stand up to the bullying from Ruth, your company is now suffering from diminished profitability, you have risked your business reputation, and your wife has had enough.

"This situation might not pose the same level of physical danger as a crocodile or other wild beast, but there is still a true and present danger to you and your livelihood," I added. "Furthermore, your wife was not protected from this possible threat, and now you might lose everything you hold dear."

I could see that the wheels were turning rapidly inside Liam's head. He fell silent once again, and once again so did I. It was obvious that we had done quite enough for one session. Liam and I agreed to reconvene in two days' time.

He needed time to process what he had learned about himself and I wanted to help him with a plan to move forward with his business and find a way to reassure his wife. She was going to need to witness a solid action plan from him in order to feel convinced that she and the children were protected. Liam had to prove that he had changed his attitude in relation to their family.

Taking Action Brings about Change

Liam remained a mild-mannered, immaculately dressed gentleman, but he was able to change his internal polarity quite dramatically by employing a few new tactics. Once he was aware of what needed to happen, he mustered the courage to implement the necessary changes across all areas of his life, including firing Ruth.

When Liam did ask her to leave the company, she did not go quietly. She threatened Liam with all kinds of retribution and he was mortified, but we got him through the process. He stood firm and Ruth was gone. She really had very little power to hurt him once she was out of his office because the industry already knew her reputation. They knew she had been the problem within the company, not Liam or his other senior team members.

The results of his decision to fire her were very gratifying: his home life improved exponentially and his business life was far more harmonious. In fact, better than he remembered it ever being. Almost immediately his employees had a lot more respect for him and he was able to regain several of the lost contracts so horribly sabotaged by Ruth's reckless actions. Most importantly, Liam's wife was happier after Ruth's departure.

That meant that our next immediate challenge was to help him in the process of interviewing for a new senior architect to replace Ruth. He made it quite clear that he did not want to find himself in the same situation as the one he had just dispensed with. He realized he was in danger of hiring the same type of person with a different face if he did not make a conscious effort to look for the warning signs he had missed with Ruth.

Liam was fortunate that his own good name in the industry and the reputation he had built for his company stood him in good stead. He received many recommendations from reliable colleagues and headhunters. He found the right person, and this time around he was the one in charge, not his new employee.

Liam remained a client of mine for the following year. During that time we gradually shifted his polarity from a heightened feminine orientation to more balanced level, which meant he could access his masculine essence much more readily. That shift was evident in his workplace because everyone settled down; there was not as much drama once Liam proved he would no longer put up with it. He was comfortable with the way things were at home too. Fortunately, he managed to keep the balance of the polarity between himself and his wife in a good state, so their relationship and family life were saved.

The prospect of nearly losing everything was enough for Liam to make the necessary fundamental changes within himself. He even came to enjoy his newfound masculine energy; using it made a significant difference to his leadership abilities both at home and in the office. Never again would he be prepared to endanger his livelihood and his family because he could not stand up and confront an obvious antagonist.

TRUE LEADERSHIP REQUIRES ACTION

Liam's story is not unique. I have found in my practice and in life that it is very common for a Highly Feminine Man to let things slide because he does not want to confront situations that could potentially take an ugly turn. It is easier to do as Liam did and hide in his office and pretend nothing was going on or that it was not a big deal. The problem with this attitude is that the people who get hurt are actually the people who do not deserve to be hurt. For example, Liam's senior architects were doing an excellent job; they were bringing in business and were clearly loyal to Liam. Liam repaid their loyalty with a weak management style. The seniors were forced to put up with an intolerable situation that was starting to damage not only Liam's reputation but theirs as well.

As the leader of his company, Liam had a duty of care to the whole of his company, which included all his employees, not just Ruth. The duty of care called for him to step up and man up to protect his business and those who worked in it. For years he did not step up because he simply could not; he was deathly afraid of Ruth the bully and unaware of what his inaction was costing him. It is my experience that the Highly Feminine Man has very poor leadership abilities due to his diminished capacity to confront and to act. These qualities are part of the masculine aspect. In Liam's case, it was not until he almost lost everything and he agreed to get help through coaching that things actually began to improve.

Whether we are men or women, leadership requires the masculine aspect within us to be in a healthy state because action is required when leading a company or a family. You have to be able to fire the person who is not behaving appropriately or reprimand a family member who is out of line with the family value system.

SHIFTING THE PULL OF POLARITY

Liam was actually afraid of Ruth. Why was he afraid? Because Ruth's masculine energy was so high and so strong. She was bombastic and arrogant, traits that highly masculine Andro women very often carry. In the face of her masculine arrogance and his former association with her, Liam felt powerless. And he was in fact powerless given the state of his inner polarity, which for the years Ruth worked in his company was on the high side of feminine.

This sort of scenario plays out in people's personal lives just as easily as it does in their business lives. It is the principle in play when two opposing internal aspects come into play in any given situation. High feminine to high masculine can cause high attraction and just as easily, high levels of fear. Liam's favoritism of his feminine aspect caused him to be derelict in his duty to his wife as well. Not only was his business under constant threat but so was his marriage. He seemed oblivious to the pain and discomfort Ruth's presence in his business life was causing.

I found out later, when I met Liam's wife, Christine, that she had been unhappy about Ruth's presence in the business because of Liam and Ruth's prior relationship. Christine's archetype was a Good Doer and so although she was quite male-oriented too, she was also a sensitive person and for a long time had made excuses for Liam's "gutless" behavior. But when Ruth's actions got completely out of control, Christine decided she would no longer be disrespected. She decided that either Liam had to step up to the plate and do something about Ruth or she was going to leave their marriage. All the ramifications of Liam's high feminine aspect came to a head at one time. An event will come along and highlight all the elements of a person's life that are out of alignment, thus illuminating the full truth of the situation.

SURROUNDING YOURSELF WITH THE OPPOSITE POLARITY

There is another element that needs to be pointed out with regard to Liam's life. The Highly Feminine Man very often attracts many masculine-oriented people around him for the simple reason that he is accessing so very little of the masculine inside himself. So if we look around Liam's world, he had a male woman who was his personal assistant, a male woman colleague in the form of Ruth, and many male colleagues who were quite masculine. Then at home he had a male woman in the form of his wife Christine. This is not a bad thing. Without all that external masculinity work and at home, Liam would have been left with an enormous amount of highly feminine traits, namely his extensive creativity and his talent, but no way to implement any of that talent and put it out to the world. That requires the masculine.

Furthermore, when it came to his personal life, for many years Liam had left his wife to duel it out with Ruth. Ruth had a high masculine aspect, so she was very definitely an Andro Woman. Christine had a high masculine aspect too, since she was a Good Doer. If we strip away the casing of the physical bodies of all three people involved in this story, we find that the two women were using their internal masculine aspects to duel over Liam's internal feminine aspect. In ages gone by men dueled for the honor of a woman. Today masculine women routinely duel against each other over the attention of feminine-oriented men because they are looking to fill what is missing from their own internal genders.

Liam progressed well over the year I coached him. As he grew more familiar and comfortable with his newly discovered masculine energy he came to realize, quite astutely, that he was still a work in progress. He had to continue to remain conscious and diligent around other people so as not to fall back into his old ways and allow someone new to polarize him back into his feminine. By heightening his masculine aspect and learning how to keep it in balance, Liam knew how to protect Christine from a similar situation ever occurring again. It was this promise that actually kept them together. The last time I saw Liam and Christine they were doing well and they and their daughters appeared to be very happy.

With this section on the archetypes complete, let's move into a more detailed discussion about how our polarity affects intimacy in our lives.

PART
THREE

CHAPTER **14**

What Happened to Intimacy?

SHE SAYS: "I'M DRAWN TO YOU LIKE A MAGNET."
HE SAYS: "FUNNY, I'M NOT FEELING IT."

THE MAGIC ELIXIR OF LOVE

Attraction is a wonderful force of mystery and magnetism. If we could bottle it and sell it, we would never run out of customers for this magical elixir. Everybody wants that special something that will deliver to him or her that special someone. They want a special attractive someone they can love and be loved by for all eternity. That is the image the world of romantic novels and movies creates in our minds. And we believe it.

According to *The Shorter Oxford English Dictionary on Historical Principles*, attraction is "the action of a body in drawing to itself, by some physical force, another to which it is not materially attached." But to us the very word *attraction* conjures up a sense of expectation, pregnant with hope and possibility, that a unique someone is out there somewhere, if only we could find them. So in the case of men and women, what is the force that causes them to draw toward each other? It is the tension created between the poles of their internal energy. The attraction we feel is the tension created between the dominant internal pole of the person we meet and our own dominant internal pole.

Attraction is essential because it drives the masculine within us to go and seek that special person. Men are the embodiment of the masculine principle, and nature decreed that men would be the hunters, not only of food but also of a mate. Once a man found his desired mate, he would pursue her until she gave him a yes or no for an answer. She made the choice. This is the natural way mating was meant to occur, with the man taking the lead, following the natural laws of polarity and attraction.

Contrast that with what happens today. Masculine women have become the hunters. We all know couples that were formed by the woman chasing down the man she had set her sights on. "What's wrong with that?" I can hear you asking. Absolutely nothing, if both people in the relationship are happy with that kind of dating and if they are willing to live in a relationship based on reversed internal polarity. I will explain further in this chapter about reversed polarity, but let's just consider the modern-day mating rituals first, because that is where a lot of the current strife between the sexes arises.

WHAT'S WRONG WITH AN ANDRO ON THE PROWL?

For four thousand years the old system of dating and mating worked well and was in keeping with our natural states as men and women. However, since women in their newfound maleness have taken to hunting for their mates themselves, they can be relentless in their task. The woman decides whom she wants and then pursues him until he succumbs like a wounded animal, or he turns around and bites her, again like a wounded animal. That bite might not be literal but it is just as painful, and it is natural! The man's response to the bite and to hate being pursued is natural to our species because the act of hunting a man emasculates him; the act of pursuit by the woman is against the natural order. Men should be the hunters because as primary owners of the masculine principle they are the natural directors and initiators. When a woman initiates the chase and catches her prey, she will always end up with a disempowered man. But let's consider: if she is a highly male woman that might be exactly what she wants and sure enough, she will get it.

However, if she is a woman who wants to know that her man is genuinely in love with her, or genuinely interested in pursuing a relationship with her, then she needs to allow him to pursue her. It is the only way she will know for sure the depth of his true interest in her. If she wants a man who has any amount of access to his own masculine essence, she will not find him by being the hunter herself. Just because she is not involved in the physical act of the pursuit does not mean that the woman loses any power. She is in no way meek, mild, or vulnerable; instead, she is active in her own way. Her activity is based on the internal magnetism of her feminine aspect, as nature intended it, and she is fully in control because she always has the right of refusal if the man's advances are not what she wants.

But today we are operating in a world where the process of dating and mating has been turned on its head. Men have become so disabled in the past few decades that few of them have the "muscles" to pursue a woman. That's because so many men have been burned and hurt by a masculine woman, to the point where they have become innately afraid of rejection and humiliation. It has gotten so bad that men can't seem to muster the effort to approach a woman, even if they are attracted to her. The humiliation many men fear is different from the right of refusal, which is a woman's prerogative. A woman's refusal is a gracious act of saying no, without seeking to damage the person being refused. Unfortunately, too many women have lost this graciousness and that is why men rightly fear undue humiliation should they be refused.

And while the right of refusal is a very powerful feminine tool when used with honor and integrity, it can be misused and can become a tool of manipulation. So a woman may refuse a man simply to keep him on a string. This is a game to her, not any kind of trust-building behavior. Women who act in this way sully the case of the feminine woman and anger men who are aware of being manipulated. Therefore, with current role reversals men are in danger of becoming fragile and womanly, something we are already witnessing. And women are becoming ever more male, with many of them resorting to intimidation and bullying to get their way. This behavior leads the female to behave as male subjugators did in the past.

WHAT REVERSED POLARITY DOES TO DATING

If a woman is highly masculine and chasing down her man to create a relationship, then it follows that her man will have to be predominantly feminine in his internal energy. In other words, she would be in her external masculine hunting mode and he would be in his internal feminine receptive mode. This is the process of polar opposite attraction in its simplest form; there is always a hunter and a receiver. Today the natural roles are reversed, creating the opposite of what nature intended. Reversing the process this way puts the woman in a weaker position, even though she may well feel superior and fully entitled to choose her man. The reality will always be that she was *not* the one doing the choosing, he was. And that is simply because he was the one who got to say yes or no to her advances, rather than the other way around.

It is helpful to think of the levels of attraction on a sliding scale. The far end of the scale was discussed above, where the woman who was highly masculine would end up attracting a man who was highly feminine. But as the scale slides away from the extreme case we just mentioned, we see that a woman can be quite male but still be able to access a healthy amount of her own internal feminine energy. In that case she can attract a man of high feminine energy but who still has a decent amount of masculine energy active within him. The concept that we are energy first before we are flesh makes the process of attraction a lot easier to understand. In other words, attraction is largely an unseen process. That means that even though we cannot actually see our energy or our vibration, it is what draws us to the people and the things we want in life. So if your polarity underpins your vibration and your vibration is the element that causes what you attract into your life, then is it possible to change your polarity?

Yes, it is possible but we have to fully understand the principles. Because this is an unseen process we often don't know why we are attracted to a person. Perhaps they are not physically what we had in mind. They may be shorter than us or they might not have the right color eyes. There is no accounting for how couples are formed. But the people receptive to the possibility of happiness are available to it when it turns up, even if it arrives in what might seem like the wrong package. This would explain why we see some pretty strange relationships. Family and friends might not understand how or why a certain couple is together, but the couple themselves always seem to be clear. They might not fully understand it but they feel comfortable, and in their hearts they know they are right for each other. Attraction is at work.

WHEN NATURE DOESN'T FOLLOW ITS RIGHT PATH

The whole process of a woman pursuing the man has another deleterious effect on the woman. A woman who thinks it is normal to pursue a man often finds herself maligned by the man, treated badly once they are in a relationship, or frankly just used by the man without any respect given her in return. When love is replaced with the desire for power in an intimate relationship, the relationship is held together with an unsustainable brittle tenuousness. There is an inability for either party to be vulnerable to the other because trust does not exist, leaving both partners feeling empty, alone, and isolated. So what is the point of being in a relationship if there is no heart connection and no true companionship?

It is important to note that because the masculine and feminine have largely reversed themselves, feminine men should follow the same rules. If you are a man operating strongly out of your feminine side, exercise your right to refuse the unwanted advances of a masculine woman. This will be an important step to finding your way back to your masculine self. If you refuse the advances of a woman you do not desire, you have the opportunity to rebuild your bravery and regain the strength to pursue a woman you do have an interest in. Saying no to the woman who may be bullying you or chasing you is a big first step to reclaiming your masculine power.

THE PROCESS OF CHANGING YOUR POLARITY

Recognizing that polarity is at play in relationships is crucial to understanding who we are as human beings. Whether we are aware of it or not, polarity is a key component of what we attract into our lives. The main reason people want to change their polarity is because they don't like what they are attracting. Would you be willing to change in order to get more of what you want in life, or to finally connect with the right person? To do this you would most likely have to change the degree to which you currently operate through your masculine and feminine energy. And that is accomplished through changing your thinking. In other words, you need to revisit how you see the world.

When we break this process down to its simplest level, we attract what we *think*. So to change what we are getting we have to first change our thinking, and that is not necessarily an easy process. There are so many factors at play, including deeply ingrained cultural and familial ways of being. And the process of change is not without its risks. It is not straightforward to suddenly change your thinking. There are many things to consider when you wish to make a significant change in your life. For example, you may have to admit that you were wrong in your previous thinking and accept that some of your past choices were ill advised. That can be tough.

And what if your family and friends don't like your new way of thinking? You could end up lonely and bereft of friends. Then at work things could change. What if your new thinking is no longer in line with the company's ethics or mission statement? What would that mean for your career? Perhaps most significantly, what if you are in a relationship and your polarity shifts because you have changed the way you think about yourself? When you adjust your thinking about what you want out of a relationship, you might wake up one day and find you are no longer even remotely attracted to the person you share your life with.

ADJUSTING YOUR THINKING TO FIND LOVE

These are some of the consequences that can arise when you shift your thinking, but there is no way to attract the right person for you without doing so. Many, many people know deep within themselves that they are not happy; in fact they might be desperately unhappy. But unfortunately most people make the decision not to change. They feel that the risks are too high; they are not prepared to expose the lives that they have, however flawed, to any level of risk. Even when the full truth is staring them right in the face, some people will still choose the path of denial.

That's why it is often said that change is not for the fainthearted. Change is for the warriors of the world, the ones who choose to be bold and who are in a constant state of wanting a better life for themselves and those they love. It takes courage to make the decision to change and then implement that change. You need to be brave because people who implement change always encounter opposition. That is a given. But if you truly wish to find someone to love you, someone you can love in return and spend a lifetime with, then change is necessary. The serenity you seek, that special sense of belonging you will feel when you share your life with the right person—that outcome outweighs all the risks.

You may feel you know exactly what you want, what kind of man or woman will make you happiest. Women in particular very often have a clear idea of what they want their intended partner to look like, or what he should be doing to earn a living, or which part of the country he should come from. I have even had women tell me that he should be a vegetarian, live in a particular suburb in their town, and be a lawyer! While all of these things can play a role if you want to be that superficial, the bottom line is that the person you are actually attracted to will ultimately be the one who is compatible with your current internal polarity status.

ROXANNE SHIFTS HER STATUS

In our case study of the Villainous Andro Woman, Roxanne was what we would call a masculine woman on the high end of the spectrum. She operated out of her masculine energy so comfortably it was as if she did not have a feminine side at all. She is a good example to revisit here, so we can understand how she shifted the status of her inner polarity.

It was only when Roxanne started to examine her life and when she formulated new goals that she came to the conclusion that she was unhappy. She accepted the fact that she was not getting the outcomes she wanted out of life because she was so highly male oriented. Most importantly for her, she recognized that she was very unhappy with the men she was attracting into her life. Through working on her own personal development, Roxanne arrived at the conclusion that she *would* like to have a father for her baby. She was a highly intelligent woman and she realized that a family unit was best for her future child. And as our program together progressed, she decided that not only did she want a father for her baby but she also wanted a companion for herself. She thought she wanted a high end of the spectrum masculine man, but you'll remember that I had to explain to her that this was not a match that would come about through the attraction process if she stayed the way she was.

Accepting That She Had to Change

Masculine has no polarity with masculine. So if Roxanne wanted a man with any active core masculine energy, she was going to have shift her own polarity status to accommodate the kind of mate she desired. Roxanne was brave and did just that. She actively started to engage with her feminine energy, and over the period of a year she managed to be comfortable with that part of herself: her internal feminine essence.

Roxanne was so far away from her feminine energy when she started out on her program that she honestly had little notion of where to begin. But since she said she was ready to change, I made a rather bizarre suggestion to her one day when she was bemoaning this very fact.

"Roxanne, would you consider getting a dog?"

I thought she was going to leap off the sofa and run out the door. "Are you seriously suggesting I have an animal?"

Yes, I assured her and for very good reasons.

This is the way I saw it. Roxanne had never taken care of anybody or anything in her entire life. Growing up, her mother doted on her and did for her. Roxanne had never lived with anyone she needed to care for nor had she been responsible for a pet. I explained that her nurturing abilities were seriously stunted and they needed to be en-livened if she was going to connect with her feminine energy in any real way. I was surprised that she not only took this advice but she did so almost immediately. She adopted a little dog and cared for it for an entire year as if he were her little son. And miraculously she attracted her husband to her. Imagine that!

Why Did This Process Work?
The man who came her way and was attracted to her was a man still very much in touch with his masculine aspect. If Roxanne had not shifted her own internal polarity more to her feminine side, he would almost certainly not have been interested in her. But the truth is that her beautiful little animal showed her many things. This little dog taught her that everything was not always about her. He needed to eat and it was not always at convenient times. He needed to go the vet. When she went away on business she had to make arrangements for his care. She did all of these things willingly, not realizing that she was effectively in training to care for a small human person.

This was just one technique of several that I recommended to Roxanne and which she embraced. She became more serious about learning yoga and meditation. Through these practices she managed to rediscover what it was like to experience her feminine energy. She tapped into her intuition and creativity and was delighted by the new ideas that were coming to her. She learned to trust and love herself. All these processes combined to enable Roxanne to shift her polarity status significantly. She was still an entrenched male woman, but she had shifted enough toward her feminine pole to be able to attract a man with a significant amount of masculine energy. Ultimately her shift allowed her to give up her major contributing masculine activity, her job at the legal firm. She listened to her inner voice and wisely swapped corporate life for motherhood, the most feminine activity she could ever commit to.

Inner Work Is a Continuous Process
While Roxanne had a very good outcome in her attraction process and she got everything she had set out to achieve, there was still more to be done to keep her life in authentic balance. For example, she did not give up working altogether. When her daughter was about a year old, she opened an online children's clothing store. This was a smart move. She was still engaging her feminine energy by

taking care of her daughter, her husband, and her little dog at home while simultaneously maintaining balance with her innate masculine energy through her new business.

Another part of her program designed to keep her polarized to her feminine energy was to start up a mother's club. This reinforced Roxanne's internal desire for her feminine aspect to remain strong because the club provided ongoing female company. She came to enjoy the interaction with other women and little children, which was not easy at first for a woman with such high masculine tendencies.

We had discussed all of these processes in her program. Our aim was to keep her attraction for her husband strong by making sure she stayed at a healthy place in her feminine energy while still satisfying her masculine drive. Maintaining the balance of polarity within a relationship is a job in and of itself. Life events will always cause the polarity of the individuals in a relationship to move around. You have to be flexible.

RYAN UNDERSTANDS HIS PREDICAMENT

To illustrate this process in another way, we can look again at Ryan, the Sensitive Man with a high level of masculine energy. When I first spoke with him he did not understand why he and his former wife had lost their way in their marriage, but I was able to help him get some perspective. In the early days of their relationship his wife, Maria, had been a fairly high-level masculine career-oriented woman. However, she still obviously had had enough feminine energy to activate Ryan's masculine energy when they met. Looking at Ryan, on the other hand, he would have been a lot more feminine in the early days of their relationship. In those days they would have had a natural attraction and compatibility. They would have started out their relationship through the attraction of her masculine energy to his feminine energy. This was the starting-gate position for Maria and Ryan.

Sensitive men tend to be quite flexible through their polarity. That can be a problem for them if they are not aware of what is happening when they fall in love. A high-end masculine woman will almost certainly polarize him more toward his feminine aspect. In

Ryan's case, however, his masculine energy intensified when he became the sole breadwinner for the family and his company started to do really well. He worked harder and harder and traveled extensively away from home. When Maria became a mother she shifted more noticeably into her feminine energy, which allowed Ryan to own more and more of the masculine space within the relationship without any challenge.

They still enjoyed a good level of polarity with this switch in polarity status. Ryan was extremely comfortable with that shift. In fact, he enjoyed being responsible for his family. It was clearly not stressful for him at all. This was where he felt most fulfilled and where he was at his happiest. Being the breadwinner and the full masculine person in the relationship was where he felt at his most valuable. Because he felt so good, he believed that Maria was just as happy too.

Another Polarity Shift Rears Its Head

As the children grew up, Maria became less and less happy herself. She was slowly shifting back into her default polarity status, which was predominantly masculine. When she went back to work as a solicitor, the fate of the marriage was sealed. Ryan was confused. Why was Maria not happy? He was providing for her and the children so well. He was extremely successful. Everything he did was for the well-being of his family. It was all he ever wanted.

What happened to the intimacy between this couple? Where did it all unravel? Here's what was going on with them internally, which severely impacted their day-to-day lives. Ryan was well established within his masculine energy by the time his children had grown up. Maria was reentering into her masculine energy, and when she went back to work she dropped into her most comfortable space. For her that was her masculine pole.

Suddenly Ryan and Maria seemed to have little common ground except for their beautiful children. Because they were both operating out of their masculine energy, they had lost the spark that had carried them through their early years of marriage. Over time they had slowly migrated to their masculine aspects.. By the time the children were grown, Ryan and Maria were both firmly ensconced in their individual masculine essences. It was disconcerting because Ryan and Maria still loved each other and that is why it was hard for them to let each other go. But they had lost their polarity to each other and the natural result of that was the loss of attraction and intimacy. Without realizing that fact, they lost their way in their relationship and as we saw, sadly, they lost each other.

What Could Ryan and Maria Have Done?

Unlike Roxanne, Ryan and Maria had not been aware of what was happening to their relationship. They allowed life to carry them along without taking stock in a considered way of where they were in the relationship. They did not know that they needed to work at maintaining their attraction and connection to each other. Roxanne, on the other hand, was such a goal-oriented individual that she came seeking help and was quick to commit to a process of change in order to get what she wanted. Her awareness of the reality of her situation caused her to gather her courage to actually do something about her predicament, and she did it well. She found solutions. Even though they were not easy to implement, she did them anyway.

It was different with Ryan and Maria. Like so many couples, they coasted through the years, probably hoping things would work themselves out. They rarely do. Relationships require constant work and that is especially the case in today's environment. Divorce rates are so high because we are simply not paying attention to our individual changing needs, the needs of our partners, and our changing circumstances. When we do not take conscious and considered action to maintain our most precious relationships, they are in jeopardy of falling apart. Even for highly intelligent people such as Maria and Ryan, it was not obvious to them how much work a relationship takes.

Had Ryan and Maria been more aware of their changing circumstances and the rules of attraction and polarity, I believe their marriage could have been saved. Maria would have spoken up long before the relationship got to the point where her resentment toward Ryan became too entrenched. She had given up her career and was stuck at home while he got to travel, make deals, and build his business. And if Ryan had really been paying attention to his wife, he might have noticed that she was less than happy as the children were growing up. Assuming that she was happy because he was turned out to be shortsighted and as a consequence he lost the love of his life.

Polarity is fluid and thoughts are powerful. In Maria's case her thoughts were powerfully resentful and her resentment was directed toward Ryan. Her polarity status shifted and he failed to notice it. In fairness, not many people would have noticed. But Ryan could have asked more questions. He could have been more present to Maria and her plight and he could have made more of an effort when he was at home. That way he would have found out what she was thinking. Together they could have figured out a way to change Maria's thinking, perhaps by doing something to give her relief from her frustration. She could have perhaps found a way to return to the practice of law part-time while the children were in grade school, and he could have supported her in that.

As it was, however, Maria's thoughts drove her further and further into her masculine pole and Ryan's lack of attention to her needs kept him firmly locked within his own polarity. Through their lack of awareness and poor communication, there was no possibility to develop the fluidity required for them to regain the critical attraction between them.

ATTRACTION AND POLARITY FOR TODAY'S COUPLES

Using the laws of attraction and polarity within a relationship is a tool that today's couples can use to keep themselves together. Gender roles are not cast in stone; each person in the relationship needs to be clear on what his or her needs are to be happy. The couple needs to realize that whenever life circumstances change, the polarity status of their relationship can change and go out of balance. We are not as static as the generations that have gone before us because we live in a fast-moving, constantly shifting world. If a couple is not taking stock regularly of where they are in their thinking about themselves first and with each other second, then their relationship is going to be in potential jeopardy. Relationships are never perfect, and romantic love alone will not sustain the levels of polarity and attraction needed to keep a relationship vibrant.

Once you are aware of any issues that might be brewing, have the courage to discuss them and face them head-on, no matter how challenging they might be. Remember that denial can only lead to more problems in the end. If you can't do it between yourselves, seek out a counselor to help you, and have the courage to implement the changes needed to reestablish a workable polarity within your relationship. Roles within the family can be fluid and you might find that a new arrangement is in order to keep both of you satisfied and healthy within your internal polarity.

For example, the man can stay home if the woman is truly fulfilled as the main breadwinner; provided his own inner self is healthy and balanced, this can work. Or if the only way the wife will feel fully happy is to stay home and care for her family, then the couple needs to do what they can to make that happen. There are creative ways to have part-time, home-based businesses, and when the man is helping with that and fully supporting the wife's choice to stay home, this arrangement can work well.

We have gained a lot of knowledge through the past decades of role reversal and full gender equality. Now it is time to for women and men to return to right order inside themselves and put equal energy toward maintaining right order within their relationships. The principles of this inner male-female paradigm work for everyone and in every kind of relationship. First move your own internal masculine and feminine essences into correct balance and then work diligently to keep a balance of polarity within your relationship with your partner.

The couples landscape has a wide variety of types of pairings that work. One of the most fascinating I discovered in my practice is the Split Couple. This is a good time to introduce and explain how this concept works because there is much to learn from the dynamic natures of men and women in this kind of intimate partnership.

CHAPTER **15**

The Split Couple

HE SAYS: "I'VE JUST MOPPED THOSE FLOORS!"
SHE SAYS: "OH, YOU'RE JUST LIKE AN OLD WOMAN!"

SPLIT COUPLES KNOCKING AT MY DOOR

Over a period of time a certain type of couple kept turning up for coaching. Their relationship was the result of a distinct pattern: a highly feminine-oriented man paired with a highly masculine-oriented woman (usually an Andro). These were not random matches; the couples seemed to have chosen each other quite specifically but probably not consciously. The immediate strong attraction between them was due to their being extreme polar opposites with regard to their internal gender.

I called them Split Couples for the simple reason that each person appeared to have entirely forsaken one of their internal genders. So when they formed a relationship, it seemed as if they projected their forsaken gender completely onto the other person. Since their chosen partner carried the missing gender fully, it meant there were only really two genders at play for that couple, not the usual four a regular couple would have, which is two apiece.

Just to clarify, even though the woman in a Split Couple appears to be totally masculine in her behavior, her internal feminine gender is not missing entirely; it still exists deep inside in a dormant state. The man's masculine essence is still inside him too; it just becomes inactive. Interestingly, the Split Couple setup can work very well for many couples. The ones I see in my practice are seemingly happy with these internal arrangements and it filters out into their physical lives quite well, all things considered.

How a Split Couple Forms

There are two ways that I have observed a Split Couple forms. The first is described above, where two highly polarized individuals find each other and it is love at first sight: a strong initial attraction. The second follows a more organic process: two people do not set out to be a Split Couple but they end up that way because as the relationship progresses, they find a groove perfectly suited to their individual natures. Life happens and they shift with the circumstances life presents them.

The Split Couple that forms over time seemed to me to experience a little less bliss in their partnership. Through years of marriage, circumstances changed them and their relationship substantially. Without even realizing it, they formed different habitual behaviors that ended up polarizing each partner into their most comfortable internal gender, almost always the opposite to the one they were born into. In other words, the man tended to become more feminine and the woman more masculine. What I found was that when these issues arose yet remained unaddressed, over time they became an entrenched part of the relationship—the "elephant in the room."

It was this organically formed type of Split Couple who turned up for coaching over and over again because they were looking for ways to end their discomfort. As I worked with them, I found that the offending elements in the relationships were subtle and easy for the couple themselves to miss. These subtleties needed a witness in order to be revealed, and I was witness to many strange yet beautiful relationships.

INTRODUCING: SIMON AND LISA

Simon and Lisa arrived at my office together and I immediately took note that they appeared to be a happy connected couple. As we said hello, I noticed what good communicators they were and that there was ease and comfort between them. The mystery grew. This couple did not appear to be in any need of assistance; they seemed to have a relationship most couples would envy.

I started the ball rolling. "Would one of you like to set the scene for me? How can I help you?"

Lisa jumped in and said they were looking for someone to bounce things off so they could look at their situation from a different angle. They had attempted relationship counseling, but it didn't work. They felt they needed someone who could look at their situation from another angle, a little outside the box. They had heard this was what my practice was about.

Lisa continued. "You see, we're actually very happy together. I know that sounds bizarre, but we are."

Simon nodded in agreement with his animated, attractive wife and carried on where Lisa left off. "We found that the relationship counselor was at a loss to help because we don't appear to have any obvious issues. We felt she was more geared for couples heading to divorce court."

This was intriguing, so I asked Simon to start by telling me some basic details about them as people and about their lives together. It turned out that this was a second marriage, they were a childfree couple who ran their own businesses, and they enjoyed a full life with plenty of friends. Simon had a successful interior design business. It was a good partnership and he and his male partner got along really well. Lisa had a business consultancy with four employees serving a large portfolio of clients. They were a successful professional couple committed to each other with what appeared to be a balanced and happy life.

Exploring Background Influences

Lisa informed me that she had lost her father when she was twenty; she had always felt responsible for her mother and younger brother. Both Simon's parents were alive and well. From what he told me, Simon had had a pretty good childhood. Not perfect, but as the youngest of four children, three of them girls, he had always felt nurtured. He also admitted that he often avoided making decisions because he had had four women in his family and they were only too happy to tell him what to do.

Simon was very happy with his interior design business and his business partner of fifteen years, Tim. They worked well together as co-owners and friends. On the other hand, Lisa, along with her four employees, was working quite hard in her business consultancy firm, serving a large portfolio of clients; she was under nonstop pressure and faced constant deadlines. Her work environment was okay, but her employees were not her friends. They too worked under enormous pressure on a daily basis to get things done. She wished she had more free time, but it just never seemed to happen.

"So how can I help you?" I asked.

Lisa responded a little reticently. "I don't really know how to articulate this and if I didn't think you'd understand, I probably wouldn't say anything at all." I encouraged her to share whatever was on her mind.

Finally she began. "I've said this to Simon before so it won't be a shock for him. I'm the one in the relationship who's a little on edge at the moment. For the past few months I've felt an agitation within me that I just can't explain, but I'll try. Here goes. I have this sense that I have all I want in all areas of my life, but I just don't think I have what I *need*."

That was a curve ball I did not see coming. "Interesting, Lisa. Tell me more about this feeling. Where does it sit?" I asked.

She thought for a moment and then responded gently, "It feels like a hole in my heart." She lowered her head as if she did not want me to see her face. "I know that sounds ludicrous. There is absolutely nothing wrong with my heart. I went to the doctor and he ran numerous tests."

Simon sat there peacefully. He was not fazed by this conversation at all. He told me that if Lisa was feeling this way then it was valid and he would support her in any way he could so that she could get to the bottom of her feelings of discomfort.

A Bottomless Pit of Longing

"Lisa, just speak to me about this feeling. Whatever comes into your head, just say it." Lisa was quite a direct person and I felt she was reliable. I was confident she would give me as honest an answer as she could about this strange malaise afflicting her.

"I feel it's something to do with our relationship," she said. "I love Simon, and even more importantly, I like him. I don't feel the problem's with him, and yet it is. I just have this longing in my being. I'm longing for something. I'm aching for something and I wish I knew what it was. And somehow I expect Simon to make it right."

By this stage I had evaluated their archetypes and saw Simon as a Highly Feminine Man and Lisa as a Good Doer. They were being honest and truly wanted a new way to look at things, so I thought I would give them the truth from my point of view.

"Lisa, Simon, you know that I don't look at things literally, so with your permission we're going to take a look at this situation from a whole other perspective." They nodded, so I continued. "Simon, I see you as a Highly Feminine Man and, Lisa, you're a Good Doer."

Simon responded that they had heard of this way of looking at relationship issues from the friend who had referred them to me. "So that means that my feminine side is quite strong in comparison to my masculine side, correct?" said Simon.

"Yes, exactly right," I replied.

Lisa said nothing.

"Lisa, I have identified you as a Good Doer, which means that your masculine side has no difficulty coming out to play. From what you tell me about your job, you have to use your masculine energy quite strongly with all your deadlines and the type of clients you service."

She responded bluntly with a little more sadness. "I do feel like a man sometimes," she said.

I hastened to reassure her that this was okay. "I understand that very well and there's a very good reason for that too," I explained. "You're just not in a space at work to ever have the opportunity to relax into your feminine energy. Simon, on the other hand, has a good deal of opportunity to do that at work. I imagine that each night when you get back from work, you get straight into organizing everything at home?"

Lisa nodded that she did. I turned to Simon and asked if he allowed her to do that. He looked at me and said yes.

Relaxing into the Feminine Aspect

I could see that Lisa was struggling a little with the concepts I was using. She said she didn't know what it meant to relax into one's feminine energy, so I did my best to explain.

"Lisa, we're always in a state of play with our internal polarity. So when you're doing masculine tasks, you activate your masculine energy, and that's a good thing. Without it you wouldn't get much done. The hurdle I've observed with Good Doers is that they need to access their feminine energy sometimes as well, in order to feel a sense of balance and internal happiness," I said.

I went on quickly to add that there was hope, that of all the different types of masculine-oriented women in the world, it is Good Doers who like and enjoy their feminine energy the most. "What this means is that you'll miss your feminine self if you can't access it on a regular basis. You won't even be aware it's missing, but I'm wondering if it's possible that the feeling of loss you feel, the hole in your heart, could it be the loss of your feminine energy, which seems to have gone astray?"

Lisa sat silently as tears fell down her cheeks. She wiped them away and said nothing for the moment. However, Simon had a question.

"If that's true, then why and how did Lisa's feminine self go away?"

I told him this was a good question with a rather lengthy explanation and that first I wanted to check in with Lisa to see how she was feeling; she looked so forlorn.

"I know this is right," she said. "I just haven't felt very feminine for years now. In fact, I've even said out loud how manly I feel. It doesn't feel right and then I blame Simon."

"Well, Lisa, you're way ahead of the game, for two reasons. One is that you can feel the difference and sense the loss and second, you know what you're doing. You do realize now that blaming Simon is not going to fix this feeling?"

"Oh yes, I've just been so frustrated and sad for so long, and now I've noticed that I've become quite angry about it all," she said.

Identifying a Process of Evolution

Simon looked relieved. It was as if we'd had a revelation and it was fixable. He had been so worried about Lisa and she'd had so much difficulty articulating how she felt that they both were tired of going around and around in never-ending circles.

"Shall I give you my take on what I suspect has been happening for you, Lisa?" I asked. "Are you okay with that?"

She offered an enthusiastic yes.

"Well, first let's discuss how you became a Good Doer, and we'll go from there. I suspect that from a young age you've been the care-taker of your younger brother and that role extended itself to include your mother when your father died. So you have no problem nur-turing people, which is your beautiful feminine side."

She said yes, that she'd had to hold everybody together and be the rock when her father passed away. Apparently, her mother fell apart and her brother, Jimmy, was still just a young teenager. Lisa de-scribed it best.

"There was nothing for it but to step in and do what needed to be done. That's just the way I am. I do that all the time in all kinds of situations," Lisa said.

This was so typical of a Good Doer's behavior. When everyone else is falling apart, they pick up the slack and do what needs to be done. The problem is that if she keeps doing this, it can become a habit and she starts to fall into the trap of always picking up every-one else's pieces.

I summed it up for Lisa and Simon. "Before you know it, you're such a busy person and there's just no time left for yourself or for those you have close relationships with, like your husband."

"Amen to that," muttered Simon.

"So what's been happening, Lisa, is that slowly but surely you've been activating your masculine energy more and more. This process leaves your feminine energy unattended, and over time it has been slowly lulled into a kind of slumber because it's not required."

Lisa looked at me sadly and said, "I can see how that happened after my father died. I've been extremely busy since then. If it wasn't Mom or Jimmy then it was my job, and I always feel there aren't enough hours in the day to keep our own home running smoothly and for us to have any real quality time together."

Who Can I Blame for This?

As the reality of this was settling in, Lisa said she was wondering about something else too. "Why do I feel this sense of dissatisfaction with my relationship? It isn't serious, I just feel like something's missing and I don't know what it is," she said.

I turned to Simon and asked him if it would be fair to say that when Lisa was at home, she never sat down. He nodded.

"Does she have strong opinions about many things—would you consider her to be quite bossy at home?"

He nodded and smiled. Lisa did not look in the least perturbed; she was agreeing with everything I was saying too.

"So, Lisa, here's the thing. These are very clear signs that your masculine energy is highly activated. You've become angry with Simon because you're silently begging him to pick up the masculine part of the relationship," I explained. "The problem is that you don't allow him to do that. You're so quick and efficient yourself, used to doing everything most of the time anyway, that if he doesn't respond at lightning speed, it's too late. Would that be about right?"

This time they were both smiling and nodding.

"But you still want Simon to be more manly so you can relax into your feminine, and I'm going to explain some ways you can try to do this. Lisa, your journey now is going to have to be one of *allowance* and *receptivity*. Simon might not be as efficient as you at home but you have to allow him to do what he wants to do to help you."

Learning to Be Receptive

I gave them some examples to help them understand this new dynamic. "If Simon wants to take you out to dinner or wants to buy you something special, you have to receive what he offers. You may not criticize his choice of restaurant or the color of the blouse he's bought you. Receive and accept graciously all that he wishes to shower upon you. That's your homework." I suggested that *grace* could be the word to emblazon on her mind as she went forward with this new approach. As modern-day women, we have lost the high art of graciousness and with that loss we have become male.

Next I suggested to Lisa that she needed to get out for some "girl time." Lisa said she couldn't imagine having time to do that. She did not have any extra time as it was, and when she did have a few hours here or there, she wanted to spend them with Simon. I understood her concerns but, at this point I felt that I needed to explain a bit more about this inner male-female paradigm so she could see the value of what I was suggesting. I went into some detail of what was occurring for her.

Needing to Recharge One's Feminine Energy

When she had met and married Simon fifteen years ago, Lisa had not been as committed to her career as she was now. But now she had owned her own business for the last five years and that meant a much larger workload than when she was working for someone else. Her mother was aging and was not very well, so Lisa had been looking after her finances and all the things her mother did not understand, which her father would normally have attended to. Lisa was also on call if her mother felt lonely, and she served as taxi driver to appointments and for daily chores with her mother, like shopping. Lisa effectively was highly masculine at work, in her caretaking tasks for her mother, and at home with Simon. I knew she had very little time for her girlfriends, which meant she did not get a chance to recharge her feminine energy.

Simon, on the other hand, had quite a laid-back nature to start with; his business had pressures but they were quite different from the intense pressures Lisa was under at work. Simon loved his business and he and his business partner, Tim, another Highly Feminine Man, were very good friends. Effectively, Simon and Tim were creating and designing all day together. They were both feeding their masculine energy through their companionship, and strengthening their feminine energy through their creative projects for clients. Simon was satisfied at work and had no need for many other friends. His best friend was at work and the love of his life was at home.

It was too bad that Lisa did not enjoy the same scenario. Her colleagues tended to be tough corporate people, all very masculine in their approach, whether they were men or women. Her job was very deadline oriented and that meant she had to use masculine energy all the time to meet the deadlines. She did enjoy a very small amount of her feminine energy through her yoga classes, when she had time to attend. I was trying to show them that the majority of Lisa's time on all levels of her life was very task oriented and those demands required her masculine energy. She was drowning in her masculine self and crying out for her feminine side.

It was so obvious that this disconnection of her feminine aspect left Lisa feeling bereft. The hole she felt in her being, the feelings she could not account for, were signs of this disconnect. Lisa was a very aware person and she had wisely taken note of her feelings. She could have dismissed them or gone into denial. Busy Good Doers are good at denial. But Lisa had decided to investigate the signals she did not understand. Somehow she knew the signs were warning bells that something was not working for her.

Overcoming Guilt and Letting Go

Lisa had listened pensively as I explained my take on what was going on for her, and she had a further question. "Am I just behaving like a spoiled person? I have everything anyone could wish for, including a wonderful husband who is kind, considerate, and loving. We have a wonderful life. We want for nothing and we have great people in our lives too."

I assured her that she wasn't selfish and told her that I saw this scenario all the time. My clients tend to be people who are well off financially so they do not have day-to-day survival issues, but that does not make them any different from people who do. When basic survival issues have been met, deeper inner feelings tend to surface. I feel that today life is inviting us to investigate who we are on a completely different level, and I assured Lisa that she had taken the brave step of confronting her discomfort head-on. And with that I continued to point out another common element in this situation.

"I think there's a gift but also a curse in living as part of such an affluent society. The gift is having the awareness to devote to your internal growth, but it becomes a curse of dissatisfaction if you feel something is missing and keep denying it. The truth is that not everyone will take the brave step. Some people will simply cover up those niggling feelings with another holiday, another shopping trip, or another Hermès handbag."

Lisa nodded. "I have friends like that," she said. "They have everything and nothing. I don't want to be that way."

A Marriage in Constant Movement

I knew that if Lisa reconnected with her feminine there would be every chance to turn the unhappy aspects of her life toward a more positive direction. I continued to explain a bit more so they could both stop feeling guilty, worried, or sad about their life together.

"As your marriage matured, you settled into your default natures: Simon into the feminine and Lisa into the masculine. Because Simon's life didn't change much throughout the relationship, his polarity did not waver that much. Lisa, on the other hand, kept feeling the pull toward her masculine from every direction. As she traveled further and further into her masculine self, Simon was left with little option but to find solidarity with his feminine self.

"Simon, do you think maybe you were a little unhappy at the beginning of your life together, but you were willing to compromise since that's what a relationship's about?"

"Yes, that's right," he responded.

"Then after a while it became a habit. Lisa did this and that and you did nothing. Lisa made more and more of the decisions about your life together, and you didn't challenge her. Lisa worked harder and harder and you didn't question her time away from you. Is that right?"

"Yes, correct," Simon answered.

"You both accepted that this was the way things were. You were lucky you loved each other and it has sustained you throughout the evolution. But now Lisa has identified her dissatisfaction, not knowing exactly where it's coming from. Her soul was telling her that she might want to create a different and perhaps more balanced life. It's really an evolutionary process to rediscover parts of yourself that you've neglected and to want to be better than you already are. It's a move toward wholeness."

Determining a Course of Correction

"I feel better already," said Lisa.

"So where to from here?" asked Simon.

"Honestly, a small program should be all you need to get you both into a new groove. Breaking the old habits can be challenging, but if you're committed to a more balanced life, it won't be too hard. It will require both of you to participate. When we enter into the polarity of couples, we cannot shift one and not the other. Invariably if we do that, the person not being coached will feel the effects and not have any tools to counteract them."

Simon said he was happy to join in the process, so I outlined some quite specific instructions to get them started. "Simon, in the short-term, you are going to have to break the habit of allowing Lisa to assume the lead in all things in your relationship," I began. "You'll have to break the habit of complacency and step up into more of a dominant role. Luckily you won't meet with much opposition because Lisa is craving a rest from her masculine energy. The time has come to bring your masculine back into the forefront, not only in the relationship but for yourself too."

My suggestion for Simon was to start with himself. "Demand more of yourself in terms of leadership and being proactive with small things. This will help you rebuild your masculine muscles," I explained. "Gradually start taking the lead when it's appropriate, while being sensitive to Lisa's needs. Our aim is to put Lisa into a state of *allowing* and *receptivity*. She's lost this ability and needs to regain confidence in her feminine self. With a loving partner, this state will be so much easier to achieve."

I warned him that since Lisa was so used to doing everything herself and making all the decisions, I would not be at all surprised if she battled him a little in the beginning of this process. It was her habit. She believed that if she didn't have a hand in something, then it probably wouldn't be done right, or done at all. "You may have to work hard to break that stranglehold that her controlling nature has on her. Control is her friend and makes her feel safe. Your job then, Simon, is to usurp the position of leader and take control."

My next suggestion got them both smiling again. "Simon, I know it sounds quaint, but you have to create surprises for her. She has to be confused about your next action because she has to learn to trust you and your judgment. You're in a good position because she loves you. Start off with simple things like having dinner prepared when she returns after a long day at the office, but not every day. Remember, surprise is everything."

I told Simon that I knew he had some long days too, but for now we would focus on doing for Lisa so she could begin to feel nurtured again. But she had to be able to receive that nurturing. Receptivity is everything when one is trying to reconnect with the feminine self.

Lightening the Load

"Another idea would be to perhaps hire someone for a short time to go over and help Lisa's mother, since Lisa really needs a break from the constant list of things to do," I continued. "I would also suggest a break from the office, a short holiday to start the whole program off. A break from your businesses could only do both of you an enormous amount of good. You could view it as a retreat for the relationship, some quiet time away so that you can reassess your value system for the relationship and how you wish it to continue into the future."

I explained that healthy internal growth requires the ability to constantly check on your behavior, then make the changes necessary. You need courage and persistence. Just before we wrapped up, I suggested that Simon take the leadership role in the relationship without becoming domineering or overbearing.

"Remember that leadership in a relationship is not about dominance; rather the focus should be on developing a sense of responsibility toward those you love," I said. "Simon, since you have an innate sensitivity already, when you combine that with the strength of your masculine energy, I think you're going to be very surprised at the results you achieve."

Finally, I checked in again with Lisa to make sure she was willing to allow Simon to take the leadership role for a while, to help her break the controlling stance she had developed over time.

Lisa responded with enthusiasm, "You know, I've felt trapped between the need to control absolutely everything in my life and wanting to relinquish all control at the same time," she said. "But I just didn't know what was going on for me. I think this is exactly why I've secretly been blaming Simon for my hollow feelings. I just desperately need a break from all the responsibility."

I was happy she felt ready to give up some of it, but I cautioned her that she might experience a feeling of grief in letting go of such a strong habit. The process sounds simple but it is not easy to accomplish. However, Lisa and Simon were motivated, and I felt they would do very well. I was right.

The Paradigm Reaches Another Couple

Simon and Lisa enjoyed their program and they made amazing progress. Simon discovered that he enjoyed reconnecting with his masculine self and found he wanted to share his discoveries with Tim, his business partner. With Lisa's permission he also shared what had been happening between the two of them. The result of that conversation was that Tim and his life partner, Matthew, soon became clients of mine too. They had silently been experiencing similar issues in their relationship and were in a desperate search for relief.

The results were wonderful because the four friends happily embraced the coaching process and shared their pains as well as their successes. In fact, they noticed that they became much closer as friends because they had a new language that allowed them to express themselves in a more logical way when facing difficult inter-personal situations both in business and at home.

Tim and Simon told me that they had noticed their friendship as a foursome had taken a turn for the worse over the years, when Lisa had shifted with the demands of her business and become more male. Matthew had experienced significant trauma through a car accident during the time they were friends. All of these changes had created distance among them and had had quite an impact on how they all got along. But no one really knew what to do about the changes in their friendships. Using the new relationship tools they learned through coaching, they all embarked on personal journeys that took their friendships to new levels. They were all able to enjoy different degrees of satisfaction and much deeper levels of collaboration with each other.

It has been my experience that the Split Couple is quite common. Relationships change automatically with the experiences any couple inevitably endure throughout the course of their relationship. In that process, it is quite easy for one or the other party to take up the reins of the dominant role if that is their default position. The problem is that it usually ends up being domination instead of leadership. That in its turn results in a relationship completely dominated by one party, which can work quite well as in the example of the first type of Split Couple; you'll recall those are the two who meet as complete polar opposites and fall madly in love.

But for the second type of Split Couple, with the kind of relationship that develops organically over time, the evolutionary process can sometimes turn their loving relationship into a poisonous one, and then dissatisfaction ensues. However, as we learned with Simon and Lisa, transformation for the better can occur. It just takes love, kindness, a strong desire to have a fair and equitable relationship, and a definite willingness to relinquish power and control.

While I have coached many people in mature relationships like these, sometimes younger men and women are struggling even more intensely with matters of intimacy, balance, power, and control. They have different challenges due to their youth and the society they are growing up in today. That realm is where we are headed next.

CHAPTER 16

Getting Hung Up on Hookups

SHE SAYS: "SEE YOU AT *MINE*."

HE SAYS: "I'LL CALL YOU . . ." (*NOT*)

SEXUALITY IS EVERYWHERE

The loss of the feminine in young women has led to an unprecedented level of promiscuity. Never before has it been socially acceptable for women to be so predatory that they could make "booty calls." Today they can and they do.

The Internet has made hookups and booty calls a normal part of life. Many of the women reading this book have not known another time and may not understand why I even mention it. This aspect of our new world order, namely underground sexuality, is rarely spoken about because to a large extent it is considered normal behavior. It's no big deal. Hookups are just a standard part of modern life. And that is true. However, what does it actually mean in terms of how the balance of your internal self is affected?

I have had young people come to my practice and tell me that when it comes to men, women, and sex in today's society, anything goes. Women can be predatory and call up men for their own use—no strings and no commitment of any kind attached. Men can play coy and have women pay their way and look after them—nobody bats an eye. These examples of the reversal of internal polarity may be considered normal but this new way of socializing is also causing many, many young people to feel used and abused. Most of all, they feel empty.

To make themselves feel better too many of them turn to sex, a new drug of choice. The more you have the more you want, and it is easy to obtain. Could this situation be further exacerbated by the proliferation of pornography, which is only a click away? Websites cater to every target market; there is no shortage of ways to connect with people who want to have casual sex or an occasional fling. Young people have free access to online porn and we are seeing them become addicted. It is commonly accepted that viewing too much explicit pornography correlates to a much lower inclination to connect with real people for sex and intimacy. I am witnessing a downward spiral that leaves me worried for today's younger generation.

CASE STUDY: ANNA

As I sat waiting to meet Anna, I wondered what her concerns might be. She was the twenty-five-year-old daughter of a friend. Her mother had asked me if I would talk to her, so Anna and I agreed to meet for lunch.

Her mother had put it quite candidly. "Jen, Anna needs to speak to you. She's miserable and she won't communicate with me." Anna had stopped speaking to her mother on matters of her private life a long time ago. She was fifteen when she became quite private with regard to sharing details of her day-to-day life, so I wondered if she would open up to me, or maybe we would just have a polite chat over salad. It could go either way.

As she approached the table, I was a little taken aback. I remembered her as such a beautiful intelligent girl with her whole life stretching out before her. Her career was starting to take off. But today Anna was looking thin and the pallor of her skin told me something was radically wrong.

"Anna, how wonderful to see you. It's been too long," I greeted her warmly.

She smiled shyly and said, "Thank you for making the time to have lunch. I really needed someone to talk to."

I assured her it that was my pleasure, that I was more than willing to listen and help if I could. She seemed to squeeze herself into her chair a little more, as if she were trying to make herself smaller and replied sadly, "Well, I hope you still feel the same way after lunch."

Her comment seemed a little strange, but I let it go for a moment while we ordered lunch. Then I decided to leap straight into any problems she had on her mind. No point beating about the bush because her body language was showing me that she was retreating. I was worried that she might be losing the courage to discuss whatever had her so upset.

FINDING LOVE IN ALL THE WRONG PLACES

"Anna, we've known each other a long time, so let's dispense with any more pleasantries and get down to it. What's troubling you?" This no-nonsense approach worked.

She burst out crying and haltingly answered, "I'm so miserable and I just don't know why." I let her cry and waited for the sobs to subside.

I gently urged her to just start anywhere. She played with her napkin and nervously picked at her bread roll. "I don't think that I'll ever find anyone to love me," she said sadly. Looking at Anna from my end of the table, I could not imagine why she would say that. She was a lovely looking woman, so smart and with a very good heart.

"Anna, what's given you the idea that you're unlovable?" I asked.

She was still sniffling but the sobs had subsided and she was calming down. "Well, I've slept with so many boys and no one seems the least bit interested in being with me on a permanent basis."

I felt sad for Anna. There was no reason for her to feel so poorly about herself. "Anna, why were you sleeping with all these boys if there was no possibility of a more stable and permanent relationship?"

"What do you mean?" she responded.

I tried to ask the question again. "You need to help me understand. Why would you sleep with a boy you had no commitment from and whom you had no intention of being with for a longer period of time?"

By the look on her face, I got the impression she thought I was from the Dark Ages. "Everyone does. It's the way you do things nowadays." I could tell she was mildly impatient.

"Is that right? So tell me, Anna, how is that working for you?"

She began to sob again. A few more tissues later, I got an answer. It sounded rather catastrophic.

"I don't know. Nothing seems to be working for me. Everyone hates me and my life is a disaster," she said.

LOVE HURTS

I tried to give her some perspective. "Anna, dear, I don't think your life's a disaster. You're young, beautiful, and you have a promising career. You might want to better understand a few things and change a few actions, and I think you'd start to feel quite a bit better. Why don't you start by telling me exactly what's causing you so much sadness."

I could see that coming clean was not going to be easy for Anna. She was reticent and the waiter bringing our lunch saved her from delivering her confession for a couple more moments. Then she got to the point. "I think I'm in love."

"Oh, but then why are you so miserable? Love is a happy thing, Anna, especially if you're young, with your whole life ahead of you."

She knew what was wrong and began to explain. "You don't understand. He doesn't know and I'm sure he doesn't want me anyway."

Anna met Jeff through friends and it turned out that she had slept with him casually on and off for about a year. But he didn't seem to have any particular interest in her. Then one night they were the last to leave a drinks party and were hailing a cab when they decided to share a ride together. When they got to her apartment in the city, Jeff again availed himself of another casual tryst; he left in the morning as usual without making any further plans to see her.

After this particular occasion Anna felt desolate and heartbroken. She realized that she had fallen for Jeff. She was smitten, and from that moment on she felt tormented. Anna saw Jeff fairly regularly through their social group but he never made any mention of their last night together, nor did he make any attempt to see her alone again. My feeling was that Jeff had probably picked up on Anna's change in feelings for him and did not want to get involved in a real relationship with her. It was better for him to keep his distance.

Anna brought me back to the moment. "What's wrong with me? Why doesn't Jeff even know I'm alive when I love him so much? Why can't I be happy? When will it be my turn to have a happy life?" It sounded like a string of childlike questions, but I could see the pain in her face and I made sure my expression did not reflect the dismay I felt.

THE COST OF CASUAL SEX

"Anna, maybe you're looking at this from back to front. Perhaps the question should be, What's right with me and why am I not valuing all that's right with me?" She was not exactly in the space for this level of introspection, but I decided to press on. "You're living in a time and space that seems to have lost the sacredness of sex and meaningful intimacy, so it's not necessarily just your issue but a societal one that's impacting you in a big way. I don't believe you enjoy this kind of sexual lifestyle, but you don't seem to know how not to be in it when everyone around you is. Would that be correct?"

She looked up at me with tears rolling down her cheeks, like a sad cherub, and said, "You're right. I don't know how to do it any other way, because that's how it works in my social group."

Her story continued and it did not get any prettier. With every sentence Anna uttered, there seemed to be a new level of previously unacknowledged pain. Anna had had many, many hookups with people she met on Facebook, Twitter, and Internet dating sites. She related one story of a man she had thought could be quite suitable for her. She liked the look of his photograph and he seemed to have a lot going for him.

She met up with him when he flew into town and they had dinner. She felt he was a little disappointing compared to what she had built up in her mind about him. He was actually successful, so there was nothing wrong with him as such, but she was simply not attracted to him. Yet within two and a half hours of meeting him she was in bed with him. She wasn't attracted to him but now she had slept with him. She confessed her remorse. "All I wanted was for him to leave my bed and leave my apartment."

By the time she had completed the story I found myself feeling a little heavy of heart, and a weighty sadness came over me. Why would this beautiful young woman sell herself so short? Anna said her friends behaved in exactly the same way. Booty calls were quite normal for the young men and the young women she knew; nothing appeared to be sacred anymore. Sex was like having a cup of tea, plain and simple. There was certainly nothing special about it; it was simply part of the interaction that went on between young adults.

But Anna could not get Jeff out of her mind, and no matter how many people she had hooked up with since then, the emptiness in her heart never went away. In fact, it seemed to be growing. She had fallen in love with the wrong person, sharing with him the most precious part of herself very quickly and on multiple occasions. But he clearly did not reciprocate her affection.

MANAGING THE PROCESS OF CHANGE

I gave Anna a chance to catch her breath by asking if she was okay to keep talking about this or if she would prefer to meet in my office another day. I felt that she was quite upset and probably needed time to process the feelings that had just come up. She seemed relieved. "You know what, I feel exhausted. I'm happy to see you next week at the office."

We wrapped up our lunch and Anna assured me that she would like to look at everything she was going through from a different perspective. She had gone around and around in her head until she was now quite depleted thinking about it all.

When we reconvened the following week, I decided that Anna was a young woman who was intelligent enough to see the value of taking herself a lot more seriously than she had been. We picked up our conversation and I explained the situation from my point of view. I made it clear to her that it was just that: my point of view. There would be many other viewpoints on the subject, but if she got a few different perspectives, she could make up her mind on how she wanted to conduct her life in the future.

"Anna, I've given our discussion a lot of thought and there are a few points I want to bring up to you. Please stop me if you feel I'm too old-fashioned in my views, but my position is that we are humans first, and we adapt our behavior to our environment. Sometimes that's not a good thing when the environment is not serving us."

She nodded in agreement. "I've thought about it too. My life isn't working for me and I'm not getting any younger. I realize now that I actually do want the normal things I grew up with, even though I've fought against that for a long time now."

VIRTUAL LIVES VERSUS REAL LIVES

So I continued on. "With so much technology in our lives, and especially in young people's personal lives, it appears as if you and your friends might be losing the ability to be physically in each others' company in true friendship. That in-person friendship is a form of intimacy. It feeds your soul, and when you don't have that kind of physical connection you can find yourself on Facebook and Twitter and all the other platforms putting forward a life that's not real."

She nodded and I could tell she was following my train of thought. "You can pretend to be happy and carefree in that virtual environment even when, in fact, your heart is breaking," I said. "But you should realize that the 'mask' that you put out into the virtual world has a cost. It costs you by draining your physical and emotional energy and most important, your soul energy."

Anna looked at me in agreement. She said, "You have no idea how exhausted I feel all the time. I feel compelled to update my status on these platforms all the time. All my friends do, but frankly my heart is not in it."

I asked her why she bothered then. "Well, everyone does and I'll feel left out of the loop if I drop off and out of the virtual world. Everybody's there and everything happens there," she insisted.

"But that's exactly my point," I said. "Everyone is online and no one is actually connecting with anyone anymore in the real sense. Connection is lost. If we lose connection with each other in a very deep and human way, surely that would explain how you could feel isolated and lonely."

Again Anna agreed that that was exactly how she felt.

"Anna, let's keep going. I'm wondering why you're sleeping with people you're not committed to. Are you doing it to form some kind of connection?" I wasn't ready for the next answer.

"Well, I don't really think about why I'm doing it. It's just what you do. It's pretty normal. If I wasn't doing it too, being open to hooking up I mean, I wouldn't be considered normal."

"Sleeping with people because your friends behave in that way is not really a good enough reason for an intelligent young woman, I wouldn't think," I said. "I think you're open to questioning your actions. If you don't feel good about something, it's time to become conscious of why you're doing it, so you can assess if it's worth continuing to do so. Self-enquiry will lead you to another part of yourself and then you can make different decisions."

Who Is Really in Control?
She smiled and lowered her eyes. She sat quietly for a moment and I knew Anna well enough to know she had realized that feigning ignorance was not going to work with me. She looked up at me and replied, "I can't believe I'm going say this, but I do it so I can control men."

Bingo, I thought. "So if you sleep with them, they come back to you and they're always circling in your social group," I suggested. "Then you feel you're in control of the situation?"

She admitted I was right.

So then it was my turn to deliver the rather unpleasant truth. "But that didn't work very well with Jeff?"

"No, and that surprised me, and now I can't get him out of my head," she said.

I asked if it was love or maybe she was upset because he was the one who got away. I could see she was getting uncomfortable.

"These are really difficult questions. Frankly, I don't know what the answer is to that one. You see, most of the time when I sleep with people, I'm quite detached."

I told her I thought maybe that detachment was a symptom of the process of sleeping around. "Eventually anyone would become numbed by the experience because it's no longer a special act. It's just another body, another time, and then that's it. The dance that's integral to the interrelatedness of men and women is just that: a dance. I don't believe you've ever experienced that process in your sexual life and my feeling is that you're longing for that process. Jumping into bed with anyone and everyone with little regard for the deep feelings of either party can only leave both parties empty and detached."

Again she replied with a silent nod.

Our Internal Structures Are Different

"Anna, I believe men and women are equal in every sense of the word, but they're constructed differently, which makes them vastly different from each other. If we're different then it has to follow that we need to fulfill different needs to keep us satisfied in life," I explained. "If you're in a female physical body and if you honor the feminine part of yourself, you'll feel honored and respected. When you feel honor and respect for your feminine self, you'll be in a receptive position for others, particularly men, to respect you as a person."

I went on to say that for men, hunting and being the predator is a normal part of their nature. Men require a clear feminine "no" to create strong boundaries, especially when they step out of line. This process creates a sense of security and happiness for their masculinity. It is also natural for men to need to make a woman feel happy and fulfilled. If that does not happen, then men tend to become unhappy and are more liable to disrespect women. The result is that the women in their lives become extremely unhappy.

She seemed to follow along, although this was obviously a new take on things for her.

"Unfortunately, from what you've told me, this process is not at play in social circles these days," I said. "Young women are coming on to young men and the men feel free to do what they like because they can. Nobody is giving them a firm 'no' to their bad behavior. And we can't even say their behavior is bad because it seems that women are perpetrating the very same behavior as well. So who are the men and who are the women? There don't appear to be any clean lines here anymore."

Anna sat quietly, processing this new information. She asked me where she should go from here and I suggested it was time to re-connect with her feminine energy. "You don't seem to be in touch with how that feels and what you need to make you feel happy and fulfilled, would that be right?"

She admitted that she was well and truly miserable and that she did not like the feeling.

Breaking Bad Habits Is Not Easy

I took it to the next level with her. "So the question is, How will you feel if you're *not* participating in all of this behavior with your friends?"

She was trying to be honest but still struggling, knowing there was a lot to lose if she agreed to change her ways. "This has been my life since I was a teenager," she said. "It escalated at university, and here I am at twenty-five and I feel like I don't know anything about relationships. I don't even have one! I do need a change, because I want more."

Brave Anna. We discussed a little action plan, nothing too stren-uous, and she appeared grateful that there was a way forward. I sug-gested she conduct an audit of her dating experiences and the life she had with her friends. Once she sorted out the elements, she could better determine which ones she genuinely enjoyed and dis-card the ones she did only because of peer pressure and behaviors she had fallen into without much thought.

The things she discarded readily were hookups with people she had little interest in and people she did not know very well. That pretty much got rid of the casual sex. Anna was on a mission to clean up her life. She started to feel better. Once she put up boundaries for herself, she started to feel her feminine energy. Suddenly she had no desire to be there for other people's convenience.

We worked on her control issues. In my experience, control tends to be an issue that all male-oriented women battle with. As the weeks went by, Anna and I stayed in touch by telephone and email.

She was a dedicated young woman. Her masculine energy was in very good shape, so she enjoyed having a project and she was diligently seeing it through.

Committed to the Process

Within just a few weeks, the change in her demeanor was evident. Her mother told me Anna was far more communicative now; they had even enjoyed a shopping trip together recently. Her mother felt that her daughter was returning to herself after an absence of many years. Anna became joyful. *Joyful* may be an old-fashioned word, a word that in the past would have routinely described the exuberance of the young, but today that is not an emotion that can be taken for granted.

After about three months, Anna asked me to lunch to catch up once again. She suggested a lovely little café in the botanical gardens. I thought that was quite telling. She was feeling comfortable to be out and about in a natural environment. The feminine aspect loves nature.

"Anna, you look so well," I said and she smiled, responding happily that she *was* well.

"I have a lot more energy and I've taken up a drawing class. I've always loved to draw but I'm just not very good at it, so I decided to go and learn a few techniques. I find it really soothing, and something happens for me when I sit down to put a sketch down on paper."

I was so thrilled that she had discovered an outlet for her creative expression. "Anna, that is just the most wonderful news. You realize that you've automatically found a way to connect with your feminine self? That's what I tell everyone. If you sincerely want to reconnect with your feminine, you'll find a way back to that neglected part of who you are. For you, the path is drawing."

She was animated, telling me about her newfound hobby. She said she had also joined a walking group and they did a nature walk once a month. These activities had been the perfect bridge from hookups and loneliness to the joy and peace of reconnecting with her feminine self.

Taking Stock and Making Changes

Anna continued to update me on her progress. She had reduced her time online and removed herself from certain sites. She no longer had time to waste, preferring to put her energies on her budding career and blossoming hobbies. She found that she wanted to spend more time drawing and reconnecting with her friends—in the real world.

She was finding that it took a lot more effort to physically see her friends and no longer had time for two hundred virtual friends anymore. She had whittled her real-world friends down to an inner circle of four. They had decided they would have a weekly dinner to catch up, and her girlfriends were very interested in her new way of being. Anna said they were now reevaluating their lives and feeling liberated to be away from the pressures they used to feel.

It was great to see her so engaged in life again. "Anna, this is astounding progress, and I'm in awe of how much you've achieved in such a short time. Has anything else come up for you while you've been doing this life evaluation and change process?"

She smiled at me and responded in an almost shy manner. "I realize that I just want to be loved and I want to be able to love somebody."

What an eye-opener that was! She had hit on a fundamental need whose fulfillment would make her happy, and arrived at that conclusion in record speed. I found myself filled with admiration for this young woman.

"Anna, to be loved you need to be lovable, and you're already that. It's just that you spent a number of years masking the real you with behaviors that were imposed on you by society," I said. "You were always lovable, but your past behavior sent a different message out into the world, and the real you was hidden by all the fraudulent activities you were participating in."

She laughed and agreed. "I'm feeling quite different since I've just been living my own life in a way that works for me. I've lost the need to compete with friends and I've noticed that I no longer need to constantly seek their approval."

Clearly Defining Your Life

I marveled at what could be achieved with a few conversations with a really switched-on young person. "Anna, you have no idea how huge this is. You've taken steps to accomplish something that many people will never achieve by the time they're fifty, never mind twenty-five. Not needing approval from others frees you up to live a life that's truly yours, one that's in integrity for you, and you alone. Good job, Anna."

She explained a technique that worked well for her and was keeping her focused. "I started a list of things I wanted to achieve and that were in keeping with the kind of life I would like to live. Writing it down helped and now my chances of achieving these things are so much better."

As we ended our lunch, Anna asked me how she should continue on this path. I told her that she was already doing very well indeed, honoring her feminine self, where it all begins. Her masculine would take the direction that she gave it through her feminine energy. I told her to continue to honor the key differences between men and women.

"If you want the love of a man who will honor you as the beautiful woman you are, you need to honor and respect yourself, and you're doing that beautifully now," I said. "The process will become like a well-sculptured muscle. The more you exercise it, the better you'll be able to feel your feminine self until it's naturally who you are once again. Then you'll no longer need to be so conscious of your behavior. Respect yourself and you'll be surprised at the level of respect you receive from men and the world."

We said our goodbyes and I knew that Anna was well on her way to a new kind of life. It appeared to be one filled with promise, and I hoped she would find true happiness in all aspects of her life: at home, at work, with her friends, and within herself.

I believe that being happy in work relationships contributes to our overall well-being, so our next point of exploration takes a look at the various archetypes by visiting them in the workplace. It will give you a way to figure out who to avoid at work and how best to work around the realities you find as you advance on your chosen career path.

CHAPTER **17**

Workplace Minefields

SHE SAYS: "I TOLD YOU *NOT* TO GET IN MY WAY."
HE SAYS: "I WON'T MAKE *THAT* MISTAKE AGAIN."

WHAT TO DO ABOUT CORPORATE CHAOS

Over a period of many years, I noticed that not all male women were equal. In fact, they really only had their maleness in common. As I became adept at understanding more about these women, it became easier for me to help them. And in the 1990s I was also able to help many large corporations plagued by emerging issues concerning this type of woman.

Increasingly, senior managers were becoming aware of significant problems arising between senior female executives and their co-workers. The top-level women I was asked to coach were often very unkind, competitive, and downright subversive when it came to other women in the work environment. This was disruptive to the companies because many talented but less competitive women became distraught under these harsh conditions, and when they could not stand the bullying and bad behavior any longer, they quit.

The loss of all these talented women proved draining to the companies, but the CEOs and board of directors could not seem to pinpoint exactly what was going on. In companies where it was suspected that a senior woman executive was causing some kind of serious friction, I would get a call to work with her, to see if the situation could be resolved. When doing corporate coaching I would sometimes call on the client at her workplace. I can recall the day I met an executive named Melanie; that meeting and so many others like it were so eerily similar that it gave me a feeling of déjà vu. My experience with Melanie is a good example of how the process usually went.

I was always well ahead of the appointment time, so I waited in the impressive foyer of a major company, quietly pacing. As I paced I felt dwarfed by the enormity of the marble pillars and saddened by the hardness of the marble floors. The world of corporate employees is often housed in magnificence but cloaked in a chilliness that pervades the atmosphere, a reminder that they are prisoners by day of something so much larger than themselves. This *thing* called a corporation controls their working life, often with very little room for self-expression.

My thoughts while I waited there were always the same; if you were an employee or executive and you had no understanding of your own inner being, then you were always going to be susceptible to the controlling ways of the corporation. That train of thought led me to a rather terrible discovery: the type of woman I coached, the Andro Woman archetype, was devilishly controlling of the people around her in an attempt to gain some control over her own life.

Recognizing the Corporate Andro
So while still standing in the foyer, the elevator doors would open, spewing people out of its giant mouth like ants from a disturbed anthill. Everyone looked the same in their corporate clothing, but I would spot my client long before she saw me. Even though we had never met, I instinctively knew who she was.

I was pretty certain she was the tall slim woman who was mildly overdressed, her skirt just a fraction too short and too tight, and her heels just little bit too high. She was as immaculate as she was statuesque. Melanie fit the image I had seen so many times; she fit it to a T. I knew she had been warned that I could be confrontational so she would be unlikely to let her guard down. I waited before greeting her, to let her find her composure, but I did not really expect her to be successful in her attempt. The Andro Woman is always on high alert and sure enough, this day Melanie's eyes were darting around before, as I expected, they dropped to check her phone. She immediately began clearing yet another message and checking to see if anyone else needed a response.

I knew how uncomfortable it would make this woman to just wait. By now confident that she was my client, I would walk up to her and greet her warmly, introducing myself. I would feel dwarfed yet again, this time by the height of Melanie's heels. She was so typical of what I had come to describe as an Andro Woman. All Andro women seemed to carry significant similar traits. They were ambitious and quite fearless in the face of their desire for power. Melanie was one of a long line of Andros I had coached. These clients had become quite predictable. My interest was piqued, however, when I started to notice that as well as these tough girls, there was another kind of male woman in the workplace.

Working Hard for the Greater Good

This other style of woman was infinitely kinder and not nearly as ambitious. Power was not that important to her, since her main goal was to get the job done well. She was quite masculine and yet had another side to her that I found appealing: she genuinely cared about other people. I could see that for this archetype, which I named the Good Doer, her masculine side was heightened yet her feminine side was still in evidence. I liked this woman, but she seemed to be at risk. The Good Doers are the worker bees of a corporation, and these talented souls are also the ones corporations cannot afford to keep losing. So I devised a program that dealt with the Good Doers' types of issues at work as they came to light, and that program worked well. I found a way for a woman like this to value her contributions to the company but still earn a few more rewards for herself. One of the key rewards was less stress and a return to good health.

ARCHETYPES IN THE WORLD OF WORK

I believe the female of our species has experienced so much oppression over the centuries that it is as though a virus runs through the collective female brain that says, "It's our turn to be top dog now!" Many male-oriented women long for the experience of feeling the masculine power that traditionally you could only access if you were born into a male body.

It is as if all the nuances of power that were exercised badly through the ages have been stored in women's collective mind and a signal has gone out to them saying that these wrongs must now be righted. And while these imbalances are being righted, we are seeing terrible abuse perpetrated by women upon men, especially by those on the extreme end of the spectrum. The battle continues to rage between the sexes because some of these highly feminine men do not honor or respect women at all, especially not the new brand of male woman.

However, there is some good news. In the cases of the Sensitive Man and the Good Doer, we see an exciting level of evolution. These people have the ability to use power well. They can elevate others and they can behave in a secure fashion. They have enough balance through their internal genders to own enough personal power, therefore they don't have the desire to lord it over others; they are not threatened by others' power. The interesting thing is that the Sensitive Man and the Good Doer Woman often do end up in positions of leadership, even though they might not necessarily seek to lead. Their compassion and integrity usually elevate them despite their reticence to take on leadership roles.

But this scenario is not true of all of our men and women. The Pseudo Masculine Man and the Andro Woman are two archetypes particularly toxic in corporate life because they have such a strong desire for power. For these archetypes, tasting power acts like a drug. They become addicted to it because they do not have a solid foundation of internal personal power. They will do anything not only to hang on to power but to obtain more. Corruption and tyranny are often the drugs of choice to satisfy their power addiction. No part of their lives will remain unscathed by their obsession.

For the Pseudo Masculine Man and the Andro Woman, the relentless craving for power is founded in their poor vision of themselves. They don't have much self-acceptance and they have virtually no ability to see what they are doing. They also have a deep-seated fear of discovery by others. This potent combination drives them to seek more and more power, figuring that if they are high enough up in the company, the chances of someone discovering they are fakes is less likely. But you guessed it: no amount of power can ever quell their insatiable need to be okay with themselves. They tend to live in internal torment that spills over and causes them to wreak havoc on anyone who gets in their way.

Andro Women in the Workplace

For the most part, Virtuous Andro women understand the responsibility of the choices they make as leaders. This breed of woman is comfortable with power and comfortable with the ramifications of that power. She is trustworthy, and if the ax has to fall she puts her own head on the chopping block. She makes intelligent decisions based on their merit and stands by them. Her decision making is not done by committee. That is the route of her cowardly Andro sister, the Villainous Andro.

It is the Villainous sister who enters a corporation and surreptitiously begins her quest for power with the patience and precision of a primordial being edging toward a higher level of evolution. She can wait because she has her endgame set in her mind and she knows how to go about her devious plans. First up, to protect herself the Villainous Andro disarms any mechanisms built into the organization to detect those who do not fit into the corporate culture. Cultures can be consciously designed or simply develop as the company matures. Either way, an upset within the cultural process can cause disruption to the smooth running of the corporation, and most companies will weed out the people who do not fit within their parameters.

The Villainous Andro Woman will circumvent these procedures, however, by appearing compliant with all company regulations. It would be rare for her to criticize anything about the organization until she is well and truly ensconced at the top of the ladder.

Compliance is a part of her elaborate veil of deception, a veil she uses to disguise her true intent. She will have few contradictory opinions that could alert the cultural detection mechanism within the company.

The Villainous Andro very quickly befriends the key people in power positions in the company, and her main prize will eventually be the person running the company. If the owner is a feminine-oriented man, she will quickly know what to do. The ultimate battle will not be with him but with any others who might have similar ambitions to her own. If it is another woman, she will fight her mercilessly until she bullies her out of the way. If it is a man, she will play whatever game she needs to in order to gain advantage.

Calculating Her Next Step

The actions of the Villainous Andro are calculated; every step she takes and every meeting she attends is all about her and her goals. She has little truth to uphold so she can bend like a reed in the wind. She can go with the flow on any given day, not making any waves until she is very, very secure within the company.

This woman is astute at assessing which are the very best coattails to ride. She makes that decision quite early on and then maps out her steps to the top. The truth is that there will be a number of coattails she will ride on her way to the top prize. There is some real evidence of this in the media at the moment. This woman—and she can range anywhere from a cleaning woman who wants power over her employees all the way to the senior executive of a corporation—has little consideration for the legalities of her actions. If she can get away with what she's doing, she will. We are talking about someone at the extreme end of the spectrum here. The only difference is the environment.

Her kinder and gentler sister, the Virtuous Andro Woman, is all about doing the *right things* to accomplish her goals. Those goals are usually for the betterment of others. The Villainous Andro Woman is all about doing *things right* to divert the gaze of those who might be watching her. The distinction is slight, but the contrast in the resulting ramifications of their actions is huge.

At the extreme end of the spectrum, once the Villainous Andro is deeply ensconced within a company and she has all the necessary power, the result is very often the demise of the corporation. Her process is like a cancer. It lies undetected, moving with stealth throughout the body of the organization. Every action takes from the host, the host being the company or the country, if she has managed to get herself to that very senior level of political control. Slowly but surely things start to disintegrate. One bad practice follows yet another bad practice because there are no compliance checks or balances on her if she is in charge. The fish always rots from the head. Very soon the company, the country, or the home is severely off track.

The employees around her usually notice bad practice, but may feel they do not have the power to say or do anything. They usually need to safeguard their incomes and many will take the line of least resistance. They also know that this woman is ruthless and if they go against her, their actions will result in dismissal. The Villainous Andro may say very little but her menace is felt and few will challenge her authority.

Therein lies the problem and also perhaps the potential solution. Few people realize that the average Villainous Andro Woman is a fearful person and that much of her bravado is just a smoke screen to hide her fear. Within the smoke screen is a really small person who feels victorious at having managed to fool so many people. The answer for you as a co-worker is to be truthful and confront her fearlessly. More often than not she will withdraw and regroup her energy to fight another day. That is the next problem. If she manages to regroup you will need to be ready once again to face her bravely. You could lose your job, yes, but working under her is a nightmare anyway. If enough people bravely take a stand against her, they can win. I have seen it happen. Not often but a few times.

The Good Doer in the Workplace

The first thing to remember is that the Good Doer has one main difference that distinguishes her from her other masculine sisters. The Good Doer has not lost the ability to migrate between her masculine and feminine aspects. Both her essences are usually in good shape but not in excellent condition, so she can still be vulnerable to polarization into either her masculine or feminine, depending on who is close to her.

So imagine that you are in a business meeting and of course there is at least one Good Doer present. What do you think happens when the time comes to delegate all the odious and difficult tasks? What are you going to do? I bet you anything that you will keep your hands firmly by your sides until one of the Good Doers puts hers up for what you would deem the ugly tasks.

If a Good Doer is present, you will automatically feel the energy of the doer and that excuses everyone else from taking on any more than is absolutely necessary. You know she will pick up the pieces and the extra workload. You feel it in her presence and you respond by shirking what you could so easily do. In fairness, even if you did try and relieve her of her load she probably wouldn't allow you to do so.

Remember that the Good Doer is neither lazy nor power hungry. Her motivation is to get things done and her reward is the internal satisfaction of being needed and doing the job well. She does not need visible power, so in fact she is an amazing backroom person, the hidden engine of an organization. She is not the person grandstanding and having people fawn all over her while she collects accolades.

She is a wonderful partner to a careerist. She is often the power behind the throne as it were, in marriages and corporations. Even if she is in a position of power in her own right, and this does occur quite often, she still gets things done with minimal fuss and disruption. She will elevate others to get the job done. Her satisfaction comes from those whom she helps and those whom she works for; her gratification and reward is that they do well.

Along with her good male side, the Good Doer's feminine is in relatively good shape in terms of her ability to problem solve and innovate. She is less of a creator and more of an innovator, as her creative feminine does not often see the light of day. She works hard to find solutions to the problems created by other people.

Her weakness is not her feminine aspect. Rather it is her masculine side that can let her down rather badly. She has a tendency to overwork her male side and that takes her to negative usage of the masculine. If she allows her feminine aspect to support and inform her masculine, she can bring the will of her masculine aspect to the fore without harsh consequences. She will then be in a much better position to take control of her life. She can concentrate on her own happiness as opposed to always trying to make everyone else happy.

The Faux Fem Doesn't Like Work

The Faux Feminine Woman wants the good life without having to work for it. She enjoys reflected power from her partner, and through him she is seen as someone important. Her own feminine side is paralyzed, so the feminine persona she puts out to the world is made up; it is a mask behind which she can hide her true polarity, which is highly masculine.

The Faux Feminine Woman has seen the traps that the Good Doers and the Andros have fallen into and she has no intention of following in their footsteps. This woman has always been adept at managing those around her so that she ends up with the power. This system works for her and she will not be changing it any time soon. All the talk of women being able to be anything they want to be leaves her feeling somewhat exposed. She does not want to *be* anything in particular. She has no high ambition for herself. Her ambition is for the person bringing in the money to support her. Feminism has become almost a dirty word for her. She's had the system worked out to her advantage all along.

The Cougar archetype is similar to the Faux in that she doesn't really wish to work either. The traditional Cougar is an older woman, quite often divorced, and if she also has Faux Feminine traits she will be enjoying a sizable divorce settlement. That makes her financially independent, so she does not need a man or a job for financial security. If the Cougar skews more to the Andro Woman's traits, then she might or might not be working, but she is probably financially independent either way. If the Cougar goes hunting at the office for the younger men she prefers, an office romance could ensue. Young men beware!

The Sensitive Man at Work

When you meet a Sensitive Man at the workplace, you soon realize that he is a very good worker, co-worker, and leader; a man of action and usually right action. He does not just accumulate knowledge but also follows through and does what needs to be done. The Highly Feminine Man, by contrast, does not have this ability to get things done, and that is one of the key differences between these two types.

The Sensitive Man is reasonable and logical. He can implement processes and he uses his innate sense of creativity and wise masculine decision-making skills to become a solid leader. Because he is secure within himself, he is free to be collaborative and fearlessly lead by example. He has the preparedness to lead from the point of view of service. He can be almost valiant in his leadership style. He is competitive, but does not need his competitors to "die," as many testosterone-fueled leaders do.

A typical scenario in a business environment when you have a Sensitive Man leading the group is that he will choose an inner circle of other men. They will be his trusted advisers and his right-hand people. The next level of executives below that group will be the people he regards as the most able for the job at hand. He does not discriminate or care if they are men or women; he just wants the best person for the job. Very often the best man is a highly male-oriented woman and that is fine with him. He will respect whoever does a good job for him. That is his agenda.

The Power-Hungry Pseudo Masculine Man

The number of these men has exploded exponentially in the last few decades. Of our feminine men, he has been the most threatened by the rise of women through the corporate ranks and indeed all throughout the workforce. The Pseudo Man loves power and authority, and before the days when women were equal to him on all levels, he could lord his masculine authority over them through the legal system or societal norms. But today he is under a huge threat everywhere he goes: at home, at work, or out socializing. He cannot escape the woman he fears most; the Andro is everywhere.

Still, the Pseudo Masculine Man will compete for a position in life, and he will play dirty to get it. Fair means or foul, he does not care and he usually takes the latter approach. He does not operate out of a legitimate masculine aspect but rather an artificial persona designed to hide the fact that he is actually highly feminine in his orientation. That makes things really difficult for him in more sophisticated workplaces. He can often get away with the charade of his masculine in a more basic workplace, but when intelligence and a refined sensibility are required, the Pseudo Man is actually at a significant loss.

His preference is to become a skilled office politician, a role he fits rather well. He is already the ultimate sycophant and a masterful flatterer. Since his drive is to have position, he craves the feeling of authority that comes with having power over others. The terrible reality is that he does sometimes arrive at the top, but he does it by using conniving ways and a Machiavellian approach, not through any real intellectual ability or talent. Once he is at the top, it can be very difficult to get rid of him. He weaves a web of people around himself to keep him safe. You guessed it: that circle is composed of weaklings like him, also lacking in true intellectual capacity, so they stick together like a band of misfit brothers and try hold their positions as long as they can.

The Pseudo Man has a built-in envy of the true masculine man, especially the Sensitive Man who has ability. He does not want to be confronted with true masculinity, so he prefers to hire masculine women to take care of the things at work that require masculine traits. When the Pseudo Man is in a position of authority, he will gradually hire more and more male-oriented women into senior positions. He places them strategically around him to keep the real men at bay, forming a ring of feminine fire to protect him. Then he can strategically play them off against each other; while they are busy dueling and challenging each other, he is safe at the top. He is a master of the dictum "Divide and conquer."

The Highly Feminine Man at Work

On the other end of the same spectrum as the Pseudo, we have a man who is not what he appears to be. The Highly Feminine Man is most comfortable in the world when he is hiding behind a mask; his behavior is rarely sincere simply because he is so fearful. Remember, he is missing a very big part of his internal self and without his masculine aspect to protect him, he is in a state of constant fear. To compensate for his lack of masculine bravery, he responds to life by being extremely affable. His ingratiating ways help him get what he needs and wants but never in any direct way. The Highly Feminine Man is the one in the office who wants the promotion but is usually too afraid to do what is necessary to achieve his goals.

Regretfully, the Highly Feminine Man has no leadership skills and low confrontational ability, which preclude him from taking the stance of leader in most situations. This man's general lack of vitality makes him more suited to a quieter working life, such as in the halls of academia and scientific laboratories. The bravery he requires for leadership and warrior duties is not developed because his masculine aspect is so severely impaired. There are occasions when this man does rise to the top, because is he is often an intelligent person. He is usually intellectually suited for a top position, but not from an emotional or psychological perspective. Positions that require leadership are not ideal for this man.

The Highly Feminine Man, who is a good person, unfortunately can have a few problems with the types of masculine energy he pulls to himself. This man is often the target of bullies. He has few protective skills so he is at great risk of abuse and bullying, which can range from mild to very severe. This man may carry a very high degree of sensitivity that adds to his risk factor. And his masculine energy is so weak that it puts his feminine aspect at risk. The masculine aspect needs to be in a healthy protective state for the feminine to function properly; without that key ingredient, the feminine is at risk of taking on the traits of a doormat.

This man is operating in the world without this protective element and that can make him a pleaser in the extreme. His ingratiating ways manifest quite differently from those of the Pseudo Man.

Whereas the Pseudo Man has an agenda, the Highly Feminine Man is afraid; he wants people to like him so they will not hurt him. So he expends an inordinate amount of energy in the pursuit of being accepted, approved of, and liked. Why doesn't he just develop his masculine aspect? He would have a lot more spare time on his hands. But he rarely does.

You'll find all these people in the workplace, and most of the time you don't really have a choice as to whom you have to interact with. Fortunately, when it comes to your personal friendships, those are within your control and you do have a choice. It's time now to look at how the various archetypes present within close friendships and social circles.

CHAPTER **1 8**

The Friendship Landscape

SHE SAYS: "THE GIRLS ARE COMING OVER FOR BOOK CLUB TONIGHT."
HE SAYS: "I'LL BE IN THE SHED."

THE WAY FRIENDSHIPS WORK

There is an old Japanese proverb that says "When the character of a man is not clear to you, look at his friends." I think you will agree this is true, and it is a good point to remember if you have to figure a man out, or a woman for that matter. Friendships add so much to the fabric of our lives, yet we don't always value or protect our friendships the way we should.

It is important for men to have friends, but not in the same way as women. Men might play on sports teams, watch matches together, or go hunting or camping. As long as they are *doing* something and they have some kind of common ground, men tend to get along pretty well. In this way their friendships are very often related to activities they share or projects they work on together. Men might be linked because their wives are sisters or friends and they find things to do while the women talk. Or they might work together and sometimes meet for a golf day or for drinks, but only occasionally would a deep personal friendship evolve. In general, adult men don't feel inclined to pour their hearts out to each other or spend endless hours talking and analyzing their lives; the latter is far more the pattern in women's friendships.

It is really women's friendships and the new friendship landscape women operate in that concern me the most. From my practice and my life, I have learned that maintaining healthy friendships is critical for women today. And it is the friendships women share that I feel are most at risk in our modern society, for a number of reasons.

THE VALUE OF FEMININE CONNECTEDNESS

Wouldn't it be wonderful to rest in the knowledge that you have a blanket of true friendship to pull up to your chin when the world is cold outside? Imagine the security of loyal support and the kindness of a word spoken at just the right moment that suddenly makes everything fall into the right perspective. One of the most precious aspects of feminine life that we have lost due to our newfound maleness is the gift of true, connected friendship, one woman to another. These are the kinds of friendships all women need but too few actually have.

To be male is to be naturally competitive. When we as women embrace competitiveness in its full masculine extreme, there is little room left for feminine friendships. Many women have developed their male aspect to such an extent that it cannot sustain the level of feminine energy required for the old female model of friendship. If we compete with each other on every level of our lives, then something has to be sacrificed and it is usually that. When the choice is between power and friendship, friendship loses out too often in this new world.

In the past women were able to strengthen and polarize their feminine aspect through the friendships and the communion they enjoyed with other. It is still possible to achieve this to a certain extent; there are friendships among women where there is genuine love and care for each other, and the traditional affect holds true. But not that many women have the time, or take the time, to develop these kinds of close and nurturing relationships with other women. With the monumental changes women have experienced in these modern times, it is only logical that their interactions with each other have also changed significantly.

One of the best ways for women to strengthen their feminine aspect is to reconnect with their female friends. When women gather in friendship, they have the ability to polarize each other back into their feminine birthright. Or if they are healthy in their feminine, it helps them keep things that way. As more and more women find a way back to each other, they will leave a better legacy of true feminine friendship as a model for their daughters and granddaughters. Feminine connectedness is what keeps the world safe from brutality. We cannot afford to lose this essential caring aspect of our feminine natures.

LEARNING HOW TO BE A GOOD FRIEND

Given how mixed up and disconnected we have become with regard to our friendships, I recommend that we establish some new rules. These rules would not be new exactly but more like a refresher course. In days gone by social rules were strict; our rules today don't need to be as rigid, but a return to being gracious and respectful is way overdue.

Stating and adopting some rules will provide a solid ground and mutual understanding of what female friendships could be about. It is our chance to revisit the old ways and adjust them accordingly to take into account our current state of evolution. It is exciting to create a new destiny for women and it's about time! If we take no action to improve this situation, most women will face a lonely and isolated future.

I know some people will say they do not have time to tend to their friendships because we live in a time-poor society. Women are under a lot of pressure, but they need to make the effort to keep in touch, especially with their women friends who make them feel good and whose company is inspiring and comforting; the women they trust to always have their back.

Trust is critically important. Without trust, there can be no genuine friendship. It is the first key element needed to build a solid and enduring friendship.

Between friends and within a group of friends there has to be a *spirit of equality*. Everyone is equal within the group. If this element is not present, there will be competition, which is what you don't want. The spirit of friendship should be less about what you have and more about who you are. Remember the important point: competition and friendship are mutually exclusive.

Because everyone is equal within the group, everyone deserves *equal time*. Grandstanding from a few very vocal friends often leaves the quieter women without a voice. Equal time requires the art of listening generously to all members of the group.

There is *no room for exclusivity* within a genuine friendship. If there is a need to exclude anyone, then spite and competition rear their ugly heads. Exclusivity has no part in the world of friendships.

Friends must be *accepting and tolerant* of each other. These traits call for a generosity of spirit from each person. Since none of us is perfect, a true friend accepts others and their faults without reservation or judgment. And if there are unintended hurts and misunderstandings, a friend will try to find forgiveness rather than give up too early.

A friend recognizes that everyone brings themselves to the table of friendship, and what each person brings is enough. When you can *recognize the special gifts each friend brings* to the table of friendship, you are in the privileged position of being able to honor your friend.

Compassion and empathy go hand in hand, and these two qualities live together in any caring friendship. Remember that loving kindness is not a quality that can be faked. If it is not genuine, it will be exposed pretty quickly.

HOW TO CHOOSE FRIENDS WISELY

Friends tend to choose each other for numerous reasons, but today there are even more nuances to the word *friend*, given the influence of social media and the high levels of competition among women. Having a large number of friends is seen as admirable, but ask yourself, How many of the people I know in my life and online are true friends I trust and love and who trust and love me back? And which are the ones I connected to for other reasons such as peer pressure, networking, or whatever?

Women need to connect with each other for their own sakes and not for any advantage a friend might bring. Unfortunately, so many younger women today have never experienced core fundamental friendships. Theirs is the generation that arrived into the world of social networking; some have never really found a circle of close friends they can really count on.

If you are ever left out of a group activity or subtly excluded in other ways, you need to watch out that you are not being bullied. Bullies are extremely skilled at tormenting their prey and as we have seen, several female archetypes are masters of it. Make sure you are not being set up to be bullied within any group you belong to; this applies to young as well as older women. No one is immune. If you feel depleted when leaving a group of friends or even one friend, be on the alert. If your energy is being siphoned from you for their needs, then you are giving too much and it is likely to your detriment. You don't need friends like that.

What friends don't do is often more indicative of the level of friendship you are enjoying with them than what they actually do. For example, do your friends step up in times of trouble when people close to them are facing some challenge, or are they suddenly among the missing? If you detect a fair-weather friend, someone who is only around for the good times, then know that you do not have a genuine friendship. We don't need friends only when we are stable and in good spirits; we also need them to be there when the chips are down. Loyalty is a precious and rare commodity these days.

You will know you have a true friend if they say they are happy for you and your success, your new relationship, or simply because you are content with your life. When there is a tinge of something sly in their voice, be alert to it because jealousy or envy may be presenting itself. Jealousy and envy have no place in a true friendship.

HOW COMPETITION KILLS FRIENDSHIPS

Being feminine is being a good friend. The male woman struggles with the concept of true friendship because she is often in competition with her colleagues and friends. Living in a constant state of competition can make her feel threatened. But to be fair to our male-oriented women, many of them are breadwinners chiseling out a place in the world for themselves and their families. The ability to operate out of their male side gives them a good living but it can also make them lethal in the workplace and in their social networks. It is destructive when they carry the competitiveness of their work life into their personal world without making any adjustments in their behavior. Male-oriented women tend to see everyone as a competitor. The danger is that if everyone is a competitor, no one is a friend. Competition causes female friendships to wither and die.

Social media has not helped the cause of female friendship. This is just another mechanism that divides women with its competitive edge. How many Facebook friends do you have? Many of them are not true friends at all; they are merely numbers and photographs on a screen. Social media engenders superficiality. Most online friends do not understand you on a deep level. The whole concept of social media is fake; you can write whatever you like about yourself, true or not. Too many people blatantly lie to make themselves appear more interesting or popular. When they do that they are actually creating more loneliness for themselves.

I have had many clients with hundreds of Facebook friends, who are still lonely and quite often sad. Ironically, it is the false friendships that leave many women feeling even more forlorn and unhappy. We have abandoned our truth in exchange for a pretense of popularity on the Internet. We need the truth and support of genuine friendship if we are to find our way back to the traditional style of sisterhood bolstered by connection, companionship, and deep open-hearted conversation. The love and care women were able to share with each other in the past has become a rare privilege these days.

FRIENDSHIPS IN THE WORKPLACE

It is helpful to look at an example when thinking about how the Andro Woman reacts to office friendships. Let's start with an Andro Woman who perhaps grew up as the eldest in her family. We know that two things will impact her friendships: her place in her family group and the degree of masculine energy she holds. These form the basis for her vibration and determine how she reacts to work colleagues and personal friends.

At work the Andro Woman is always on guard and ever watchful for other Andro competitors. She will not befriend other Andros because their male-to-male polarity precludes her from forming close workplace friendships; Andros are not able to shift into their feminine so it just does not work. It is the Good Doers at work that she will watch for and befriend. They pose no threat and can be convenient for dumping extra work and tasks on. The Good Doers seldom complain; it is in their nature to get on with whatever work is on their plate. The Andro Woman is canny enough to hire these women because she instinctively knows they will get the job done.

Faux Feminine women, on the other hand, are not that fond of work so the Andro won't have much to do with them in the workplace. Their vibrations will not jell in the workplace anyway because these two archetypes have quite different agendas. Andros desire power and position and will find polarity with those who can assist with that task. Fauxs go to work to find someone to serve them eventually and forever! They are also quite male, and since male to male does not attract that explains why Andros and Fauxs keep their distance.

Depending on her own life situation, however, an Andro may befriend the Faux outside of work. Those two energetic types do have a few general things in common. They can both be quite insincere. Faux Feminine women are very amusing so they tend to be good company if you are not looking for anything too deep. And the Andro Woman is not looking for a deep and meaningful friendship. She is looking for advantage and power and the Faux Feminine Woman can be quite helpful in this respect. That is because the Faux woman is an amazingly skilled social climber and the Andro finds this attribute quite handy in a superficial friendship. This works particularly well if the Andro had a Faux mother and watched her maneuver her way through social circles. She is familiar with the game and understands its necessity. However, if the Andro had an Andro mother, she will be probably be focused on work and these little social ramblings won't hold much interest for her.

GOOD DOERS DO FRIENDSHIP REALLY WELL

Outside of work, Good Doers like to hang out with each other. As we have mentioned a few times, Good Doers are more flexible in their polarity system than other archetypes. They can easily migrate from their masculine to their feminine. That is why they make such good friends to each other. When one is having a "feminine" moment, the others around her can polarize and fulfill the masculine role. If one is having a "masculine" bout and requires nurturing, the others can switch to their feminine essence quite easily and readily to give their friend the required feminine support. Good Doers are the only chameleons among the masculine women of our time. That is because Good Doers understand each other, they have very little malice, and they really enjoy the company of women similar to themselves. They are comfortable and skilled at switching polarities to accommodate others. The old adage "Birds of a feather flock together" certainly applies to these women.

While it is beneficial for Good Doers to be part of a group, they must remain aware that joining a friendship group can leave them vulnerable to interlopers who would seek to take advantage of their good nature and flexible polarity. Enter the Andro who has her own agenda.

AN ANDRO IN OUR MIDST

The Andro Woman finds Good Doers quite nurturing when she needs kindness and a sympathetic ear to listen to her from time to time. And the Andro usually needs friendship because most women are not going to give her any kind of true allegiance. Good Doers can offer undemanding and loyal friendship. But watch out. The Andro Woman will ingratiate herself to the Good Doer, then shift the Good Doer's polarity to gain whatever she needs from her—and the Andro wants anything the Good Doer has that she can use to further her own advantage.

There is another interesting instance when an Andro will seek out a Good Doer for friendship. It happens sometimes when an Andro had a nurturing father or sibling in her past and she now seeks to

replace that element of energy by befriending a Good Doer or joining a friendship group with Good Doers in it. The Andro Woman
can keep any number of groups of friends happy simultaneously, for
a sound energetic reason: she doesn't actually invest any of her own
energy into any group. The group is just there for her and her needs.
So in the case of the Good Doer group, the Andro Woman scoops
up the members' energy without investing anything back. They don't
need her to because they are so happy being the givers. They will
listen to her, nurture her, and take care of her because that is what
they do best. It is easy for them and they do it with a glad heart.

In return, the Andro takes them for a ride. It might take a while
for the Good Doers to realize that the Andro never really recipro-
cates their good will. If this group ever needs the Andro Woman's
help or assistance, she will probably not be there for them. They are
not a group she finds advantageous to her bigger picture. She knows
that she can step on them and therefore she has little respect for
them as people because she does not fear them. If she feared them
the way she fears other Andro or Faux women, she would be more
gracious. But almost without exception, the Andro will have no difficulty going missing in action when the chips are down for a Good
Doer friend. The Andro will eventually resurface, but only once
there is no possibility of demands being made on her.

A GROUP OF FAUX FRIENDS

Although a group of Faux Feminine women or Andro women will
discuss their issues, as friends they remain quite superficial. No one
is required to place too much energy into the needs of the others;
Fauxs and Andros cleverly manage to stay on the periphery of just
about any group they join. The Faux does have a healthy respect for
the Andro. They are similar, but the Faux is only too aware that the
Andro is capable of turning on her in a heartbeat. So the Faux tries
to look like she is participating but does not get involved in anything
that requires her to give anything of herself. That is her pattern.

The Faux represents predatory masculine behavior at its extreme.
This woman is not a candidate for the new sisterhood women are

forming today. She is not a friend and should never be trusted; she is capable of unplumbed levels of deceit. She cannot even trust herself because she does not know who she is.

THE STRENGTH OF THE NEW SISTERHOOD

Collectively speaking, women are the single most powerful answer we have to the current state of our civilization. They have always ruled the world but mostly from behind the scenes. In the past women accepted the responsibility of being the voice of reason; they brought the balance of their feminine energy to situations of all kinds and were often the catalysts behind peace negotiations.

The quintessential example of a woman as a pacifist is Baroness Bertha von Suttner, who according to the *Encyclopedia Britannica* was not only the first female recipient of the Nobel Peace Prize (1905) but was also credited with influencing Alfred Nobel to establish that prize in the first place, a year earlier. Born in Prague in 1843, at the age thirty-three she got a job working for Nobel as his secretary. From what was arguably a lowly clerical position, von Suttner went on to become a committed peace activist and world-renowned author, remaining dedicated to the cause of peace for more than thirty-five years. She even attended the Hague Peace Conference in 1899 and influenced the delegation toward initiating the Permanent Court of Arbitration (PCA), a court aimed at replacing armed conflict with arbitration. The PCA still operates today.

Women have traditionally been peacemakers and we need them to be that again. One of the best ways to achieve this is for women to first reconnect with their invaluable feminine essence and then reconnect with each other. There is strength in numbers; women in right order, with strong friendships among themselves, can once again bring balance to our chaotic world.

But we know that it is hard today for women to develop the kind of strong friendship groups that could span their whole lives. They are missing the kind of friendship that is truthful, kind, and supportive; without that kind of sisterhood, women can become isolated. True nurturing friendship is absolutely essential to the feminine soul. As women, we need a place to commune with our sisters in trust and love, fully willing to take care of each other and even each other's families when needed.

I am excited at the prospect that women reading this may take better heed of their actions and invest time in true friendships. Now that they know the incredible value they will get in return, they can feel motivated to make changes to bring true female friendships into their lives.

I would like to ask you to join me in looking to the future. Knowing now how polarity impacts all aspects of our lives, I want to paint a picture of what the world can look like when we achieve an honest internal balance within ourselves and forge true connections in our romantic relationships. I propose this is possible for men and women when we welcome the return of the champion and a return to grace.

PART
FOUR

CHAPTER **19**

Return of the Champion

SHE SAYS: "I'M LOOKING FOR A GOOD MAN."
HE SAYS: "DO I QUALIFY? I'M TRYING . . ."

CHOOSING TO BECOME A CHAMPION

What is a champion? Is he a defender? A protector? Is he still the upholder of right order? And what is right order today? Men are confused. They no longer have a clear picture of who they are or what is expected of them. In the past a champion had clarity about who he was. He might have been a gladiator, a soldier, or even a crusader: a real defender of the faith. He was the provider of food, killing prey to feed his family. Often he found himself serving as a knight in shining armor, and of course he was proficient at rescuing damsels in distress.

For the most part damsels no longer need rescuing and if you come across one who does, it might be prudent to be a little wary of her motives before you rescue her. She could be a Faux Feminine Woman and you will get more than you bargained for! So if all the old champion jobs are now defunct, how can a man hold his masculinity in good esteem in this modern age? He lives in a world where a woman can take care of herself, and in many cases she can just as easily take care of her man and her family too.

With the lines so horribly blurred, men react in different ways. The good guy is still the good guy; he knows the right thing to do and he does it; he carries his share of the load. He is honorable and honoring of the women in his life. Then there is the kind of man who has seen the blurring of the lines and progression of our society toward strong male-oriented women. He has seized this opportunity to take the blurring to a whole new level and use it to his advantage. This man is and always has been an opportunist whose type has been with us through the ages. But previously such a man was easily flushed out because it was difficult for him to hide from himself or his community. Champions abounded, providing a stark contrast to the inadequate behavior of men who failed to carry out their responsibilities proudly. These lesser men were named and shamed if they did not meet the expectations the social codes of their time dictated.

PRESENT-DAY REALITIES FOR THE CHAMPION

When we fast-forward to today, things are lot more fluid; society's norms are not nearly as rigid. It is no longer crucial that men be the sole breadwinners, and they are not frowned on or shamed when they have a lesser job than their spouse, or even no job at all. There is more room for interpretation of what is correct, acceptable, and even doable. Within this flexibility, many men have lost their way. They excuse themselves from being the best they can be because the women in their lives are so successful and capable. They see women's success as an opportunity to take a backseat. There are two questions we should be asking ourselves: Should men renege on their manhood in the face of their partner's success? And what is the cost to men who don't step up? I invite you to come to your own conclusion as we continue this discussion.

Looking at our culture today, champions come in a variety of packages. They range from the stay-at-home dad to the captain of industry. With the reversal and shifting of our internal genders, no one seems to have a clear definition of what it is to be a man. Strong male role models have all but disappeared. So many of today's men were raised by their mother in a single-parent situation or their father was absent or abdicated his role as protector and provider for whatever reason. With the disappearance of male role models in the home, boys and young men were raised floating adrift like a rudderless ship.

Within the jungle of new premises and expectations, it is easy for anyone to feel lost. In the case of men, they end up struggling to figure out what it means to be an upstanding man. So now they find that if they are too directive in their approach, they could be considered a bully. But if they don't give any direction for fear of being considered domineering then they are in danger of being perceived as weak. Good sensitive men find themselves in an almost impossible situation. They very much feel they are damned if they do and damned if they don't. The picture of masculinity is so unclear that all they can do is flounder in a murky sea of debatable expectations. Until now that is.

HOW TO RECOGNIZE A CHAMPION

Today our TV screens are filled with false champions. These are the sports champions society elevates to demigod status. They are proficient in their sport but their behavior outside their arena is often less than admirable. This is understandable, as most of these men have only focused on honing their athletic abilities and nothing else. Unfortunately they become role models for children and the problem is perpetuated.

We see football players behaving in ways that are very denigrating to women. The reality is that they are the complete opposite in makeup to a true champion. A true champion has his masculine energy in order and is protective and directive of both his own feminine and that of the women he encounters. Too many professional athletes are suppressive in their attitude toward women and even worse, they behave in a possessive way, treating women as nothing more than objects for their use.

The heart of the champion still beats within male members of our species, but there is need for a wake-up call and the implementation of some practical steps in order to reactivate him. The best place for a woman to begin looking for a champion is to find a Sensitive Man and hope he is up to the challenge. We need the new Sensitive Man to step up because he underpins the health of our society moving forward. It is critically important for all of us that he does not lose his way.

The Sensitive Man still has a strong connection to his masculine self. He is in balance internally and operates out of his strong masculine side predominantly. It is his internal masculine health that enables the Sensitive Man to behave as a warrior when necessary. He can defend right order in his family or at work, no matter where he finds things to be out of order. Just as important, he is readily able to tap into the sensitivity of his feminine aspect in order to discern the difference between right and wrong.

I realize that it is hard to differentiate between men in our new world. Most men have engaged with their feminine side. They have had little option because so many women have wholeheartedly engaged with their masculine aspect. This process alone has been enough to drive men to relate in a much greater way to their feminine energy. So with virtually all men today being more sensitive, it is a confusing process for women to define who is a good man and who is less than a good man.

What is the difference between a man who champions his wife in her career because that is what she wants and a man who takes advantage of his wife's ability to have a career with good earning capacity? The answer is very simple. We must look at his personal *intention* to figure out if he is truly supporting his wife or taking advantage of her. He will reveal his underlying intentions through his words, his tone, and his actions. You need only review the male archetype chapters to see what I mean.

If a man does sacrifice his own career to champion his partner in hers then he truly is worthy of the title of champion. If her career is so important that he has decided to support her and take the lead in looking after their family and, in truth, organizing the rest of their personal lives while he's at it, then he has sacrificed himself to what he sees as the greater good of their family unit. If he is truly dedicated to the good of the whole, then he can indeed be considered a modern-day champion. On the other hand, if it is his intention to use unemployment as an easy way out because he has little career success to sacrifice and a lot to gain by staying at home, he is closer to being an opportunist and probably lacking in drive. This is not champion behavior; this type of man will do very little at home to truly contribute to the greater good. His wife will not feel cherished, loved, and protected but rather used and exhausted.

EARNING RESPECT THROUGH RESPONSIBILITY

Many men in reversed roles within the family may feel a sense of inequality. A man who takes a lesser role in terms of breadwinning for the family can easily find himself in the position that women did for centuries. Women were undervalued and at the mercy of the major breadwinner. The man today who is a true champion has the difficult task of remaining masculine within the bounds of this shift of roles. It is a Herculean task that requires his partner to be sensitive to the difficulties he faces as a man in a role not of hunter but of nurturer. No one wants this good man to lose his masculinity. Both partners need to make sure that the man is valued and respected for his contribution and his sacrifice. His role as true protector and supporter to his family is of course no less valuable because he doesn't bring home a paycheck.

So what about the man who is still the main breadwinner, holding a responsible and demanding job? He is a champion by being active in the external world; provided he also treats his wife and family with respect and love at home, and supports his wife in her career success if she chooses to work, then he too is a champion.

However, the hard-working man comfortable in his masculine aspect yet sensitive when needed is becoming an endangered species! He has become weary of battling Andro women and having little support from the feminine men around him. We need this man to keep the faith and not give up the fight. We need him to increase his natural champion abilities even more at this time. And we need him to be a role model to the other men around him, especially younger men struggling to find their way. This champion must not allow himself to be polarized into his feminine energy by strong male women. We need him to stay the course of his predominant masculine pole to keep the balance of our society. He is our hope and our protector of balance.

Regretfully, his role is a lonely one and if he is not conscious of the importance of what his role demands, we could all suffer irreparably. We are in danger of a complete role reversal of the internal genders. Women are losing their femininity at a seemingly uncontrollable rate, and they appear to be at a complete loss at to how to retain it in the face of how masculine their lives have become. Ultimately, from an internal perspective, women do not want this situation. Masculine-oriented women are not balanced internally and cannot find true peace and contentment. In a world where women become too male, men lose their manliness and become unbalanced and unfulfilled. A disastrous outcome!

HOW TO BECOME A CHAMPION

So what does a modern-day man have to do to maintain his masculinity and ensure that his level of honor remains in a healthy state? The first thing he has to do is to stop blaming the women in his life. As a would-be champion he has to take complete responsibility for the state of his own masculinity. The fact that women are now far more masculine than they have ever been is not an excuse for him to abandon his own masculinity.

The champion has to find within himself the fortitude to stand up and be counted as a fully fledged masculine person. In other words, the champion does not apologize for being a man. He honors the role of being the male of the species to his fullest capacity. I have seen in my coaching practice that it is easy for men to be afraid of expressing their masculinity for fear of being labeled misogynistic or chauvinistic. But men who are champions are neither. In fact, I have yet to meet a true champion who has not managed to retain his love of women.

Leadership is embraced really strongly by women today but that does not mean that men should forgo their own leadership abilities in their favor. Champions understand the importance of the role of the *father* and they embrace all that the term means; everyone still needs the protection afforded by leadership balanced with wisdom..

The roles of leader and protector have not disappeared just because women are equal in every sense of the word. In fact, more than ever, the leadership qualities of the male champion have to be strong and viable. He needs to keep from being toppled by the sometimes more robust and forthright "leadership" offered by Andro women. As men's leadership qualities become strong and sustainable once again, the corporate world will welcome the balance this provides in that it will complement the leadership styles women offer.

Beyond these traits, we also recognize that the champion is a man of honor and conviction. His conviction keeps him immune to the vagaries of the flatterers and the manipulators. He is focused, fair, and respectful in his dealings and in his relationships, a true gem among the growing sea of feminine and highly feminine men you will run into.

DEVELOPING THE ABILITY TO BE HEART CENTERED

The champion has the ability to be heart centered, which he accesses through his feminine essence. I am speaking here of the internal feminine essence that both men and women have access to, and when he knows how, a man taps in to his feminine in the same way a woman does. Being heart centered means he is compassionate, empathetic, and thoughtful. Both of the sexes must work at keeping these very important feminine traits healthy and in balance.

I was at a seminar where a very sensitive feminine man struck up a conversation with me. We discussed this subject and he told me that many years ago he had given up wearing a necktie. I asked him why. He said he believed that whoever created the necktie had a purpose in mind: to help men separate their heads from their hearts, particularly at work.

The symbolism struck me. When men put on their suits and ties, they are ready for battle. They might as well wear metal armor. This man had arrived at his own conclusion about the need, or lack thereof, for a tie. He was not about to be dictated to by a convention he felt was counterproductive to accessing his heart, which ultimately meant *how he would live his life*. I know there are many, many men in today's world that have absolutely no difficulty accessing their heart center. This is reassuring since they have a big role to play as society moves forward.

MENTORING THE NEXT GENERATION OF MEN

One of the major roles of the champion is to exemplify to younger men how to treat the women in their lives. If his example is weak or in any way devoid of the honor that should be accorded women, then we head back down the slippery slope that leaves women dishonored and unprotected. Vulnerable to abuse simply because they are physically weaker than the average male, if women are abused either physically or emotionally we endanger the whole of our society. If women are not protected and honored as the feminine life-giving co-creators of our society, the very fabric of who we are is endangered.

It is the champion who holds in his hands the balance of how we move forward with the revolution we find ourselves engaged in. He safeguards the balance between men who have deserted their masculine energy and women who have abandoned their feminine energy. He has the unique ability to be the guiding light for a return to correct balance between the sexes as we settle into a new way to doing things. The question is, Will he take up the challenge? And what do we lose if he does not?

CHAPTER **20**

Return to Grace

HE SAYS: "I'M LOOKING FOR A GOOD WOMAN."
SHE SAYS: "DO I QUALIFY? I'M TRYING . . ."

THE LOSS OF OUR COLLECTIVE FEMININE

The women of today must wonder sometimes, Has forsaking our feminine side been worth the pursuit of full equality between men and women? Or is there a better way of being, not yet fully considered? The biggest issue in all of this is that today's women do not appear to be in balance with their energies. The collective feminine mind has been tormented for so long that women no longer know how to be at peace. There always seems to be something more to fight for, something more to be done—no rest for the weary.

Women will find peace and harmony when they gain a true sense of security, something that will come when they truly believe they are equal and move forward from that strong base. Imagine a world filled with secure women! I mean secure in every sense of the word, with nothing more to prove, no more battles to fight. Women who have arrived at a point of knowing that they are equal co-creators on this earth—equal in every way.

A GRACEFUL NEW WORLD

So what would this actually look like in the real world? Well, first the war between the sexes would end almost immediately. What would be the point? The games men and women perpetrate on one another would be pointless. They would have no meaning. And we wouldn't need all the books and seminars on "How to Catch a Man" or "How to Catch a Woman." They would have no relevance.

Then imagine the fashion world! It would have to rethink its stance since the constant search for the next provocative fashion statement would no longer be needed. Designers' next season's line would be made up of clothing meaningful to the women they design for, instead of being targeted at the men women used to be trying to "catch." Women would fully own their worth and there would be no debate about the value they bring to the world as individuals. That would be grace personified.

When women honor themselves first and no longer need reassurance that they are okay, they will be able to gain the full respect of men. When women have that respect, men will be able to give up their fear of the feminine. Eliminating this fear is so important because as history has shown, where there is fear there tends to be violence.

And imagine if women found forgiveness! First, women would need to forgive themselves for the anger and hatred coursing through their veins for all the wrongs they have suffered throughout the ages. They also need to forgive themselves for the anger and hatred they feel as a result of years of suppression and persecution. In essence, women would be forgiving the other half of themselves. Men in our world today would be forgiven and they would feel that forgiveness. This would be the salve men need to heal their own wounds endured in centuries past. Women need to forgive both themselves and men for all these past wounds, and men absolutely have to feel this forgiveness. Once these matters are achieved, both genders will be able to move on.

WHAT DOES IT MEAN TO BECOME MORE FEMININE?

To be feminine is to be inspiring. When the feminine aspect of a woman is active, she is inspiring; she has the power to breathe life into the world. She can be the inspiration not only for men and for her children, but also for herself. To be inspiring is to elevate others to heights they never dreamed possible. Embodying the graceful feminine, a woman has the ability to shift perspective on just about anything. Inspiration can cause change through a group of friends, a family, or just a couple.

Since the feminine is the spark that is creation, women need to reconnect with that part of themselves and when they find it, protect it with all the strength they can muster. As we become aware of all the uninspired men around us, perhaps we need to investigate a little further why that is. Without the inspiration of the feminine, who will be the wind beneath men's wings? Will they be that for themselves? To be their own inspiration, men would have to go deeper and deeper into their own feminine aspect. The danger with that is that they may never resurface and women will be left bereft of external male companions.

A man comfortable with his masculine essence responds well to the true feminine in a woman. She has the power to enable him to understand his feminine aspect, a part that may be hidden from himself. The same concept holds also true for a woman. If a man has a healthy masculine within and behaves in an authentic masculine way, it can be enthralling for her. She is then encouraged by his example to find that upright man, the healthy masculine essence, within herself. If a man is in his true masculine, a woman can safely inhabit her feminine self when she is with him. Men and women are fascinated with the opposite pole of their physical reality, but they need that opposite pole to be in right order so their own predominant energy is not corrupted.

We have the opportunity now with this knowledge to re-create women of power, integrity, and authenticity. We can shape a new world inspiring to all women and men. We can do better and be better and we can breathe new life into our emotional lives and the lives all those around us.

BE COURAGEOUS ENOUGH TO BE NURTURING

To be feminine is to be courageous—courageous enough to nurture. Nurturing is a fundamental feminine trait, whether you are a man or a woman, and with more and more masculine women in our midst, this essential trait in women is in danger of disappearing. It is crucial that women and men reconnect with it to save our children, our animals, and our planet. The world would be a sad place without a dependable source of nurturance. The role of nurturer has traditionally fallen on the shoulders of women, but more and more men have responded to the challenge in recent times because women are not as available at home to nurture their families as they once were.

But first it is essential to nurture yourself and that, again, takes courage, especially if you are a male-oriented woman. The belief is that if you are tough you do not need nurturing, and that is where the problem lies. If we cannot nurture ourselves, how are we to nurture others? If we do not realize that nurturing ourselves allows us a free flow of caring energy to others and that energy in its turn returns to us, then we are all in danger of feeling devoid of love and support. We feel abandoned and aridness overtakes our lives like a drought desperately in need of alleviation.

Therefore it takes courage for the graceful woman and the champion man to travel deep into the feminine self and find the peace that lives there. This is the space of rest and sanctuary. This is the place free of competition. It is the place of possibility. It takes courage not to be compelled to compete. When you can arrive into this space within your feminine self, you will have created a safe harbor from the external world. When this ability is mastered, you can provide that safe harbor for your fellow human beings when they are distressed. If you have the courage to access your feminine self and nurture it, you will provide a springboard for your masculine side to travel out into the external world in safety and security. It is that security that provides a confidence that is real and not based on a false sense of ego. It is a sense of security based on trust: the trust of self. None of this is easy, but it is an admirable ideal to aim for. It is a benchmark and a guiding light for a truly feminine life.

HOW TO BECOME MORE HEART CENTERED

As we mentioned in the previous chapter, accessing the feminine allows a person to become heart centered. This is the ability to be compassionate, empathetic, and thoughtful; to be able to take others into account rather than solely focusing on our own self-centered needs and wants. When I ask women to operate from their heart, many of them say, "What do you mean?" It can be difficult to explain that first you need to *feel*—to access your gut feelings. That will lead you to your heart center. Being truly feminine means that you can be authentic in your feelings and how you convey them through your spoken words. Don't shut yourself off from what your gut, or intuition, is telling you. It is coming from your feminine self.

Many male-oriented women have cut themselves off from their feelings. It is understandable; they are under so much pressure in their work lives today. They are constantly working toward deadlines, balancing the pressures of running a family with the responsibilities of a full-time job. The luxury to take a moment and check in with themselves to make sure they are flowing from their hearts isn't always an option. Too many male-oriented women just do not have the awareness or the time. When life was a little less harried we had time to contemplate, and contemplation is the key to becoming heart centered.

NOT ALL ANSWERS ARE CLEAR AT ALL TIMES

Accessing your feminine aspect means to live in a constant state of possibility. The feminine is vast and unformed, chaotic, and often not easy to understand. It is a world of intuition and beauty just waiting to be molded into reality, the raw stuff waiting to be given form and brought through into the physical world. It is really important to understand that if we lose access to this feminine aspect of ourselves, we are in danger of being molded by forces outside us. We lose touch with our creative abilities. We lose the inspiration that can drive our masculine selves. We lose the integrity of who we are at our core and become copies of someone else.

This is evident everywhere. People model their lives on rock stars and celebrities of dubious standing, or mimic dictators on micro and macro levels because they have no sense of their own inner creative process. Without discernment you have little personal power because you are not creating yourself from within. Instead you are following the leads of people you perceive to be powerful but who are in fact just good imitators and manipulators. Fortunately, you can tap into your feminine, which provides you with an inner compass that guides your way to integrity and authenticity. There is nothing authentic about mimicking the behavior of others, which is why the courage of the feminine is an invaluable asset to your inner guidance.

ACCESSING YOUR INTERNAL NO BUTTON

Change is obviously required to become the New People. The New People will discover tools: strengths, and abilities they did not know existed; or if they had an inkling of their presence they did not know how to access them. One powerful tool that exists within the feminine, available to both women and men, I call the *internal no button*. In ordinary life when you say no to someone, depending on the circumstances, you may be effective but sometimes not. You will not be effective if the energy behind your no is not as powerful as the demands made by the other person. However, when the feminine is accessed properly, this internal no button allows you to command a very powerful energy that in most cases will overcome the other. When operating from this level you don't have to put up with bullying or manipulation from masculine-orientated women at work, or the attentions of a man you have no interest in.

Having a healthy sense of your internal no button is absolutely essential if you are seeking grace. First you must be very clear about who you are and what you stand for. Then you can be clear about what you see in the behavior of others and decide what you will and will not tolerate. It is important to not reward or agree with behavior you do not approve of or it will recur until you press your internal no button and say no from that deep feminine to put a stop to what you don't want around you. You will then be very clear as to who you are as a woman, and that clarity will be obvious to those around you. You can stand by your convictions and say no when you need to. Like a mighty tree that is deeply rooted, your convictions can't be uprooted, for you will be firmly and deeply connected to your feminine.

Once you have that level of energetic clarity, your internal no will grow in power and will protect you. This is one way back from the current social state where most women are seeking approval and attention rather than staying rooted in their own convictions. Rooted in your convictions, with clarity about what you want and protected by your internal no, you will no longer send out any mixed messages or present an oversexualized version of yourself. As your internal no grows in strength and presence, you will become more confident. You will tap into the grace that is naturally yours as a woman connected to her feminine. You will then be able to confidently manage the changes occurring within you and your immediate environment. Knowing who you are, knowing what you want, and being backed up by the very powerful feminine, you become a powerful force—a powerful magnet drawing what you want to you without manipulation, bullying, or deceit.

STAND STRONG FOR YOURSELF AS YOUR SHIFT HAPPENS

Once you begin your ascent into grace, be ready for the changes that start happening in your world. Shifting your internal energy will create a corresponding shift in your external world. Be well prepared for the disapproval of those around you. If they are not changing like you, they will not understand your process and may feel threatened because you will be altering the balance in their social or work group. They may be subtle or not so subtle in trying to get you back to the way you were, in a space where you could be influenced once again. My advice is stay your new course. Keep listening to your inner guidance—following your intuition—so you know what is right for you. Keeping your energy in right order will keep your life in right order.

As you steadily develop the ability to gracefully individuate and honor yourself, you will ultimately divorce yourself from the mass consciousness of pretense and showwomanship. Old relationships may well run their course; if people are not willing to accept and love the graceful, confident woman you have become, then let them go. Grace will be yours and you will cease to need the approval of others. Your soul will sing because it knows you are in complete control of determining what is right for you. You will be taking responsibility for the whole of your life at home, at work, among friends, and within your birth family. Who you are as an energetic being goes with you wherever you are and wherever you go. And you are fully responsible for the vibration you send out and the image put out into the world.

BUILDING A NEW SISTERHOOD

Grace takes courage, but it is also contagious. If every woman and girl can begin in just a small way to support her fellow sisters instead of tearing them down at every opportunity, very soon there will be a critical mass and a new sisterhood can be born. That new sisterhood won't be perfect because the feminine never is. The feminine essence is far too large and unruly to be perfect, but sisters in this cause will recognize each other and support each other in remaining in good order.

In that new order children will be protected by not only their mothers but also her relatives and friends. Pretty soon we will have the village we need to raise the child. The pressure can then come off single parents who, faced with the enormous task of raising small children, feel isolated and alone. Mothers in general will feel supported, benefiting from the relief and security older women in their circle can bring to their parenting.

Through collective grace women will have their internal no supported by the sisterhood. It will be a resounding no to bad fathers who do not participate in the financial security of their children. We will say no to men who feel free to terrorize the mothers of their children. We will say no to bad bosses, both male and female, who exploit mothers and the vulnerable.

The feminine energy that resides within every woman is a powerful force to be reckoned with and it can be used for good or evil. All through history, right up until our present day we have witnessed bad feminine behavior. Too many women are used to operating out of their shadow rather than through their full and glorious feminine selves. I believe this bad behavior has become a collective habit after centuries of dealing with patriarchal behavior, but women no longer need that level of subterfuge to get what they want. Power lies within themselves. All they have to do is reconnect with the seat of positive power within.

Through a return to grace, individually and collectively, the new sisterhood can break the habit of shadowy feminine behaviors. We have our rights now. We just need to step into them in a full and positive way.

BLESSINGS FOR ALL THE GRACEFUL MOTHERS

A woman of grace understands the enormous responsibility that rests on her shoulders when she brings new life into the world. Parenting is the responsibility of both parents but the mother is the embodiment of the feminine energy, which is the nurturing energy. The positive expression of her nurturing will ensure the best possible outcome of children growing into positive, balanced adults.

A graceful mother ensures that children of either gender are raised with honor and respect for each other. If a boy is brought up to respect his mother and his sisters, he will be incredibly well set up to function as an adult man in the company of women.

The raising of graceful and respectful children is easier said than done. It is particularly hard for women who are sole parents to demand respect from their sons and daughters, but graceful mothers lead by example. A graceful mother honors her own feminine energy and in so doing ensures that her children see the feminine aspect as something precious and honorable.

A graceful mother will draw on her own masculinity if need be, to ensure that her sons will honor her feminine and the feminine of all women whom they come into contact with. As a graceful mother, she is adept at drawing upon her masculine energy without forsaking her feminine essence. In this way she also serves as a model to her daughters that females deserve respect and that women can be strong when they need to be.

A woman of grace demands respect and demands to be honored. In the process of demanding respect, her children are themselves changed. The child of a mother who is respected and honored can only be respectable and honorable. The child sees the world through secure eyes and behaves in secure ways. Everything falls into place, even if it is not perfect.

A graceful mother does not disrespect the feminine by undertaking actions that are manipulative or deceitful since these actions can and do cause irreparable harm to the feminine essence. These kinds of bad behaviors are always first learned at home; children are very susceptible to the behavior they witness. Children do not do as we *say*; they do as they *see*.

Therefore a graceful mother shows the best way to conduct oneself by her own actions. She has to be both the honorable man and the moral woman. Graceful mothers know that they are women first and masculine second. They demonstrate daily to their children the power of the feminine energy that exists within each human being, and therefore the children will see and feel this feminine essence within themselves.

A woman of grace sets her sons up so they can honor the true feminine and her daughters so they can honor the true masculine. If that could become the new way to raise children, we could eliminate pain and suffering and look forward to peace and harmony in the homes of the future.

A SOCIETY IS HOW ITS WOMEN ARE

When a woman of grace functions from a healthy feminine energy in harmony with her internal masculine, she is at peace and in a place of receptivity. She is in an active state of drawing into herself all that she needs to continue a life of balance. This woman will be protected as she is protective. She will be honored and respected by the partner she attracts and his energy will be in right balance with hers. This harmonious union will generate a chain effect of grace that passes down the generations.

Since women in harmony with their feminine are the nurturers, they are in a broader sense the nurturers of society. The wisdom of the feminine is essential to provide balance with the masculine. The well-being of any society is dependent on the well-being of its women. Where women are disempowered, society is out of balance and often ruled by violence. Women must step into their feminine for their own health, their children's health, and the health of society.

CHAPTER **21**

Embracing the New Way

SHE SAYS: "THE DIRECTIONS SAY TURN LEFT HERE."
HE SAYS: "HEY, WE'VE ARRIVED!"

How often have you driven home and not had the vaguest notion of which route you traveled to get there? You and your car were on autopilot. Maybe your whole life is like that: like living in a trance. You know what? It's time to wake up! The alarm is going off. What you are hearing is a call to arms for men and women to get moving, to get out of the path of the crocodile. I really worry about what will happen to the state of our relationships and the state of the world if this dangerous predator keeps gaining on us. The predator in this case represents the danger we really face—the danger of a loss of self, a loss of hope, a loss of love, and a loss of legacy.

Surely we will want to be remembered for something important. Each generation contributes something lasting and indelible to the fabric of history. What kind of role models are we being to the generations to come? How do we expect our descendants to relate to each other when we can't seem to talk face to face anymore about our own lives?

Young people are increasingly living in a virtual world. In fact, we all are. We have constructed elaborate lives online where we have hundreds of "friends," many whom we've never met and others whom we hardly ever see in person. I think that we have all grown so comfortable living in our virtual realities and in our heads that we forget there is a physical world and real people we could actually see and hear and touch and laugh with. We can share food and good times with real people. We can count on them and they can count on us in good times and bad.

Humans were never intended to become isolated individuals living life through a keyboard and computer screen. It is our connection with others that makes us complete. It gives our lives purpose and meaning. When we connect with our family, our friends, our work-mates, and especially when we spend time with our intimate partner, we come alive. We have fun. We learn and grow. We laugh and cry. We are no longer in trance or on autopilot, and we overcome the desperate loneliness that often lurks just below the surface of our being.

The good news is that we don't have to live lives of quiet desperation anymore. There is hope. There is a different and deeper way to live. You just have to choose to take responsibility for yourself. Patterns of behavior are tough to change but it is not impossible. Why not take an internal audit of where you stand right here and now and think about what you would like to change?

Knowledge is power. Through reading along with our case studies, you know much more about the motivations inside yourself and inside the people around you, in relation to polarity and attraction. With this new knowledge, you have every reason to be hopeful. You have discovered some new tools and techniques to balance your internal yin and yang. As you try new ways of behaving and relating to others, you will see that these ideas work. You will become more at peace within yourself and receptive to attracting the right intimate partner to share your life.

Now that you know which archetypes to avoid, you can choose a workplace or career that doesn't have as much drama and stress. You can be open to trying new activities you enjoy instead of sitting by the sidelines of life, surfing the net one more Saturday night. As you engage with the world, doing things that fulfill and challenge you, you will attract friends and friendship groups that will help keep you on your new positive path. Why keep moving through life as if you were sleepwalking? All it takes to get started is one small step. Have the courage to envision that step and the bravery to take it.

Men and women, it is the same call to arms for us all. All we have to do is access our feminine courage to determine the change we would like to make and engage our masculine bravery to go for it! Embracing this new way of thinking allows you to become the graceful woman or the champion man that dwells inside you. Use your internal courage and external bravery to become an agent of change and role model for the next generation.

That will be a valuable legacy. Imagine if twenty years from now our descendants can say we were the generation that broke free and chartered the course back to personal relationships that actually work and are sustainable! That under our watch people learned how to feel loved and fulfilled and that no one ever looked back.

I believe that embracing this new way of being can be the most exciting process we will ever have the privilege of participating in. Men have an opportunity to be the best men history has ever seen, engaging with their feminine side while maintaining a healthy male essence. Each man then has the unique opportunity to connect with women in a mutually respectful way and find a suitable loving partner he can trust.

Women gained many choices through their struggle for equality and the reality is that men gained choices too. The liberation of women actually liberated men as well. Each of us is now free to show both sides of our internal structure without fear or shame. Masculine and feminine, yin and yang, we are equal but different, inextricably linked to each other.

The time has come for women to wholeheartedly embrace their equality. Women have never had such an opportunity to access their masculine essence and express it in the world. As long as they also keep a strong hold on their feminine essence, women have the best of all worlds. Embracing equality means taking it to the next level and fully integrating it into ourselves. When the equality integration process has matured and been fully embedded in the collective psyche of women, we will no longer question who we are.

To cement this process, which is still in its infancy, in the big scheme of things women now have the added responsibility not only to themselves but to each other to embrace this challenge fully and with all the internal grace within them. It is so clear that women have the opportunity now as never before to be the magnificent creatures they are. We can change how we think about each other, how we treat each other as women, and how we interact with men. When we embrace each other rather than always being competitive or confrontational, life becomes tremendously better in so many ways. Each woman will find the right partner for herself, someone who will love and support her through thick and thin.

Truly, the time for excuses is over. The trance has lifted. We have heard the alarm and are ready for action. The new way is quite simple. Here's what it looks like in its ideal state. We are equal. We are in right internal balance. Our polarity is healthy and we attract the exact mate and the loyal friends that suit our new lives. We support each other and move forward, fully integrated, fully equal, happy and in peace, as graceful women and champion men.

Bibliography

Atkinson, William Walker. *The Kybalion: The Definitive Edition*. New York: Penguin, 2008.

Bailey, Alice A. *Glamour: A World Problem*. New York: Lucis, 1978.

Berg, Yehuda. *The Power of the Kabbalah*. London: Hodder & Stoughton, 2003.

Cross, Robin, and Rosalind Miles. *Warrior Women: 3000 Years of Courage and Wisdom*. London: Quercus, 2011.

Haanel, Charles. *The New Master Key System*. New York: Atria, 2008.

Johnson, Robert A. *She*. New York: Harper & Row, 1976.

Jung, Emma. *Animus and Anima*. Putnam, CT: Spring, 2008.

MacDonald-Bayne, Murdo. "Lecture Notes, 1948–49." In *Life Everlasting*, 2nd rev. ed. Christchurch, NZ: Mystica, 2008.

Mares, Theun. *The Quest for Maleness*. Cape Town: Lionheart, 1999.

Lao Tzu. *Tao Te Ching*. Translated by Stephen Mitchell. London: Frances Lincoln, 1999.

Neville, Gregory O. *Our Emotional Links to Disease*. National Library of Australia, 1996.

Salaman, Clement, Dorine van Oyen, William D. Wharton, and Jean-Pierre Mahe. *The Way of Hermes*. Rochester, VT: Inner Traditions, 2004.

Acknowledgments

A wise person once told me that nothing worthwhile is ever accomplished on your own. I experienced that wisdom over and over again as I traveled through the process of writing this book. Without the amazing support and belief of those around me, I doubt I would have been able to complete this somewhat difficult journey.

To my wonderful editors, thank you. Amanda Murray, your calm approach was soothing. I always felt I was in safe hands. To Simone Graham, it was an epic journey that we traveled together. Thank you for your talent in structuring this book in such a readable way. To Peter Guzzardi, thank you for your gentle and sage advice on the direction we needed to take and your deep insight that provided clarity.

To my agent Bill Gladstone from Waterside Productions, your constant presence was so reassuring. Thank you for believing in this project and thank you for your support in the times when I was feeling less confident.

My heartfelt thanks and gratitude to Jan Jacobs at Johannes Leonardo New York for the generous contribution of the book cover. Thank you, Andrea Gustafson, a talented artist who kindly produced more beautiful covers than we could have hoped to choose from. Thank you from the bottom of my heart.

Without my wonderful friends I would not been have been able to achieve so much in such a short time. To Sophie O'Shaunnessy, one of my earliest clients who became a wonderful friend. Thank you for always believing that this book should be written.

To Sue Fennessy, who constantly pushed me to write sooner rather than later. Thank you for believing in the process and in me. To both you and James, thank you for providing me with a base in New York. I am so grateful for your support.

To Corrie Perkin, my darling friend, you sustained me through this process with your wonderful professional insights. I am blessed to have a friend who is a writer and a bookseller. Thank you for all our breakfasts and for all our coffee breaks and for your enduring friendship.

To my friend Rob Cromb, who came up with the ingenious name of the Faux Feminine Woman. Rob, your insights into this woman were invaluable and I thank you for sharing them with me.

To my darling friend Nicky Whelan, thank you for your unswerving belief in the work and your generosity in sharing your experience with others. Your bravery in embarking on this journey with me is remarkable for one so young.

To all my amazing clients, thank you. To the extraordinary men and women I have had the pleasure and privilege to work with over so many years, thank you for journeying with me. And thank you for having the courage and the bravery to implement what you discovered.

To my son Rob. I was desperate to find answers for you. As I watched you grow and saw the pain and heartache your generation was facing, I was determined to find answers. Thank you for being my constant inspiration to find deeper solutions to the issues that face us in relationships today. I hope that we can all try to eradicate as much internal pain as possible.

Finally, my deep and abiding gratitude to my husband Iggy. Darling, thank you for your belief in me and in this project. You believed in me long before I did. Your unshakeable belief saw me through the demands that were inevitable. Your wise and measured feminine essence always provided the voice of reason. Your masculine bravery protected me from the world and often myself while I processed these concepts. I am eternally grateful for your support.

Index

About the Author

Jennifer Granger is a talented and intuitive transformational coach and author who started her practice fourteen years ago in Melbourne, Australia. Having worked as a corporate insider on four continents over a twenty-year period before that, she taps into both her business acumen and deep spiritual awareness to connect with her clients and help them reach their full potential. Within her coaching practice, Jennifer works with successful individuals from a wide range of creative, corporate, and entrepreneurial backgrounds who seek deeper meaning in their lives and who wish to overcome blocks that may be keeping them from being fully happy and at peace. Her worldwide client base spans from Sydney to New York, Los Angeles to Monaco, Singapore to London.

As women and men continued to seek her out for help in understanding the complexities of their personal, professional, and intimate relationships, Jennifer developed a truly unique theory of what makes people tick. Over the years she began to see more and more of the same "types" emerging, as clients explained the challenges they faced each day at home and at work. Once Jennifer began to define men and women ever more clearly by their characteristics and actions, a new paradigm began to unfold, captured now in her groundbreaking 2014 book, *Feminine Lost: Why Most Women Are Male.*

www.jennifergranger.com